Love, Reason, & God's Story

Publisher Acknowledgments

Thank you to Peter Feldmeier, PhD, of the University of Saint Thomas in Saint Paul, Minnesota, for his thorough and constructive review of this manuscript in process.

Special thanks to Julie Hanlon Rubio of Saint Louis University, in Saint Louis, Missouri, not only for reviewing the manuscript and advising the publishing team, but also for class testing the work with her students, to whom we are also grateful.

Thanks also to Joann Heaney-Hunter, PhD, of Saint John's University, New York, whose input on matters relative to the work was greatly appreciated.

Love, Reason, & God's Story

An Introduction to Catholic Sexual Ethics

David Cloutier

Saint Mary's Press®

The publishing team included Leslie M. Ortiz, general editor; and John B. McHugh, director of college publishing; prepress and manufacturing coordinated by the production departments of Saint Mary's Press.

The scriptural quotations contained herein are from the New Revised Standard Version of the Bible, Catholic Edition. Copyright © 1993 and 1989 by the Division of Christian Education of the National Council of the Churches of Christ in the United States of America. All rights reserved.

Cover image royalty-free from Shutterstock.

Printed in the United States of America

7006

ISBN 978-0-88489-945-7

Library of Congress Cataloging-in-Publication Data

Cloutier, David.
    Love, reason, and God's story : an introduction to Catholic sexual ethics / David Cloutier.
        p. cm.
    Includes bibliographical references.
ISBN 978-0-88489-945-7 (pbk.)
    1. Sex—Religious aspects—Catholic Church. 2. Sexual ethics. 3. Catholic Church—Doctrines.
I. Title.
BX1795.S48C56 2008
241'.66088282—dc22

2007044400

Contents

Part 1

Sexuality and Catholicism: Telling the Stories

Part 2

Sexuality and Catholicism: Exploring the Practices

11 Epilogue

Part 1

Sexuality and Catholicism
Telling the Stories

1 Love and Reason

Your Heart or Your Head?

We've all had to ask this question, particularly when we face choices about romantic relationships. What do we mean by "heart" and "head"? What exactly are we asking here?

This is a good place to begin our study of Catholic sexual ethics. In a sense, the heart/head problem helps us begin to understand the terms "sexual" and "ethics" in our subject. We'll get to "Catholic" later: it's probably the most complicated. For now we can start by simply reflecting on our experiences of the heart, the question of love.

Two Descriptions of Romantic Love: Completion and Sickness

Is this love? The fact that we ask this question points us to certain assumptions we make about falling in love. Most importantly, we take it as a fundamental, almost uncontrollable human experience. We "fall" into it. Something happens, and we are drawn to another person. Yet students of Western culture have, for some time, reminded us that our experience of romantic love is shaped by the language and cultural expectations of our time. For us, in a world where practically every movie, TV show, and song has at least a romantic subplot, it is no wonder that we "fall in love."

So let's look at two descriptions of romantic love that do not come from modern culture. These descriptions should help us name our own experiences with more attention to detail.

The first is drawn from the discussion of love in one of Plato's dialogues. Aristophanes, one of the characters, suggests that romantic love happens because lovers are two parts of an original whole that has been separated. The human race was originally created as large, four-armed, four-legged creatures with faces in both directions. However, these creatures proved extremely powerful, so much so that they sought to assault the gods. Yet Zeus and the gods did not want to kill off the humans, for that would mean no one would honor and make sacrifices to the gods. So Zeus devised a plan to weaken them: cut them in half, and then turn their faces around to face the cut (an explanation of the belly button), so that they would not forget the gods' power.

This did in fact weaken the humans considerably, but caused them a lot of trauma. They went around searching for their "other half," and when their other half was found, they would throw their arms around each other in a tight embrace and refuse to let go. Indeed, the embrace was so total that they began to die of hunger, since they would not leave each other. What to do? Zeus devised the perfect solution: turn their genitals around. That way, when they embraced, it would lead to new generations, and the race would not die off. And so it came to pass that romantic love, which was the force that arose from their sense of being incomplete and separated from themselves, would also function for human regeneration.

Compare this story to the attitudes and practice of the Fulbe, a people who live in the northern part of Cameroun, in West Africa. Helen Regis writes, "The ability to control emotions lies at the heart of the Fulbe construction of personhood" ("The Madness of Excess," 142). The highest value is placed on poise and on one's general availability to fellow villagers. The people show a remarkable generosity and attentiveness. However, this spirit of solidarity is threatened by the "madness" of love. Hence the Fulbe, along with other African peoples, regard romantic love as the result of being possessed by spirits. In one example a man who refuses to find a second wife after his first wife is found to be infertile is constantly criticized: "Her charms are too much for him. He has lost his head completely!" (p. 144). Men who spend too much time at home with their wives, and not enough in public, are said to be "sick" and "under the power of a spell" (p. 145). The Fulbe tell a story in which a man falls in love while traveling, only to find that the woman is a member of a tribe who can turn into hyenas and eat humans. The story illustrates the fate of those who are unable to control their emotions, and instead give in to them. As Regis writes, "It would be difficult to construct a more frightening scenario. Her kin, as hyenas, literally tried to eat him alive" (p. 146). Only a madman would seek such a fate.

Romantic Love among the Loves

It is evident from both these stories that whatever "falling in love" is, it is understood in descriptive contrast to certain other kinds of feelings and experiences. For example, love is somehow different from lust. The love of which we are speaking is not the same as a practical relationship of usefulness. It is not a love bestowed on everyone. It coexists with friendship relationships, but is not necessarily the same. Indeed, it is potentially a threat to friendly relations in the community . . . or even with the gods! These contrasts invite us to develop our description by considering how this experience fits into the entire web of human relationships in our lives.

That phrase—*romantic* love—suggests that more is going on here than what the word "love" alone conveys. Surely we love a great many people: our parents, for example, or friends or roommates. You may love a favorite teacher or a celebrity. So what makes romantic relationships distinct? What makes them "romantic"? And why do we feel this way toward some people but not others?

The immediate reaction to this question is predictable: sex. I would suggest that that conclusion is premature. Are romantic relationships just about sex? Are the best romantic relationships simply the ones with the best sex? Most people are likely to think that there is more involved. But what?

The best way to approach describing the distinctiveness of romantic relationships is to compare them with other sorts of relationships. To do so, I will enlist the aid of the famous writer C. S. Lewis, whose classic book, *The Four Loves*, offers us extensive descriptions of four types of loves: storge, philia, eros, and agape. These Greek words cover some of the different meanings we intend when we say we love someone. Lewis didn't make up these distinctions—they have been around at least since ancient Greece—but by following him, we may grasp more clearly how romantic love (eros) compares and contrasts with other loves in our lives.

The first love Lewis discusses is *storge* (pronounced STORE-gay). He describes storge as "the humblest and most widely diffused" of all the loves (p. 31). Lewis uses the English word "affection" to name this love, but we might simply describe this love as neighborliness or "being nice." The primary characteristic of this love is that "almost anyone can become an object of affection" (p. 32). There is no need to match age or interests or personality traits. You can have this sort of friendly, neighborly relationship with just about anyone, from your parents to your distant cousins, from your next-door neighbor's grandmother to your local store clerk.

This may not sound much like love, but in fact it is immensely valuable in two ways. First, Lewis says storge is the love that leads to "the truly wide taste in humanity." It is the sort of love that can be on good terms with anyone. Storge sets us at ease in wide gatherings and is gracious to all. The teacher who takes good care of all of his or her students might be an example, or the doctor who works with all sorts of different patients and treats them warmly. Second, these examples should help us recognize how storge is ever-present in our daily lives, and how miserable life would be without it. Imagine, by contrast, the cold and distant doctor or the rude store clerk. Imagine the driver consumed with aggression and hostility. The absence of such neighborliness makes life difficult, but its presence can transform daily life into something good. College campuses are classic examples:

some schools advertise how friendly and warm their campus communities are. This doesn't mean everyone is best friends with everyone else. Rather, it means that daily life is permeated with a general friendliness: familiar smiles, courtesy, and the like.

The second love Lewis describes is *philia,* well translated as "friendship." There are some people we say are "friends with everyone." Strictly speaking, this isn't possible. You might say it demeans friendship. Following the Greek, Lewis says that to be friends with someone is to have a relationship based on a shared task and a shared love. Affection crosses over any and all lines of interest, but friendship does not. Friends have common interests, perhaps not in everything, but certainly in something.

Writing in 1960, Lewis asserted that friendship had lost its value in his culture, but we certainly cannot say that about our culture. In many ways, friendship has come to matter more as local ties of family and affection have become weaker. Take, for example, the show *Sex and the City*: we know little to nothing about the four women's families (even their parents), and yet have a sense that we know them. From high school on through marriage (a longer and longer period of time in our culture), friendship seems to reign supreme.

But is this friendship? Lewis distinguishes between "companions" and "friends." Companions are all the people with whom you share a task or an interest. Professors, for example, are naturally companions, as are members of most professions. Members of your football team or your drama group or your choir or your video gaming circle are companions. You enjoy talking shop, sharing the interest that you all have. But not all companions are friends. It is only when you discover, says Lewis, a particular shared vision, captured in the remark "I thought I was the only one!" that friendship begins to blossom (p. 66). Companionship is the matrix in which friendship develops.

Lewis is trying to describe what we mean when we say we just "click" with some people and not with others. What matters is that "you see the same thing"—or even that you passionately differ, but you care passionately about the same thing. In this way, Lewis might be a little skeptical about *Friends* or *Sex and the City*. What holds these people together? Is it really a commitment to a shared good? For friendships to be strong, they can't simply rest on getting along. That might last for a while, but resilient friendships (he argues) are based on a commitment to the good. For example, my closest friends from college when I graduated (in 1994) are not my closest friends now. Away from the shared context of college life, personality and support came to matter less and shared interests came to matter more. This doesn't mean I no longer enjoy seeing my old friends, but those relationships have become more like storge. In a way, I know who my real friends are. Not everyone whom we might call a friend actually rises to this level; many friendships are simply a deeper version of storge.

Helpful in this regard is the Greek philosopher Aristotle's longer description of friendship. Aristotle believed that we have three types of friendships with others. One, a friendship of virtue or character, is the kind of deep connection and shared vision that Lewis describes. The other two were "partial" types of friendships. He called these "friendships of pleasure" and "friendships of utility." These are true friendships, because they involve mutuality and well-wishing for one another, but they lack the deep ground of genuine friendship. Instead, they are based on less important goods. Friendships of pleasure revolve around simply enjoying one another's company or sharing fun leisure activities. You may have completely incompatible political or religious views, but you have a great time shooting hoops together or watching *Desperate Housewives* or hanging out at the bar. Friendships of utility revolve around some useful purpose you share—for example, a good lab partner or a co-worker with whom you collaborate on a committee. Again, your overall visions of life may be different, and yet you work well together on some specific project or task. These are friendships, Aristotle says, but they do not involve the full love of a friendship in which your friend is "another self," truly sharing what means most to both of you.

We can begin to distinguish philia from romantic love, however, by noting that Lewis suggests that friendship is, for the most part, between persons of the same sex, because men and women lack the shared matrix necessary for real friendship. Let the men get together in the TV room and get passionate about football, and let the women hang out elsewhere and talk about clothes, he claims. He allows that when men and women do share a sphere or task (much less common in his society than in ours) friendship may happen, but "the friendship which arises between them will very easily pass—may pass in the first half-hour—into erotic love. Indeed, unless they are physically repulsive to each other or unless one or both already loves elsewhere, it is almost certain to do so sooner or later" (p. 67). With few exceptions, relationships between men and women simply will not be friendships. They will either become eros or remain storge.

Is this true? To answer that question, we have to describe what we mean by "erotic love." This is what we ordinarily see as sexual or romantic love. Lewis maintains that eros, fully understood, includes sex but is not all about sex. Offering an answer to our earlier question about whether sex is the only distinguishing factor of romantic attraction, he denotes specifically sexual love as *venus* and says that it is a *part* of eros, but only a part. A man acting on venus does not "want a woman. . . . He wants pleasure for which a woman happens to be the necessary piece of apparatus" (p. 94). By contrast, someone in eros wants "not a woman, but one particular woman" (p. 94). It is a love that is not just about sex, but about the whole person: the whole person is fascinating. It is this particularity that is the hallmark of eros. Unlike friendship, where the eyes of the friends are focused on the good they share, lovers focus on each other in their entirety. This gives birth to the well-known phenomenon where those in love completely overlook the other person's flaws, or even consider them "endearing," precisely because they are part of the beloved.

Lewis argues that such a love is distinctive, not merely neighborly or friendly, because it seems to come upon us suddenly, from out of nowhere, and it speaks the language of irresistibility. It is almost as if we do not choose. Rather the beloved is chosen for us—quite the opposite of friendship. Moreover, it can come with alarming speed—quite the opposite of affection, which by its nature comes gradually over time as familiarity grows.

Indeed, the suddenness and totality of eros can also be its danger. As Lewis suggests, eros speaks with a voice that demands "total commitment," yet it is not necessarily God's voice. In another text, he quite bluntly ascribes such love to the devil. In *The Screwtape Letters*, the master tempter writes that the devil's bureaucracy has been at work the last few centuries "closing up" lifelong monogamy as a way to deal with sexual desire: "We have done this through the poets and novelists by persuading the humans that a curious and usually short-lived experience which they call 'being in love' is the only respectable ground for marriage; that marriage can, and ought to, render this excitement permanent; and that a marriage which does not do so is no longer binding" (p. 81). While eros may mark a promising beginning of a relationship, it inevitably fades. Hence, it is best seen, according to Lewis, as a beautiful beginning, aimed ultimately at something else.

Here, Lewis introduces the fourth love, *agape*. Agape has traditionally been translated as "charity," but that English word has become distorted. Charity does not mean giving to the poor. Rather it is the love that arrives when, inevitably, the other loves fail. This is the love that loves even when there is no feeling left, appearing especially as forgiveness.

This is, of course, the love God has for us in the Christian story, as well as the love we are supposed to have for God. This is what Jesus means when he calls us to love God "with all your heart, with all your soul, and with all your mind" (Matt. 22:37). It is absolute and unconditional love. The dominant characteristic of this love is disinterestedness. To be disinterested is not, of course, to show no interest, but to ignore any sense of one's own interests being at stake in love. For all the other loves, some degree of mutuality is necessary for love to be realized. Friendship is not one-sided, and unreciprocated eros is sad, even tragic. But agape is specifically about ignoring this mutuality, transcending it, and loving those who are not lovable or who do not love back.

This lack of mutuality raises the question of whether such a love is compatible with all the other "natural" loves. After all, if they are all marked by mutuality, agape would seem to be opposed to them. Lewis argues that agape and the other loves are compatible: that the other natural loves need agape to complete them. Ultimately the problem is that all human relationships end up being asymmetrical: the giving and receiving do not work out neatly. In some relationships, we may have to give a lot more than we receive. In other relationships we may need a lot more than we can give. It would be nice to think that overall, over the course of our lives, this would resolve into a happy equilibrium, but that's just not the way it works. Some people may find themselves called to give much more than they receive from others. Some may have to suffer as recipients, never able to give worthy gifts to others. In our culture, which so highly values equality and so carefully calculates the cost-benefit ratio of every transaction, this asymmetry is disturbing. Shall we abandon all relationships from which we do not profit? Some might say yes, but agape says no. God is presented in the Jewish and Christian stories as preeminently faithful and steadfast. God's love is often severe, disturbing, unexpected. It is not always tender and kindly. But it is always faithful; when we fail, as people do constantly, God's love does not fail. God's love never takes the path of abandonment. That steadfast faithfulness is the essence of agape.

While agape is a completion of the natural loves, we should not forget that it can also be a challenge to them. Quoting the nineteenth-century thinker Soren Kierkegaard, theologian Amy Laura Hall notes that "although 'we human beings speak about finding the perfect person in order to love him,' Christ speaks to us of 'being the perfect person who boundlessly loves the person he sees'" (Hall, 42). Read that again carefully. It reminds us that most often, when we humans "love," what we are doing is finding a person who seems perfect to us. That means that what we love in our best friends and our families is ourselves, which is not love at all. As Hall writes, "Even when I proclaim that I love another dearly, what I am likely cherishing is some aspect of the other that relates to my own self-centered hopes and dreams" (Hall, 44). God's love, seen in Christ, challenges the preference for self inherent in our human loves. From God's point of view, God loves us not because of what we do (or fail to do) for God, but simply because we are persons. God is not self-interested. And so agape challenges us to consider whether our "falling in love" is really directed at the beauty and wonder of the other person, or whether it is a matter of using the other person—or the parts of the other person we deem acceptable and lovable—for our own fulfillment.

For Discussion

1. Why might the experience of falling in love be thought of as seeking completion? Why might it be thought of as being sick?

2. Compare Lewis's loves to the relationships in your life. Do they fit these categories?

3. Is eros = friendship + sex? If not, what are the additional qualities? Or do you not see friendship as essential to eros?

4. Do you feel that you truly love others selflessly? Is such selfless love possible? Explain how you understand the relationship of self and other in your loving relationships.

Avoiding Ranking:
Practicing the Loves in Everyday Life

As you read through the loves and thought about different relationships in your own life, were you tempted to rank them? Even if they are all "love," can't we say that our lovers are more important than our friends, and our friends more important than those for whom we only have affection? This tendency is reflected in our language. Think of the term "significant other," which implies the existence of people that are not significant.

But reality is more complicated than a simple ranking. Imagine that your best friend is on a ski trip over Christmas break, while you are celebrating Christmas with your significant other's family. Suddenly your cell rings, and it's your best friend's sister, weeping and telling you that your friend has had a terrible accident and is in the hospital awaiting potentially dangerous emergency surgery. The friend wants you there. What should you do? Do you say, "My significant other comes first in my life, and I'm committed to Christmas with his/her family, so I guess I can't go." Sounds rather heartless, doesn't it? But when you decide to go your significant other objects, saying, "Don't you love me? Am I not your highest priority?" What do you do then?

So a simple ranking cannot account for the differences between eros and friendship. But surely friendship and eros trump affection? Again, the problem is not that simple. Consider the cry of the man lying beaten by the side of the road in the parable of the Good Samaritan (Luke 10:29–37). The whole point of that story is that priority should be given to those in immediate need, even if that relationship happens to be one of affection. For many of us, professional connections related to our jobs may at some times be genuinely central in our lives. Affection may not have the flashiness and depth of friendship or eros, but its wide coverage means that it may play just as important a role in our lives.

We ought to avoid ranking the loves. For a happy, fulfilled life, all of them are important, but in different ways. Our tendency to rank them may be most pronounced in the priority we give to relationships of eros. The immediate meaning of the term "love" in our culture is often erotic love. It is the flashiest of the loves, and besides it gets all the media hype. But perhaps we might reconsider. For example, the great theologian St. Thomas

Aquinas suggests that friendship is the love that is most like our relationship with God, and that friendship is the central category of relating to others. This is not a ranking; it simply calls us to recognize the role of all the loves in our lives.

Friendship and Romance: How Do You Decide?

In describing the different types of love, perhaps the most interesting question is how we differentiate eros from friendship. Lewis, as we saw, felt that nearly any true friendship between members of the opposite sex will eventually turn into eros, at least if both parties are available. We, however, may have quite a different perspective. Most of us grew up in a world where we took for granted that we would be friends with men and women equally. Men and women work together today in nearly every field. Just as importantly, many people expect that their romantic partner will also be their best and closest friend. This is a relatively new phenomenon. In former times the sexes were more separated in everyday life. You might have great love for your spouse, but your friends were drawn from a whole different group.

Another way to put this is to note the common observation that people are immediately attracted to those who are wrong for them, who are bad for them. Sometimes a relationship that starts more slowly, with less romantic attraction and more friendship, ends up being a better relationship in the long run. Should we just abandon our search for eros and go out with the friends with whom we feel most comfortable? Should you marry your best friend, even if you don't have that "falling in love" feeling?

Reason

This, of course, brings us back to the initial question: your heart or your head? We've thought a bit about what we mean by heart; now we have to figure out exactly what we mean by using our heads, our reason. Again, we can all recognize the experience of wanting something (or someone), but then wondering, "Is this really a good idea?" What exactly are we asking?

It is characteristic of human beings to think before acting. That is where the study of ethics begins. Perhaps there are times when you've looked at a dog or a cat or a tree and wished you could live as it does. Dogs and cats and trees are alive, but they are alive in a different way. In one sense, they are the same as us: a tree that's alive is a tree that is still growing and developing. The same holds true for us. To be human is to be growing into our potential, like moving from seed to sapling to tree. But where do these various potentials lead? An oak cannot become a walnut tree, nor can it become an animal. It's an oak tree; we pretty much know what it will be. It is alive, but it does not have a hand in its own completion.

You, on the other hand, are different. Sure, you can't make yourself into a cat. But you have a hand in determining what you become. What you do—and what the tree doesn't do—is *act*. To act is peculiar to humans, and it is the way we become who we will be. The tree moves, but the tree doesn't act. When the wind blows, the tree bends and sways; we move in the wind, too, but we also push back, keep our balance. That's more than moving: that's acting.

Ethics is the study of human actions. Chemists study atoms and molecules; ethicists study actions. So to start off, we might want to put an action under the microscope and examine it closely to understand how it works. Think of an action, any action, you have performed—say, reading an assignment. The first question to be asked about such an action is, what are you doing? But any answer to that question will really be an answer to the question, why are you doing it? For example, say I ask you what you plan to do this afternoon at 4 o'clock and you say, "I will be driving my car." This is an answer to the question, but not a complete one. A more complete answer might be, "I will be driving to the mall to buy new clothes."

Why is the latter answer more complete? In the first answer, "driving a car" is certainly a physical movement—or more precisely, a set of physical movements—but physical movements are not all we mean when we say human beings act. Remember, trees move, but they don't act. Moreover, if you answered my question by saying, "I will be fantasizing about my girlfriend," we might not be able to identify any actual physical movement, but we clearly have an action—you are clearly doing something.

Actions Have Purposes

If an action is not simply physical movement, what is it? An action has a purpose, an aim. That aim is what we are really looking for when we ask the question, "What are you doing?" Say I am walking across the campus with a friend, and suddenly, while passing the flagpole, she drops to the ground, does ten quick sit-ups, gets back up, and continues our conversation. Perhaps owing to my reserve, I will refrain from inquiring into her mysterious behavior, but then, the next day, in the exact same spot, she does exactly the same thing. I ask, "What were you just doing?" If she answers, "Ten sit-ups, didn't you notice?" I will not be satisfied with that answer, will I? What is missing? She has not told me why—for what purpose, to what end—she is doing this. Now, if it were a campus ritual to do this on certain days of the year, I would not have to ask the question. But since it is not, and since she has now done it twice at exactly the same spot, I assume that there is some reason, some purpose, some order to the action. If there is not, I will have to question her sanity.

This example should show us that most of the time we know the purposes behind our own actions and the actions of others. We naturally assume that everyone acts with purposes in mind, even if the purpose is "just for the fun of it." Every human action has a purpose, and we can only understand the action if we know what the purpose is.

Where do these purposes come from? In the above example, why are you driving to the mall to buy new clothes? You could answer, "Because I am a stylish person, unlike you and your colleagues, Professor." But suppose I reply, "Because you are a slave to fashion and to the advertising of a consumer society." Now things are getting interesting! Ethics is interested in an accurate description in response to the question, what are you doing? In other words, what you are *really* doing. Let's say you're going to the mall to buy new clothes, but you feel a tad guilty about that, so you say, "I'm going to buy a gift for my grandmother." Now if that's an out-and-out lie, obviously you've offered an inadequate description. But in fact, you do buy a little bottle of perfume for your grandmother. You also buy a couple hundred dollars worth of clothes for yourself, however, and you probably wouldn't have made a trip to the mall just for grandma's present. In that case, "I'm going to buy a gift for my grandmother" cannot be said to be accurate.

So we have competing descriptions. This is a problem because the only way we understand our actions is by describing them. In matters of ethics we are sometimes quick to identify an action as "right" or "wrong," but we should be patient: first, we need an accurate description.

Actions and Desires

So, what is behind your trip to the mall, your stylishness or the advertiser's sales pitch? Where does your purpose come from? We are interested in purposes because, behind them, we have desires. Desire gives rise to purpose. I am doing an action for a purpose because I want something. Properly speaking, ethics is a study of desires before it is a study of actions. The question, what are you doing? is then superseded by the prior question, what do you want?

What do I really want? And why do I want it? Where do desires come from? This is a complicated question. Let's start with an example: where does my desire for my morning cup of coffee come from? Obviously, it comes from inside of me, but I can say with certainty that the desire is not "natural," which is to say, I was not born with it. Rather, I have acquired this desire by becoming acquainted with coffee (and caffeine). In this example, Catholic moral theology would call the coffee an *object*. The desires that arise inside of us are elicited by objects outside of us. (Notice here that the object strictly speaking is not the coffee itself, but drinking the coffee.) But of course many people do not drink coffee—for some time I could not stand it. So how did I ever get started drinking it? My girlfriend in college drank it and urged me to try it. What did I desire? My heart was burning for my girlfriend, not for the coffee. Of course, then I figured out about caffeine, and went to grad school, and that was that.

At this point we need to head off a fallacious way of understanding action: I call it the mechanical model. Actions are not caused mechanically—movement is. What causes the 8-ball to go into the pocket? The cue ball. What caused the cue ball to go? The pool cue. What caused the pool cue to move? My arms. But what caused me to move my arms in that particular direction at that particular time? The "cause" is the purpose: to win the game, which I desire. This is not mechanical causation. Philosophers call it "final causation." That is, actions are caused by things that *pull* us, rather than things that *push* us. Now if someone is holding a gun to my head, that's a *pushing* cause, but we know that's a poor example of action, since action is ideally voluntary. It comes from within us.

But why do I desire to win the game? At some point, you have to answer this question by saying simply, "Because it is *good*." This is really the way actions get started: we come to desire an object because we perceive it as good. According to Thomas Aquinas, that is how we're made. We're drawn toward good, and we're driven away from what is evil. Now we have not yet considered what makes something good or bad, but we can say simply that we are drawn to those things that our reason presents to us as good.

Notice the crucial difference between this and mechanical causation. For example, we can imagine that our sexual actions are the result of a "sex drive," quite a mechanical phrase that suggests that our actions stem from some internal engine. But no well-adjusted human being feels a continuous, burning desire to have sex all the time. What we call "sexual desire" is aroused by encountering the good. Our desire for sex, like our desire for everything else, is forward-looking. Desire is the thing *inside* us that perceives that something *outside* us will fulfill us.

Thinking of actions as mechanical can get us into trouble as we interact with other human beings. Let's say you are thinking, "I want to have sex with my girlfriend." If you're thinking mechanically, you will think just like you thought when you were trying to sink the 8-ball: I'll make this move, then that one, and the act is successfully performed. Admittedly, this works in a sense; you can treat other people like pool balls. But then what exactly is your girlfriend doing when she's having sex with you, if you've "succeeded"? She's not really acting at all; you've simply manipulated her mechanically. When the partner is not choosing to participate from her own desire, the term for such sex is not "making love" or "hooking up"; it's "rape."

Another problem with viewing acts mechanically is that actions are not primarily about achieving certain results, but about what purposes you have in mind. Think of the common phrase, "She didn't do it on purpose." It refers to some action that caused an unfortunate result, but it assumes that what matters most is not the result, but the fact that no harm was intended: the purpose of the action was not to cause harm. Conversely, we might imagine a terrorist who plants a bomb that fails to detonate. Can he say, "I'm no terrorist—where are the dead bodies?" A prosecuting attorney will urge his conviction not on the basis of the results, but on his purpose in planting the bomb.

Returning to our original head versus heart problem, we see that we've shed some light on what we mean. To use your head is to think about what you should do, to think about what is really "the good," to consider the purpose of this or that action. Your heart is telling you that the object is good and pulling you toward it. But your head asks, "What is truly good? What is this really pulling me toward?"

For Discussion

1. Think about a recent situation in your life where you didn't quite know what to do. How did you analyze the possibilities? What did you do? Can you explain your decision-making process in terms of your desires and purposes?

2. Using actions from your life (e.g., which courses to take, how to treat a friend, what to do with money, which career to choose), explain the "final cause" that determined your actions. What truly "caused" your choice?

Ordering Multiple Desires: Narratives and the Ultimate End

When we think through actions, it's inevitable that we start to debate not just one action, but a set of actions and their purposes. If human actions were in fact isolated, atom-like units, they could be fairly complex but not particularly confusing. But things are not that simple. Going to college might be considered a complex action, which really means that it is a whole set of actions. Most importantly going to college is not usually an action with a single purpose. The complexity of our actions indicates that the desires behind them are also complicated. We want a lot of different things.

This is a second crucial role for the head. How we go about organizing or ordering our actions and desires is as fundamental to understanding them as knowing that each action has a purpose. So how do we order our actions and desires? Do we make massive to-do lists and try to schedule everything in? In a word, no. If this is the way one has to go about ordering one's actions, something has already gone wrong. Rather, we use stories (narratives) in order to make sense of actions in bunches.

A story has a beginning, a middle, and an end. The story moves because the characters act in certain ways and not in others, in order to bring the story to its destination. As children our moral development begins not with philosophy but with the stories that we hear. The stories begin to allow us to learn what it means to strive for a goal, what sorts of actions work (and don't work) in moving us toward the goal, how to deal with others who have different goals, and (perhaps most importantly) what counts as a good goal. But the story does not simply hand us these things in a list. Rather, it places them within settings and within the sequential development or failure of characters' lives.

From these stories and from the stories of the others we see around us, we learn how to shape our own life stories. Of course there are a lot of different stories we hear, too, especially in our culture. This is both a blessing and a curse. On the one hand, hearing many stories allows for a certain creativity and makes it less likely that we will blindly follow a bad story. On the other hand, we can live many different, incompatible stories and end up a mess. In C. S. Lewis's *The Screwtape Letters*, two devils are discussing a person they intend to capture for their "father" when one observes, "Your man has been accustomed, ever since he was a boy, to having a dozen incompatible philosophies dancing about together in his head. So he doesn't think of doctrines as primarily 'true' or 'false,' but as 'academic' or 'practical,' 'outworn' or 'contemporary,' 'conventional' or 'ruthless'" (p. 8). Lewis's point is that by placing at our disposal many different stories, we come to think that there is no such thing as a good or bad story. And this, of course, is fatal to ethics, for it means that Hitler and Gandhi, Ron Artest and Martin Luther King, Jessica Simpson and Dorothy Day are all equally valid stories for our lives. In the end we may submit to a bad story. Or we may give up trying to find a true story and just go with the flow, allowing multiple stories their domination over our lives.

Why do we need a single story? Without a settled story, there can be no sense of a final ending. And without a final ending, our entire chain of desires goes on without any direction or purpose. Without a final purpose or a deepest desire, we cannot end up organizing all our other desires. It would be like trying to organize the scenes of a movie without knowing what the ending is: it would be an impossible task. The only way to determine the order of the scenes is by looking at all the pieces and figuring out where they are going. As Aristotle and Aquinas put it, if there were no ultimate purpose, desire would go on without end.

In order to reason well about our actions, the final piece of description we need is an ending, a point to the overall story of one's life, what ancient philosophers called the "ultimate end." This ultimate end provides the basis for ordering everything else, for all other actions must somehow coordinate to reach this end. For example, while we may pursue many purposes in our college career, for nearly everyone the goal is to graduate. Consequently at some point all the other purposes and desires must get organized so that the ultimate end, the ultimate purpose, is attained. Here you may object, and rightly so. Sure, graduation is a goal, but is it the ultimate one? We faculty labor under the grand narrative that the purpose of going to college is simply to learn and to learn to love learning. A graduation is not simply supposed to indicate you met certain requirements, but that you have become "liberally educated" (watch the movie *Mona Lisa Smile* if this mystifies you). We may be happier with the peace studies major who never graduated but left college to devote her life to working in Africa than the career-motivated professional major who jumped through all the right hoops but will never read another book in her life, if she can avoid it.

Even at the comparatively simple level of reasons for going to college we can see the complications involved in identifying an "ultimate end," the purpose for which everything else is done. What about one's life as a whole? What is our overall purpose? Or, stated in terms of desire, what will completely and totally satisfy us? If your instinct is to answer "nothing," then you basically have two alternatives. You can turn to the Buddhists, who conclude that since our desires come to nothing, we ought to unlearn them to find peace. Or you can side with the hedonists, who conclude that because there is no point to anything, we basically need to enjoy each day as much as possible. Christians (and many others) believe these views to be false. Humans desire satisfaction because, ultimately, humans can be satisfied. We work toward an end because we can in fact arrive at a happy ending. Christians sometimes have silly ways of articulating what that happy ending looks like (e.g., a long escalator into the clouds), but that's beside the point. When we really look at what we are doing or what others are doing, we will be driven to ask, "What's the point of it all? What's the ultimate purpose? What do I really want?" The ultimate purpose is that which we most desire, that which is deepest in us, that for which we were made.

For Discussion

1. Consider a character from a story (book, movie, etc.) who is portrayed as evil or a failure. What makes him or her that way? What is the ultimate end of this character?

2. Name some stories that have helped you figure out which desires are more important than others in life. What are the morals of these stories?

3. What *is* the purpose of your life? Have you considered this recently?

One Last Piece: Virtues and Vices

At this point, we really have all we need to start doing ethics. We know we have to describe actions, that we have to make sense of them in terms of their purpose, and finally that we need to place them within some larger story that leads to an end. Before we leave this topic, I must note one other term used to understand action: virtue. Unless you are afflicted with an addiction to philosophy and theology, you don't ask yourself the questions we have been asking about your actions. Yet hopefully, when you read this chapter, you could see how you have been "doing ethics" all along. How are we able to act ethically without consciously thinking about ethics?

Ancient thinkers, both Christian and non-Christian, agreed that as people grow into adults, they develop what they called virtues. Roughly speaking, a virtue is a habitual way of acting that "automatically" channels desires in certain ways when presented with certain objects and leads to certain characteristics and regular ways of acting. They explained this as our developing a "second nature" that builds on and completes (or wrecks!) our human nature. If this second nature leads to actions in accord with goodness and truth and reality, the characteristics are called virtues; if the opposite occurs, they are called vices. So, for example, we all develop habitual ways of dealing with strangers we meet. Do we blow them off? Do we judge them by their appearance? Do we respond warmly and hospitably? The point is, over time, we stop thinking about it. We develop a stable way of responding to the presence of a new person. The fact that we don't have to think about them doesn't mean that the actions are not *ours*. Indeed, habitual actions, actions that we don't even have to think about, are the deepest indicators of who we are.

We need the language of virtue to explain why we may be good at analyzing choices, but not actually good at acting. Acting well and thinking well are not identical: compare a sports commentator to those actually playing the sport. The commentator (or manager or coach) may be able to explain the actions of the players in more detail than the players themselves. But that ability to explain, analyze, and even evaluate does not mean that the commentator can in fact do the things that the players are doing. Nor is it necessary for players to be able to articulate all the details of their actions, particularly when they are actually playing. They are not thinking. They are acting out of the second nature they have developed for the game. They are acting out of virtue.

A virtue, then, is a sort of skill, but it is more than that. Skills generally have specific application (think sports again) and can be learned by almost anyone if he or she just does the action enough. A virtue has a much more universal application—it applies to many different areas of life. Training a basketball player to win a game and training him to treat other players and fans with real respect are two very different things, but both involve training. We learn to act in certain ways and not others by acting habitually in these ways. In both cases, the more we act in correct or incorrect ways, the more we develop our abilities or destroy them. In both cases we make a choice to develop or not develop a certain skill or virtue. And in both cases, the process begins when we are young, so that a key beginning to our learning comes from having a good coach (or "role model")—or we suffer because our earliest coaches and role models trained us poorly.

Of course, being trained well or trained poorly only makes sense if we know what the object of the game is, the ultimate end, and the sort of role we need to play in order to reach it. Good and bad coaches inevitably rely on stories. Indeed, we tell stories of good and bad coaches, indicating the virtues and vices of a given role. Actually, all stories develop "characters," that is, they indicate what it means to develop a life well or poorly. They ultimately indicate what a good person and a bad person look like. If we watch movies that treat women as sexual conquests and then go to the bar every Friday with that sort of action in mind, then guess what: we will become that sort of person. Does that make us an admired and popular hero or a predatory and immature jerk? Or we may in fact watch conflicting sorts of movies and have mixed motives when we go out to the bar on Friday night, and then we are what Aristotle called *akratic*, somewhere between virtue and vice, having some idea of virtue but not yet doing it freely and happily, not taking pleasure in it. Indeed, we may be divided within ourselves: part of us may idolize the confident "alpha male" while another part is repelled by him. We wonder who exactly we are and want to be. Notice that we have now returned to our first observation: by our actions we become human, become one sort of person or another.

Conclusion

So, is it your heart or your head? You can't really choose between them. Reason needs love in order to do anything at all, but love needs reason in order to organize and direct our action toward what is good, toward what will ultimately fulfill us. You might say that reason needs love in order to get out of bed in the morning, and love needs reason in order to know what to do once you're out of bed. It is not a matter of balancing the two, but har-monizing them.

And the way we do that is through understanding our actions and lives in terms of a story. We organize our various actions and purposes and de-sires in terms of some sort of ultimate ending, some ultimate purpose in life. In light of our purposes and stories, we shape our behavior by developing habitual ways of acting called virtues and vices. And so we become a certain sort of person, more and more determined toward a particular story and end.

But which story? The pick-up artist or the nice guy? Which story is *true*? Do we tell the story of the pick-up artist as someone who is happy, or do we tell it in terms of someone who needs to grow up? As should be clear, the key question is which story or stories are we going to believe? Because to believe these stories is to believe *in* these stories, to trust them, to hope that they will guide us to happiness and goodness. And so it makes sense to turn now and ask: what love stories do you believe in? And which ones are just fictional, just fantasies? That's the next chapter.

2 Love Stories

"And they lived happily ever after." Such is the classic ending of a good love story. You'll remember that we ended the last chapter by recognizing that our belief in various stories shapes our choices. In this chapter we consider what makes for a good love story—or in terms of our last chapter, what stories shape our understanding of how eros works and what feelings are "good." We will think about our favorite love stories and analyze what they tell us. Then we will look at some of our cultural stories that operate to explain our sexuality.

Ingredients of a Love Story

The best place to start is to think about your favorite love story. One of my favorites is the movie *High Fidelity*. No doubt I like the movie because it stars John Cusack (one of my favorite actors) and because it is set in Chicago (where I was born and raised). I also like it because the main character is a music geek, the owner of thousands of albums (with which I also identify). Already we can see that we like certain stories because we identify with them, we are able to relate to the characters, relate the characters to our own lives. Their desires and actions and goals are somehow like ours. And so we identify the story with our own story.

High Fidelity is not primarily about music or Chicago—it is a love story. At the beginning of the movie we meet Rob, whose girlfriend of the past few years (Laura) is moving out and leaving him. He's miserable about it, but he doesn't want Laura to see him miserable, so he tries to put on a show of strength. He's akratic, not quite sure if he should be miserable or strong and unaffected. Indeed, he's not quite sure where his life is at.

And so Rob does what many of us do at such times: he goes back over his life, and specifically all his past relationships, to figure out the plot of his own story. Why did the things that happened happen? And so we get to see Rob sorting through the various romances and seeing that there are different plots in each one. He dated a "nice girl" for a couple years in high school, but he says, "I wasn't interested in Penny's nice qualities, just her breasts." So eventually he dumped her. In college, he dated a stunning, sophisticated woman for two years, but constantly wondered, "Why would a girl like Charley go out with me? I worried I'd be discovered as a fraud." And eventually, she did dump him for a much handsomer, cosmopolitan type, and he learned that in relationships "you gotta punch your weight, know your class." After that came the inevitable rebound relationship, in which he and Sarah bonded because they were afraid of being alone for the rest of their lives.

Eventually, what becomes clear to Rob from all this (especially after he goes back and meets up with some of these past girlfriends) is that his key problem is that he doesn't really know what he's doing. In the course of the movie he and Laura have discussions about whether it's completely over or not, and while sometimes he's possessive and passionate about getting back together, at other times he's open to a one-night stand with a glamorous singer he meets at a club. Even when he and Laura do get back together and he says, "It was everything I ever wanted," into his record store walks a young, cute, smart record critic from the local paper who wants to interview him, and he starts making her a mix tape, indicating that maybe Laura is *not* everything he wants. Laura, after all, has pretty bad taste in music.

Rob is struggling to figure out what story to live by and makes this explicit near the end of the movie, where he finally cries out, "When is this gonna STOP?!" He returns to Laura and says,

> Other women . . . they're just fantasies. And they always seem really great because there's never any problems. . . . And then I come home and you and I have *real* problems. . . . And there's no lingerie.
>
> Laura: I have lingerie.
>
> Rob: Yes, you do, you have great lingerie, but you also have the cotton underwear that's been washed a thousand times and it's hanging on the thing. And they have it, too; it's just that I don't have to see it because it's not in the fantasy, d'ya understand? I'm tired of the fantasy because it doesn't really exist and there are never really any surprises and it never really delivers.

Then he delivers the key line: "I'm tired of everything else, but I never get tired of you."

What Rob realizes is that he has been trying to figure out what the story of true love is, and that he's been mistaken by imagining that true love is about exciting pop stars and fancy lingerie and brilliant conversations about music. This is "the fantasy." He realizes it's a false story, and that the true story is about Laura. He describes their relationship at one point: "She didn't make me miserable and anxious. It sounds boring. It wasn't spectacular. It was just good. *Really* good." But at first he couldn't commit to that because he had all of these other stories about what "good" meant. It was only when he could break through those stories that he could truly love Laura.

But where did he get these fantasies? Rob sets up this question with the first line of the movie: "Did I listen to pop music because I was miserable? Or was I miserable because I listened to pop music?" The entire story forces Rob to consider whether the stories we are sold in songs are true reflections of relationships, or whether they are misleading. And that is exactly the question we need to consider when we look at the love stories we cherish most.

Indeed, some of you may think that Rob's story is not a happy ending, that he's "settling." While the movie clearly wants us to believe in this story as a happy one, we may think that Rob has given up, that he's no longer searching for "the One," and that he's just exhausted and taking the best he can get. Is that love or cowardice? But on the other hand we might wonder where we get that story about "the One" and "not settling" in the first place.

For Discussion

1. Identify a key love story that shapes your approach to romantic relationships. What constitutes a happy ending in the story? How does that story shape the choices you make? What is the "logic" of the story?

2. How do you tell the plot of your romantic life? How do you look at the past and imagine the future? Why? Are there other ways to tell your story?

Scholarly Love Stories: Biology, Psychology, Society

Love stories are not just in the movies or the drama of dorm life. There are also scholarly arguments that swirl around Rob's questions, analyses that try to get to the roots of Rob's desires, to understand what he is really after in his sexual life. These stories are not just for scholars. They shape our culture deeply and give us ways of reading stories like Rob's and like our own. Moreover, they are the stories offered by the authorities in our culture: scientists, doctors, therapists, advice columnists, and cultural critics. No century has spent more time or energy analyzing sexual love and desire than the twentieth.

We can look at three ways of getting to the "true" story about what's really going on in our sexual lives that dominate these analyses. Perhaps the place to start is Lewis's distinction between eros and venus. Eros, remember, concerns the romantic desire for the whole person, while venus is the narrowly focused desire for sex. The idea that sexuality is about things larger than just sex has been explored and embraced across the board in the twentieth century, in both Christian and secular circles. Even the Vatican has acknowledged the pervasiveness of sexuality in our lives, saying, "It must be considered one of the principal formative influences on the life of a man or a woman" (Congregation for the Doctrine of the Faith, *Declaration on Certain Problems of Sexual Ethics* [*Persona Humanae*], no. 1).

Some ancient Greek philosophers depicted erotic desire as the way to divinity, as a desire that began perhaps for some beautiful human body, but then rose through that body to other beautiful bodies and finally, to the Beauty that was above them all. The Greeks intuited what these more modern thinkers were also getting at: our sexuality is not simply about sex. It is a yearning, a desire that transcends the need for a simple act. However, the word *sexuality* itself is a relatively recent invention, used first in 1836 in reference to plants, and only coming into common use near the end of the century in the earliest attempts at a scientific study of human sexual conduct. These early "sexologists" were like all the budding scientists of their day, interested in creating classification systems that were precise enough to fix and control the world that was observed. Joseph Bristow comments that "sexuality emerges as a term that points to both internal and external phenomena, to both the realm of the psyche and the material world" (*Sexuality*, 1). Ironically, a term devised to provide precise classifications now has a vague and multidirectional meaning.

Biology

But the first scholarly story we need to tell thinks we are just making it all too complicated. In this view, Lewis's distinction between eros and venus is itself just an illusory story. The truth is that sex and the sexual drive are no different for humans than for any other animal: it's about reproduction, the perpetuation of the species. It's about biology. Our experiences of "falling in love" are all variants on this basic need for conceiving and supporting offspring. We can tell whatever stories we want as a culture, but the real purpose for constructing stories at all is biological. We have to continue the species. The basis of sexual desire, like that of other human desires, is chemical.

An example of this view can be seen in the work of Helen Fisher. A prominent anthropologist, Fisher has written widely on the phenomenon of sexual love. In her book *Why We Love* she argues that "romantic love is deeply embedded in the architecture and chemistry of the human brain" (xiv). Fisher, however, does not equate this simply with the drive for sex with any and all partners, which she calls "lust." There are "three primordial brain networks that evolved to direct mating and reproduction." One is lust, one is romantic love, and one is "male-female attachment," the "feeling of calm, peace, and security" you get with a long-term relationship, the purpose of which is to enable the partners to stay together long enough to raise the offspring (xiv). While Fisher outlines three different drives, all of them are directed toward a single purpose: reproduction of the species.

This can be seen in Fisher's investigation of why we fall in love with particular people, and not others. Fisher offers many examples. Men are more interested in women's appearance, she argues, because to a great extent they can see, on the basis of physical appearance, whether a given woman is a "good reproductive bet." Men thus respond more immediately to women. Women, by contrast, are looking for someone who can provide for them effectively through childbearing and rearing. These qualities are not observable visually, since they also have to do with a man's sense of loyalty, his courage, and his intelligence, and so women must take more time figuring out if a particular man has what it takes to be a good partner. Fisher even reports on a study that suggests women look for different characteristics based on whether they are ovulating or not (115–16). When ovulating, they look more for features of physical strength, whereas when they are not ovulating, they look more for features of sensitivity, attention, and commitment.

Ultimately, Fisher traces the rise of romantic love through evolution, explaining why partners who "fell in love" were ultimately more successful in gaining and raising offspring. She also suggests that divorce and adultery should not be seen as odd: although a strong pair-bond is necessary in the earliest years of childrearing, "serial monogamy" is likely to be the most effective evolutionary pattern, since it allows for more reproduction (132–35).

Note that Fisher is not saying what a popular song said a few years back: "You and me baby, we ain't nothin' but mammals, so let's do it like they do on the Discovery Channel." Actually, animals don't care about hooking up for sexual thrills. They don't even mate when they are not biologically in heat. What animals are aiming at is reproduction. Fisher is not saying that biologically we are all just interested in random sex. Indeed quite the contrary: the experience of sexual love *can't* just be random lust, for such lust does not best serve the reproduction of the species. Random lust does not result in pair-bonding to raise the children.

Another thing that Fisher is not saying is that there is no such thing as love. She's not against all the beautiful window dressing; in fact, she celebrates it. Nevertheless, she insists it is only window dressing, and we shouldn't mistake the window dressing for the real causes. She's simply arguing that the experience we describe of falling in love is ultimately rooted in biological desires aimed at reproduction, not in finding "the One" or the perfect friend.

Fisher and other modern scientists ironically reproduce what many ancient philosophers and theologians said about sex: that it was ordered toward reproduction. The existence of sexual desire was properly channeled into having children for the good of the family and the society. Thomas Aquinas writes, following Augustine, "Just as the preservation of the bodily nature of one individual is a true good, so too is the preservation of the nature of the human species a great good. And just as the use of food is directed to the preservation of life in the individual, so is the use of sexual acts directed to the preservation of the whole human race" (*Summa Theologica*, II-II, 153, 2). The roots of sexual desire go toward a certain end, a certain purpose: the reproduction of the whole human race.

Fisher's account, while certainly making sense of some scientific data, goes beyond the data insofar as it too tells a story. It is part of the larger narrative that we may call "the modern scientific narrative," which states that everything that happens in the world is ultimately reducible to scientific explanations. More specifically, human activity is determined by biology, and it is only a matter of time before biology (and chemistry and physics) explains everything.

It can even tell us what is really going on with Rob. Rob's male biology has, for a long time, determined his sexual roaming from relationship to relationship, but he is in crisis because ultimately he is driven to have offspring, and he has no offspring. He makes up stories about why he's exhausted and why it is better to stay with Laura, but the fact is that Laura is a "good reproductive bet"—a stable relationship, a caring person, a person whom you would want to raise your children. Biology explains his epiphany.

Most people, upon reading Fisher's account, are likely to resist this description. No, no, we insist, it's not simply about reproduction. It's not simply about the continuation of the species. Falling in love with someone is much more than this. Sexual desire is not simply about reproduction.

But is there any basis for rejecting the biological view, other than our love of romantic stories? Yes. The above worldview, taken in its totality, makes a crucial leap of logic. It goes from explaining the biological and chemical reactions *involved* in human action to arguing that such reactions *cause* human action. This is an incomplete account of human activity. A simple example: I am teaching a class at 11 o'clock and, as usual, I am hungry. My hunger is biological. It's been four hours since breakfast, my metabolism is relatively fast, and I have been teaching all morning. On the biological view, my hunger will now cause me to get food. But of course this is not what happens. I don't suddenly run out of the classroom and get food. I continue teaching. How can my action be explained? Biology can't give a complete narrative of my actions here—something else is at work. We can presume that this is true about our romantic lives as well.

Behind this story about sexual biology is the larger story about science, which is really at issue here. No one disputes the fact that science helps us understand the world better, that it explains some things about our world. The contested question is whether it explains everything. Can everything in the world be reduced to chemical reactions? It is important to recognize that this is a story, not a matter of fact—a particular way of telling the story of human knowledge. And as the hunger example demonstrates, it is a story that is often oversimplified.

For Discussion

1. Is there a scientific explanation for everything? If so, does life have any larger purpose?

2. If you could take a drug that would simulate the biological feelings of falling in love, would you? Would that experience make loving a specific person unimportant?

Psychology

In our century in particular, the most important addition to the biology story is the discovery of the complexity of the mind or the psyche. Our actions are not simply a matter of biology, but of psychology. Thus in telling a story about our sexuality we might look less at chemical reactions and more at our minds and our mental experiences. Sigmund Freud's theories about sexuality pointed in this direction. Freud, the father of modern psychology, noted early in his career that the claim that sex was simply about evolution and reproductive success failed to explain several facts about human behavior: it failed to explain the persistence of homosexuality; it failed to explain why many adults pursued other organs as objects of desire; and it failed to explain why young children would experience excited feelings and interest in their genitals (Bristow, *Sexuality*, 62). Freud therefore began to argue that the "sexual drive," even when it included "normal" male-female reproductive intercourse, had a much wider scope, encompassing our desires for pleasure and pain, our relationships with our parents, and even our desires for life and death.

Freud's key hypothesis was that of the unconscious. In simplified terms, the unconscious is the place in the mind where repressed desires go. Our conscious mind is dominated by a basic need to function and succeed in society; hence, we must repress desires that conflict with cultural norms. But these desires do not disappear. Rather they form the unconscious, which "becomes the turbulent zone where diverse sexual drives have to be repressed so that the human subject maintains its identity" (Bristow, 64). Freud believed these repressed desires appear early in childhood, and the management of these desires constitutes a crucial, even determinative, growth process. He suggested two crises through which such management takes place. In the Oedipal complex, a young boy experiences desire for his mother, thereby perceiving his father as a rival. His desire is conflicted; he wants to kill the father, and yet he also identifies with the father. The other complex, called the castration complex, occurs when a boy begins to discover that not all others have the same sexual organs he does, producing a severe crisis of identity, since his initial reaction is to refuse to confront the reality that women are "missing" something.

Such early desires and their management are necessary if we are to explain nonreproductive sexual drives, even such common ones as kissing, which is obviously not reproductive. Freud explains that the importance of the mouth as a sexual locus has to do with oral pleasures experienced by the child, particualry breastfeeding. The key underlying insight here is that, due to the many variations observed in adult sexual behavior, it must be the case that "the sexual instinct has many discrete, if not disharmonious, sources" (Bristow, 68). Reproduction is not the sole purpose. The disharmony develops because of aberrant and incomplete resolution of the complexes above. These conflicts, dealing as they do with fundamental matters early in life, therefore have the potential not only to "pervert" sexuality, but to affect the development of the whole person in keeping with his or her cultural context.

Freud's work is actually quite dark and speaks with some severity about the need for ordering our sexual drives, but its cultural influence in America often stressed its more optimistic side: the need to overcome the repression of our sexual feelings if we are to become healthy and mature adults as a whole. Freud's work, at least in its popularization, posits the development of our sexuality as essential to our happiness. A life without sex, or denial of sex, or even curbing our sexual desires, is ultimately unhealthy. The story of sexuality here, in its popular form, is a story where sexual actions are a form of therapy, a form of mental exercise in which we work out certain problems and tensions.

How might therapists interpret Rob's story? The movie doesn't tell us about Rob's childhood or family life, and therapists would likely say that we need to know about that before we can understand Rob's problem. But they would probably suggest that his relationship history exhibits a definite "neediness": Rob seems to need love and affirmation, and he looks for romantic companions that compensate for various deficiencies in his life. Rob, they might say, has "self-esteem issues." Therefore it's not really clear that he has solved his problem by suddenly settling on Laura. Maybe he needs to be alone for a while and work on becoming happier with himself.

Notice the shift here from a more biological/reproductive view. The biological view is oriented toward the overall good of the community and the species. Sex has a relatively limited purpose. By contrast, the Freudian/modern view of sexuality makes it key to *personal* health, to individual happiness, and sex affects all areas of our lives.

However, there is also a similarity in these views: each claims the larger authority of modern science, which can authoritatively tell us what is really going on. Both discourses are medical; they represent what some have called the medicalization of sexuality, where the authority delegated to control and direct sexual activity, once the province of religious authorities or the family, now lies with various factions of the medical community. This explains why it is culturally acceptable to evaluate people's sexual lives as "healthy" or "unhealthy."

For Discussion

1. Do you find Freud's explanations persuasive? Why or why not?

2. Do you think our society places too much importance on sexuality? Not enough? How important is sexuality for a happy life?

Society

But why should medical authorities, whether biologists or psychologists, have the final say over what sexuality is really about? This is the key question raised by influential French theorist Michel Foucault. Foucault's work is a touchstone of what is now considered to be "postmodern thought" or "deconstruction" or "genealogy." Foucault's work was wide-ranging, beginning with his interest in French prison reform and the mechanisms used to control prisoners throughout history.

Foucault's key insight can be summed up as follows: all of human life is governed by regimes of power and control, where some humans are attempting to exercise control over others, while simultaneously attempting to hide or mask the fact that they are exercising control. The work of philosophical thought is to unmask the way power operates, especially by exploring biased historical accounts of the origin and creation of regimes of authority. We are all, needless to say, familiar with the unmasking of religious authorities as false, but Foucault maintains that the authorities imposed by modern science are no better. In either case, the aim of the discourse is the control of the many by the few. The more the authorities say that you are free to choose, the more suspicious you should be about the ways in which their power is operating.

Foucault's ambitious history of sexuality begins with a story, the story he intends to call into question. This is the story of the movement in the West from sexual repression to sexual freedom. He outlines this story as one in which, primarily in the nineteenth century, sexuality became repressed and restricted by being placed in the strictly-bounded home. Most importantly, sex became surrounded by silence. Supposedly we have now started to free ourselves from this Victorian corruption of sex. He notes that the proclaimers of sexual revolution speak in virtually religious terms about the promise of a new day that will come from removing Victorian taboos about speech and sexual practices. Foucault terms this story "the repressive hypothesis."

However, he intends to call into question this broad story. He finds it curious that a society seeks so strongly to castigate itself for its own hypocrisy and "sins" against sex. He wonders specifically if the proclamation of the repressive hypothesis is "in fact part of the same historical network as the thing it denounces . . . by calling it 'repression.' Was there really a historical rupture between the age of repression and the critical analysis of repression?" (*The History of Sexuality*, 10). The repressive hypothesis is not mistaken, but it pretends to locate itself outside the control it critiques. It pretends to be a story of freedom, when it is in fact a story about new forms of control and new authorities.

In this sense, Foucault can be said to be the unmasker of the unmaskers. If Fisher and Freud suggest that scientific study can actually tell us what good sexuality is, then Foucault can show us how these scientific discourses similarly serve to create normative (and deviant) forms of sexual desire and action, which simply allow the biologists and psychologists to have the sort of control that priests and religions used to have. Like the older narratives of religion, it is supported and reinforced by "experts." And like the older narratives, its ultimate purpose is the same: to assure social control over sexuality by imposing a certain story, which defines certain acts and desires as normal and others as abnormal. Note, for example, that Fisher's studies clearly suggest that lifelong monogamous fidelity is unnatural. Forms of Freud lie behind the idea that a commitment to celibacy must be unnatural and unhealthy.

But how does Foucault support his argument and what alternative can he present? Foucault examines the discourses that claim to produce "the truth about sex." He argues that there are two main alternatives. One is the *ars erotica*, the tradition of sexual literature that promotes the arts of sexual pleasure. These represent a sort of wisdom literature—sayings and maxims and advice—passed on from sexual "masters" who develop secret arts for sexual pleasure. Many civilizations have this sort of tradition; the *Kama Sutra* is an example.

However, the post-repression era has not been notable for producing literature in the *ars erotica* tradition; quite to the contrary, it has been led by scientists and medical authorities. So how have these authorities claimed to produce the truth about sex? Foucault claims they have done so in the same way that the dominant Western Christian tradition has done for centuries: through confession.

Confession is the other great procedure for producing sexual truth. Foucault traces the concerns of the sacrament of confession with sexual sins, and then links these concerns to the modern discourse about sex. What has changed, Foucault argues, is not the mode of discourse, but its location and its authorities. Whereas in earlier eras confession happened in the church and was controlled by the clergy, now it happens on the psychologist's couch (or on TV) and is controlled by credentialed medical authorities. Sexual authorities continue to control and shape the discourse, even as they loudly proclaim the advent of sexual freedom and experimentation. Modern authorities (including Freud, Kinsey, and the other names associated with the wresting of sexual discourse from religion) "caused the rituals of confession to function within the norms of scientific regularity" (Foucault, 65). Far from refusing recognition of sex, the scientific era "put into operation an entire machinery for producing true discourses about it" (Foucault, 69).

Summarized, Foucault's work forms the basis and support for the idea that all notions of sexuality are culturally constructed, often by those who are in power in order to retain their power. Thus we might say that sexual desire and love are ultimately plastic, bendable and shapeable in countless different ways, with no particular normative shape, whether biological or religious. Hence, as an alternative, Foucault's project will aim at a recovery of the *ars erotica* tradition, in which both religious and scientific discourses about sex are resisted through the practical pursuit of experiences of sexual pleasure.

To get more of a sense of what Foucault is trying to do, we can compare it to three different ways of talking about food. The first would be the ancient religious taboos against certain foods, present in Judaism, Islam, and most religions. Eating is ordered by ritual regulations of the tradition, in which certain foods or combinations of food are considered unclean and are avoided. Examples of this abound in the Old Testament and in Jewish tradition generally, particularly in terms of distinctive foods for Jewish feast days, such as the unleavened (yeast-free) bread Jesus uses at the Last Supper, which is a celebration of the Jewish feast of Passover. These rules are not arbitrary, but have a purpose: to order eating toward serving God. Hence these laws "were ordained as a way of setting the Jews apart in their day-to-day life, so that they might be conscious of their responsibility as members of a priest-people" (Arthur Hertzberg, *Judaism*, 141).

The second way is what we might call the medical discourse about food. The ultimate purpose of eating is health, not religion. Foods can be classified by health. This is the reigning discourse in our society, where every day seems to produce a new report about certain foods protecting us from disease or causing it.

The third way is talking about eating food for pleasure. Here we should not think of the McDonald's addict, but the person who comes to enjoy rich, well-prepared, complex foods: the gourmet, the connoisseur. Many have pointed to the diets of the French and of the Mediterranean countries, in which pleasure in eating is the guiding principle—miraculously, without sacrificing health and longevity. Taste and creativity are viewed as the true purposes of eating.

Each of these ways of conceiving the action of eating is driven by different purposes and aims, and they each generate different virtues and different narratives by which people make choices about what to do (recall the language of our first chapter). So too is the case with sexual action. Foucault presents us with regimes governed by religious aims, medical aims, and pleasurable aims, each of which narrates our sexual lives differently. Perhaps most importantly, in the same way as with food, each of these regimes is a matter of deploying social power. The gourmet takes his taste to indicate social refinement and superiority, for example. Approaches to sexuality serve the same end: the power of those who impose their narrative upon society.

While Foucault himself regarded our society's obsession with sexuality also as a problematic cultural construction, saying that sex "has become more important than our soul, more important also than our life" (Foucault, 156), and accusing modern psychology of reproducing the lurid obsession with sexual disclosure earlier demanded by the Catholic confessional, Foucault's work has in fact become intertwined with the "repressive hypothesis" pervasive in the culture, reinforcing our peculiar interest in varieties of sexual activity and expression for happiness. Ultimately, Foucault's work is used by postmodern theorists to question any and all suppositions that there is a normative, "good" description of sexual love and desire. Instead, sexual desire of any kind is opened up as a field of exploration and play, making it almost a matter of individual taste and style, like those who eat food primarily for the purpose of pleasure.

For Discussion

1. What are the social power structures that have shaped your view of sexuality? Can you name them?

2. Do you think sexuality could ever be approached the same way as food, as a story about taste and variety? Why or why not?

Fisher, Freud, Foucault, and Our Everyday Lives

The stories of sexuality that we have just explained may not be as well-known as some more famous and popular love stories, but they have in fact shaped the stories that get told and retold in our everyday lives. These are the cultural stories, often unidentified, that contribute to our personal understanding of sex and sexuality.

Where do these stories function? An example of the biological story can be seen in some of the behind-the-scenes work at prominent online dating sites. In a magazine article profiling the efforts of various sites to devise tests that provide successful romantic matches, Helen Fisher describes how she constructed a 146-item compatibility test that attempts to classify users as one of four types, based on the levels of four different brain chemicals: dopamine, serotonin, testosterone, and estrogen. The goal of the test, Fisher says, is not to match people based on values and similar interests, but to find people who "fascinate" one another, in both the short and long term. This "fascination" factor explains why you may not "connect" or "click" with many people with whom you have much in common. As Fisher describes it, "You may have the same goals, intelligence, good looks, political beliefs. You can walk into a room, and every one of those boys might come from the same background, have the same level of intelligence, and so on, and maybe you'll talk to three but won't fall in love with any of them. And with the fourth one, you do. What creates that chemistry?" (Lori Gottlieb, "How Do I Love Thee," 63), For Fisher, it is the underlying brain chemistry, though she admits that it is difficult to identify that match in advance. As another site director commented, "If I could concoct a test for chemistry, I'd make a zillion dollars" (Gottlieb, 66). Yet all these sites are proceeding to build huge samples of test-takers in the hope of constructing a model where they can predict such chemistry. Eventually, they hope, science will direct us to our perfect love.

However, this story is not the dominant one. People do not ask for genetic information when going out on dates. Most of all, and most interestingly, almost no one suggests on a dating site that the ultimate purpose of sexual chemistry is reproduction of the species. Instead, biology is most often employed in the service of the psychological or therapeutic view of sexuality. Brain chemicals and hormones ultimately aim at fascinating relationships. And why do we want such relationships? It is suggested over and over again that such relationships will make us happy and well-adjusted and psychologically healthy.

What exactly does that mean? At this point, the therapeutic story of sexuality has more difficulty. Perhaps thirty or forty years ago the therapeutic view sought to stabilize relationships, and it still does a lot of work for those caught in what are defined as unhealthy relationships. Unhealthy relationships are usually defined as abusive in some way and involve one partner using the other, without appropriate reciprocation. Why is your roommate with that guy who treats her so badly? Why is that weird guy down the hall always on the Internet in the middle of the night? The therapeutic story will most often suggest that these "unhealthy" manifestations of sexuality are rooted in psychic causes, in unhealthy relationships from childhood or adolescence. By defining unhealthy relationships in this way, the therapeutic view silently endorses a normative view of human sexual relationships as free, equal, and ultimately in service of the development of individual happiness.

Foucault would ask, who is to define what is a healthy relationship and what is not? One person's dysfunctional hooking up might be another person's liberation and exploration. Is there anything necessarily wrong with a college sophomore hooking up every weekend? It might be a way of looking for intimacy. Or it might just be recreation. He or she enjoys it. What gives the counseling office or the residence life office the authority to tell us which story we ought to believe?

This story of sexuality as self-expression is further reinforced by the enormous variety of sexual possibilities and experiences. As we will see, the language of hooking up serves the purpose of concealing what is actually going on, since the term can cover any number of possible experiences. Unlike fifty years ago, college students with ambiguous feelings about attraction to the opposite sex are not seen as unhealthy—indeed, such feelings are encouraged as a form of self-expression. Similarly, bisexuals and transgendered are no longer seen as unhealthy. However, the alpha male who seduces women might be considered unhealthy. Foucault might wonder: is this science or merely a regime of power and control at work?

Foucault's story is insistently slippery, calling into question any kind of potential defining of sexual boundaries, other than consent (which is necessary if sex is to be self-expressive). It is a drama where the self goes from being submissive to being expressive, from being controlled by others' perceptions and expectations to being in control of oneself.

Because all these stories are going on in our culture, sexual practices and relationships have a distinct, do-it-yourself flavor, with each action and coupling being worked out by the individual parties. You might think, isn't that how it ought to be? After looking at our cultural stories, as well as working on some descriptions elsewhere, many will be tempted simply to conclude that "we're just all different."

That would be hasty. What about pedophilia, legalized prostitution, incest? These stories are abhorrent to most people, and it's hard to say that they're just a matter of personal taste. Yet when we say that "everyone should do whatever he or she wants," we're asserting exactly that: our different tastes in sexuality matter no more than our different tastes in cereals. Few will accept this conclusion in its entirety.

The idea that everyone can have a different sexuality suggests that sexuality only concerns individuals: each person has his or her private sexuality. This is simply false. Nearly every other culture recognizes sexuality as a common good, a social necessity. Most couples need communal support. They need social structures by which they can become couples in the first place. And the society needs children, born and raised. None of this will happen without some shared stories and models. We will discuss this social character of sexuality extensively in future chapters, but here we need simply note its existence.

Note also that "doing what we want" is not as easy as it sounds. Are there things you wouldn't want your children to watch? Assuming there are, you are indicating that while we might tolerate a wide variety of stories, we don't actually think all the stories are equally good. We live in what is known as a pluralistic society, a society in which multiple views of the same subject are allowed to coexist. The point of pluralism is not simply to reduce life to a series of ice-cream-flavor-level choices. Rather, our cultural ancestors assumed that we had a better chance of getting at the truth if we allowed multiple disagreements to exist than if we simply allowed one pervasive story or influence to shape the culture completely. Multiple views are not supposed to provide a shopping mall of choices, but to allow us a better chance to make good choices. Thus in a pluralistic culture the task of critically examining all these narratives is important. The Founding Fathers assumed that disagreement ultimately made for better judgment, but that means we must develop the skill of evaluating different stories. Without this skill, "what we want" will probably be derived from advertising, since our massive media culture has by far the greatest cultural power of storytelling during the formative years. These people want power over us—that's why the media are always telling us to think for ourselves, in order to disguise how the media present a single "right" view of the world.

Finally, leaving sexuality to individual preference—like ice-cream flavors or breakfast cereals—ultimately suggests that sexuality is pretty trivial. And few actually believe that. In fact, as the spiritual writer Ronald Rolheiser reminds us, sexuality is one of the most powerful aspects of human life, and hence also one of the most dangerous (*The Holy Longing*, 192–93). Treating it like breakfast cereal either means we are depriving ourselves of an important part of life or that we are playing with fire. Playing with fire can be fun, until someone gets burned—and that happens all the time with our sexuality. Few people have their lives ruined because of the breakfast cereal they chose, but the same cannot be said for poor sexual choices. Sexuality matters intensely for our lives. Sexuality and romantic attraction have this kind of power. One way or another, we pretty much agree it's a big deal. We just disagree about what the deal is.

Challenging Stories?

The importance of these theories of sexuality inevitably challenges our initial descriptions of sexual feelings, covered in the previous chapter. Those descriptions of the experience of being in love largely ignored the stories that structured such experience. More importantly, such initial descriptions function "on the surface." They do not ask probing questions about why we are having these feelings, especially about why we have them in a particular way toward a particular person. Modern theories of sexual desire challenge our temptation to regard romantic love as a given, something that is "just there."

Perhaps these stories also need to be challenged. It is possible that these theories explain far too little about sexuality, rather than explaining too much. The biological story, which reduces everything to reproduction, has already been shown to be deficient in regard to how sexual drives encompass acts that are not reproductive, and how sexual drives are heavily shaped by culture and power dynamics. These later theories, in turn, explain little about the explicit purpose of our sexual actions. Freud and Foucault, in different ways, presume that our actual purposes, the actual aims we set for our sexual actions, are something of a sham. What is really going on, they say, is the working out of the turbulence of the unconscious or the power dynamics of the culture. Is it plausible that our sexual behavior is so mysterious that we cannot grasp a purpose for it and act accordingly? This is particularly the case insofar as (unlike Lewis and the four loves) these authors focus almost entirely on sexual acts, and not on the sexual relationships that encompass them. That is to say, all these authors reflect the modern scientific tendency to extract acts from their natural ecology, the context that gives them their meaning.

These theories remind us to be suspicious of our initial descriptions and assumptions. More is going on than at first appears. Perhaps more is going on than these theorists think, as well. In order to consider that, we will now turn explicitly to the Christian narrative, in order to see how this encompassing context might explain and order our sexual desires.

Conclusion

Like Rob reviewing his relationships in the movie, this chapter has considered the love stories that shape our perceptions and choices, especially our beliefs about what sexuality is all about, sexuality's ultimate purpose. We can argue about these stories at great length, gaining further insight into their accuracy (remember, accurate description is the beginning of ethics, as we noted in the first chapter), but the ultimate purpose of a particular area of life (in this case, sexual relationships) needs also to be placed within some story about the ultimate purpose of life as a whole. We saw this in chapter 1, we see it when we stay out of relationships because we have to devote our efforts to school, and we see it when we choose a job that pays less but allows us to spend more time with our family. We see it again in Rob's story: he met Laura for the first time when he was a DJ at a club, and he notes that "meeting promising women is sorta what the DJ thing is all about." Rob orders his job story toward his love story. Why? After looking at various love stories, we have to turn to stories about life as a whole to make full sense of our actions.

3

God's Story

In the last chapter we talked about love stories, the patterns and plotlines that shape our approach to romantic relationships. In looking at some of the cultural stories, we saw that these romantic storylines were embedded in larger plots, bigger stories about the world. For example, we saw that Helen Fisher's account of love as biological rests within a larger story of modern science. These larger stories shape the smaller ones. So in this chapter we turn to the largest possible story within which our lives are embedded, for our lives are subplots within that larger story. It's as if life is a TV series, and to make sense of particular episodes, you have to know something about the overall story. But what is that larger story in which our lives are embedded? That's God's story, Christianity.

What Is a God Story?

We might also call this a master narrative, a story that orders all the other stories. Everyone acts within some sort of implicit or explicit master narrative. This is implied in the claim in the first chapter that there is some sort of ultimate end, some definitive happiness that orders all our action.

But do we really need a master narrative? Does Rob, from *High Fidelity*, have a god story? In fact, everyone has a master narrative insofar as his or her life looks like a genuine story, a coherent plot with a beginning, middle, and end. We know from psychology that people who are deprived of such stories—who no longer can see their lives as making sense and having some sort of plot—become depressed and even self-destructive. They have increasing difficulty making choices, or make choices randomly, and of course chaos ensues. But such people are exceptional. By and large, insofar as life seems to make sense, it's because it makes sense in terms of some story.

If the story is not explicit, then odds are that one of two things is happening. First, it is possible that people are simply relying on standard, culturally given stories to guide them in various compartments of their lives. Compartmentalization refers to the common phenomenon in our culture of viewing our lives as made up of relatively separate areas—compartments —which may relate to each other in some small way but mostly exist independently of one another. For most people, the two primary compartments of life are work and family, with friends or companions functioning as a third category that may or may not overlap with the first two. Most of us function with a "play" compartment, where we put our hobbies and leisure time activities. To a greater or lesser extent, we may have a "politics" compartment, where we act in the community and follow political issues. And most people also have a "religion" compartment, where they pursue matters classified as spiritual.

Compartments are also made over time—being a school kid, being at college, being a young and carefree twenty-something, settling down to have a family and a steady career, retiring—with each period having a distinct task and character associated with it. Different forms of behavior are considered appropriate for different life compartments. When I have a class discussion about student drinking habits and wonder if going out and getting wasted is a good action, some people reply that it's OK "because it's college." They imply that going out and getting wasted when you're thirty years old suggests alcoholism, but not when you're in the compartment called college.

The other alternative is that, recognizing these compartments, and rejecting any overall god story, the person orders the compartments by his or her own choosing. But notice that this is not the absence of a god story. It's a god story in which you are god. Your particular preferences at any given time organize various goods in your life. Your ultimate end is yourself. This is the social phenomenon we call individualism.

Individualism overcomes the problem of compartmentalization by justifying choices simply in terms of individual preference. There is no master narrative other than the preferences I feel at any given time. Sociologist Robert Bellah, perhaps the leading scholar of individualism, tells the story of a man who spent most of his twenties and thirties clocking long hours at work and moving up the career ladder, and then around age forty decided to change course and spend more time with his family. He didn't describe this change of overall perspective in terms of discovering that family is more important in life than a career; rather, he simply told Bellah that his feelings changed, and he just changed his action to fit his new preferences. He might change it again in ten years.

Both of these stories point to a common phenomenon in our society: fragmentation. That is, in each of these cases, you go on doing certain actions, living out certain stories, and you discover a problem. In the case of individualism, you see that while you may have a master narrative and your friend may also, there is no narrative that ties you together. You are just fragments. A similar thing happens when you look at your life and see work and a house and a vacation, and you ask, "What is this all about?" You feel like a cog in a machine, just doing the motions demanded of you in society's assembly line. What's the bigger purpose?

In *High Fidelity* we can see a god story, a master narrative without which the story cannot come to its conclusion. The story is about more than Rob and Laura being together—it has to be more because we are meant to view the story as having a happy ending. But what makes the ending happy? For one thing, as we have already noted, we see that Rob gives up certain romantic illusions, focusing on his own false desires, and comes to love and appreciate Laura. This is a sort of conversion from illusion to reality, not merely a change in preference. As the story ends Rob is making a mix tape, but not to display his own musical knowledge and tastes. Rather, he makes a tape "of all the stuff that would make her happy." The story suggests that what Rob has learned is that real happiness comes not from imposing your narrative on others, but on learning to love others' narratives—from learning to orient yourself and your story to the other person, not orienting the other person toward yourself. That's a purpose larger than the self.

The movie makes a related point about Rob's job. It is clear that a big part of the problem in Rob and Laura's relationship stems from the fact that Rob feels stuck in his job. He is the professional critic. But the turning point comes when he discovers some skateboarders outside his store who have a band. Upon hearing their music, Rob takes the plunge: he offers to produce a record for them. Laura celebrates this. Here again is a god story, this time about creativity, about how our lives are fulfilled when we are not just working for someone else, buying and selling and critiquing and consuming, but when we actually move to creating something new. Somehow this is better, something more than just going through the motions. This master narrative lurking in the movie identifies why certain choices in life are better for happiness than others.

Religions and philosophies give you something more than this, something bigger. They are bigger, more developed versions of the story hinted at in the ideas of love and creativity that shape *High Fidelity*. They affirm that your life is not just about your needs or about the various machines in which you are a cog. As human beings, we are made for something more than this. Often enough these desires in our own culture come out in the love stories we considered above, which is part of the reason we don't like having such stories deconstructed. If romantic love—our search for "the one"—is basically just about chemical reactions, we feel that we have lost something meaningful in our lives. Are our loves just chemistry and our jobs just earning money to pay the bills? Is that all there is, or is there something more? Is there "God"?

For Discussion

1. Consider your own life: what functions as the god story? Religion? A personal slogan? Creativity? What shapes your particular choices to prioritize this or that "compartment" in your life?

2. Have you ever had the sense that your life was part of something bigger? Describe the experience. Why do you think you sensed this?

The Bible as God's Story

Before we get to the content of the biblical story, we should say a few things about its form. First, although the Bible is made up of many small stories and books, it is meant to be one overall story. Often we hear the Bible in small chunks, and it is something like seeing season four, episode two of a six-season, twenty-two-episodes-a-season TV series. Based on isolated episodes we may form mistaken conclusions if we do not know the overall story. Clearly the Bible is significantly more complex than any TV series, so when we look at isolated parts of the Bible we need to have some sense of the overall story in order to know what is going on.

Second, the Bible is a story about everything. That is to say, it is not a purely religious or spiritual story. Like any story, it has a beginning, a middle, and an end. The Bible begins with the creation of the world, and it ends with a vision of the end of the world. So it is not a narrowly religious book. To say it is about everything does not mean that it literally talks about everything, of course. But it is a broad narrative that is meant to have a place for everything.

Third, and perhaps most importantly, the Bible functions on two different levels simultaneously. If we fail to see that it is meant to be a story about everything, we probably won't see how it weaves these two levels together.

On one level, the Bible speaks of the relationship between God and the world; we might call this the vertical dimension. But it is mostly not a book of theology or philosophical argument. Rather, it is primarily a history; we can call this the horizontal level, where it is a story about the world itself and in particular how humans relate to one another in the world.

A famous example will help us understand how this works. Jesus is asked, "Which commandment . . . is the greatest?" His response perfectly displays how these two dimensions of the story are not separate. He answers, "You shall love the Lord your God with all your heart, and with all your soul, and with all your mind. This is the greatest and the first commandment. And a second is like it: You shall love your neighbor as yourself" (Matt. 22:37–39). This is clever: are there two commandments? Or is the second "like" the first in the sense that the two are really all part of one larger whole? We can see these two dimensions, but the Bible suggests that they can never be separated. A Christianity that is only concerned with loving God will devolve into empty acts of prayer and piety, and neglect the neighbor. A Christianity that is only concerned with loving the neighbor will devolve into a social program and neglect God. The Bible suggests that our relationship with God and our relationship with each other are interconnected. Hence God's story is also, at the same time, the story of the world.

With these formal points in mind, we can turn to the content of the story. I will describe four plotlines that run throughout the story and give it its overall shape. These plotlines represent patterns of seeing, which then can be used to place our actions within the plot.

God's Story, Plotline 1: Idolatry

Let's begin the biblical story with the problem of idolatry. This may seem like an odd place to start, because we don't tend to spend a lot of time thinking about idolatry as a problem anymore. We don't often see crowds of people worshipping stone statues. When we hear "idol" we're more likely to think of the TV show *American Idol* or the "immunity idol" on *Survivor*. By beginning the biblical story with idolatry we're starting with the recognition that we humans are constantly getting God wrong—and we need not think about tribes worshipping stone statues to see this point.

Who is God? After all, it's God's story. Let's hear about the main character. What do you picture when you imagine God? A big guy tossing lightning bolts? That's an idol. A kindly old grandmother in the sky? Another idol.

God is neither of these things, and yet it is so easy for us to fall into such pictures. Thus the first plotline of the biblical story is concerned with training us out of these pictures and instead revealing who God really is. This is why the classic theological designation for the Bible is revelation. Its purpose is to reveal God, which is necessary since we keep getting God wrong.

So who is God? St. Anselm, a famous medieval theologian, offered a definition we can start with. God is "that than which nothing greater can be thought." Notice that he is not saying that God is the greatest thing you can imagine; rather, God is beyond that. As Robert Barron writes, this definition is "tantamount to saying that whatever you think is less than God" (*The Priority of Christ*, 213). St. Augustine said something similar: "If you understand, it is not God that you are understanding." These definitions say what God *is* by saying what is God is *not*.

Such an approach can be helpful. For example, take the stern old grandfather and the kindly grandmother. The weakness of either image is seen in the other. The stern old grandfather will be great when you want to see justice done or get some task performed, but the kindly old grandmother is there for comfort and care and nurturing. We could even say that this is why it's good that there are both stern old men and kindly old women in the world, because the world wouldn't work well if everyone was one or the other. Here, by thinking of God as the stern old man, we can already think of something beyond that—and the same with the grandmother. Therefore these cannot be God, for you cannot think of anything as great as God.

Frustrated yet? Actually, part of the point is to be frustrated: you can't grasp God. It's our desire to grasp God that is criticized as idolatry. For some people, however, this frustration leads them, quickly or slowly, to give up. If something can't be grasped, why bother? We call this point of view agnosticism.

Agnosticism can be a fine place to be, since it refuses the characteristic temptation of idolatry, but it can run into problems. In our discussion of human acts in our first chapter we recognized that we act because we desire some object, and that ultimately we are looking for something that will satisfy us; we are looking for happiness. Agnostics don't stop acting; therefore, we still have to look at what is driving their action. They are still seeking happiness, just as much as anyone else. And so through the back door, idolatry will come back in. Agnostics place their trust in something. Something is supposed to make them happy.

What the great religions of the world have recognized is that our desire for happiness is transcendent—that is, it transcends any one thing in the world it goes beyond that. This desire to go beyond what is already there leads to many great and beautiful things. But it is also what leads us to worship idols. Once we recognize this transcendent desire, there are really only two options. We can decide that nothing will in fact satisfy us, and so the only way to live is to try to get rid of all our desires, let them go. This is the central doctrine of Buddhism and the philosophy of the Stoics. Or we can claim that there is something transcendent that will satisfy the desire, something beyond any one thing in the world. Judaism, Christianity, and Islam all take this option, and name this transcendent "God."

But that is abstract, and one of the great things about the Bible is that it is not abstract. The first and most important way it portrays the ungraspable God is by having God call people. The first full story of the Bible is the story of God's call to Abraham. "Now the Lord said to Abram, 'Go from your country and your kindred and your father's house to the land that I will show you. I will make of you a great nation, and I will bless you, and make your name great, so that you will be a blessing. I will bless those who bless you, and the one who curses you I will curse; and in you all the families of the earth shall be blessed'" (Gen. 12:1–3). And this story gets repeated over and over again. God calls Moses. God calls the Israelites out of Egypt. God calls the prophets to speak to Israel. And Jesus follows in this tradition. Perhaps his most characteristic tagline is, "Come, follow me."

What does all this calling tell us? It tells us that the opposite of grasping something is not ignoring it, but trusting it. We try to grasp things because we want control over them. We want to manipulate and change them. We try to grasp social problems because we want to change them. We try to grasp other people so we can make them do our bidding. And we want this control because we are afraid, we don't trust.

Because we don't trust what is other than ourselves, we tend to create idols in our own image. That is, we make gods that look suspiciously like us—or more powerful versions of us. We give ourselves to the worship of things because we believe that we can somehow control them. So if we are a nation of consumers, we will naturally place our trust in money, because we believe we can grasp and control money, and thereby control our own lives. And so it goes for any nation or culture.

The Bible, by contrast, tells us that we are created in God's image. Notice that this is the reverse of idolatry: it's not that God is like us, but that we are made like God. This, the Christian story teaches, is why we long for God to complete us. It is why, fundamentally, we love: our capacity to love is what makes us in the image of God. Love means an ability to trust, just as God does in creating the world and placing *free* humans in it, rather than trying always to grasp them and keep them in his control, like some cosmic puppeteer.

Here we can ask, "Did God screw up?" God made us to desire God, but we desire all these other things in place of God. What gives? Why do we trust in other things, including ourselves, rather than trusting in God? Here we need to zoom in on one of the "prequel" episodes in the biblical story: God's creation of the world and what happened next. We are familiar with the basic parameters of this story: God creates the whole world, and it is all good. God is God. Day is day. Night is night. Adam is Adam. God does not have to defeat any enemy in order to create the world; there is no original competition or battle. God is even portrayed as concerned about Adam's loneliness, and so creates a suitable companion for him. The story concludes, "And the man and his wife were both naked, and were not ashamed" (Gen. 2:25). The nakedness of the man and the woman indicates how safe, well-ordered, and noncompetitive creation was. Nothing needed to be hidden; no one needed to try to take advantage of anyone else. In short, by giving us the naked man and woman, the story hints that things now are not like they were then—which brings us to the serpent.

It is important to notice that the serpent is not presented as God's rival or enemy. Indeed, the text explicitly says that God made the serpent, and we know from earlier that God created everything good. There still is no competition. The serpent says to Eve, "Did God say, 'You shall not eat from any tree in the garden'?" (Gen. 3:1). We must examine this remark closely. First, the story has already told us that God has given every tree in the garden to them for food—except one. Through a question the serpent subtly suggests something about God: that God is holding something back from them, that they are naked before God but that God is keeping something from them. By overstating the case, the serpent suggests that God may not be looking out for them, but for himself. By suggesting this, the serpent leads Eve to overlook all the things she has been given, and look instead at the one thing that she has not been given. Suddenly, "all the trees except one" doesn't look generous and loving, but stingy. It is like the child whose life is filled with toys and good things, who then focuses on none of these things, but only on what he or she doesn't have, convinced that his or her parents, in withholding something, are being stingy and not looking out for the child's good.

But it takes one more line from the serpent to push Eve over the edge. God has said, "Of the tree of the knowledge of good and evil you shall not eat, for in the day that you eat of it you shall die" (Gen. 2:17). It will be bad for you. God says that he's not keeping this from them because he's being selfish, but for their own good. And so the serpent has to offer another suggestion: "You will not die; for God knows that when you eat of it your eyes will be opened, and you will be like God, knowing good and evil." And so Eve reconsiders—it *looks* like a good tree.

The serpent is not lying, at least not directly: their eyes are opened when they eat of the tree, and they are not killed instantly, though they die eventually. The serpent doesn't so much lie about the tree as get Eve to ignore the long-term picture and look at the immediate benefits.

What benefits? That they would become godlike. And here is exactly the issue. For some reason, Adam and Eve are not content with God's order. They decide they want to be gods themselves. They introduce competition. Notice how misguided this is: the serpent says they will know good from bad, but where exactly are these bad things? As yet there is none, for God has created everything good. There is in fact no inadequacy in the situation, but it is suggested that there is, that something is amiss. And so, sure enough, what do they do as soon as they eat of the tree? They make clothes for themselves, no longer able to be naked, no longer open to one another. They have taken God's position away and started creating themselves. They are in charge, "gods" of their lives.

And of course the whole thing is a disaster. They hear God strolling in the garden and they hide from him. No longer are they open to God either, but now they fear him. Once it becomes clear what happened, God asks why, and instead of saying, "We wanted to be like gods," Adam says, "The woman whom you gave to be with me, she gave me fruit from the tree, and I ate" (Gen. 3:12). He points a finger at her, saying, "Not me, her." A chapter earlier, she was "bone of my bones, and flesh of my flesh." Now he's disowning her. She, in turn, pushes the blame off on the serpent, claiming to have been tricked. The chapter ends by describing the "new world" they have created, where there are all sorts of competitions, between man and woman, between serpent and child, between man and the earth, between the serpent and other animals. Thus begins the competitive world, all because we want to be gods rather than be ourselves.

The story is subtle: we are in fact created in the image of God, and Catholicism has always taught that we have not entirely lost that image. But it ends up confused. We might say we have not entirely lost our ability to love, but we constantly confuse love with other things. For example, we confuse love with winning. This is the key point of the story that follows, of Adam and Eve's sons, Cain and Abel. God accepts Abel's offering, but not Cain's, and the story says that Cain greatly resented this: he was "very angry, and his countenance fell" (Gen. 4:5). God asks why he is resentful of Abel; he urges Cain simply to do good, and there will be no problem. Cain can learn to bring a better offering, and God will accept it. But instead of working on his own offering, Cain decides the problem is Abel. That's why he is resentful: it looks to him like a competition, where he "loses" because Abel has "won." So his solution is to kill his competitor. And like his parent, when God asks him what's up, he separates himself from his brother: "Am I my brother's keeper?" The irony here is rich: on the one hand, Cain has decided that he and his brother have to be considered together as competitors for God's affection, but, when God asks him about his brother, he intentionally separates himself from Abel, saying he has nothing to do with his brother. In his zeal for God's love, he can view his brother only as a rival to be eliminated.

We may also confuse love with possession. Another early biblical story that depicts the fallen condition of the world is the tower of Babel, where all the peoples of the world decide it is a great idea to build "a city, and a tower with its top in the heavens, and let us make a name for ourselves" (Gen. 11:4). They reach for the heavens for their own glory. A more graphic picture of trying to possess God could not be drawn. In this case the people

are united, but united in their rivalry with God. Love becomes a human ac-
complishment, meant to "make a name for ourselves." We see this problem
often, in so many spheres of our lives. Love becomes a matter of one person
possessing another, controlling another, having power over another. Why
do we do this? The scriptural narratives make it clear: it is ultimately a matter
of fear and rivalry. If we let the other person be free to love us, we fear what
that person will do. We fear he or she will "win" and we will "lose." And so we
try to take control. And we know how well that works.

Competition and possession thus become the disease Christianity has
called sin. This sin, this fundamental disruption of the peaceful order of relationships established by God, is always rooted in some form of idolatry,
some sort of an attempt to make ourselves into god. When we talk about
the disruption of peaceful order today, perhaps the gravest example comes
in the looming environmental crisis, which is surely a matter of our idolatry
of science and technology, and of the personal ends they serve. But we can
find this disruption everywhere. What the Jewish and Christian story helps
us see is that, in every example of disorder, conflict, and violence, there is
a fear-filled fleeing from God, a setting up of some sort of false object of
happiness that ends up running the show and ruining the show.

God's Story, Plotline 2: Jesus

We can summarize the above plotline by saying that the call out of idolatry
is in fact a call out of imitation love into real love, a call that requires a caller
worthy of such a trust. And so the second plotline is that God's love actually
appears in the midst of the series, and his name is Jesus.

Of course you will notice here that God is a clever storyteller: how interesting that, in a story about rejecting idolatry, God himself shows up in
a single, particular person! It would seem like an invitation to idolatry, until
we look at the stories of the person who actually showed up. We see a poor
man, a compassionate man, an intelligent speaker, a peacemaker, and ultimately a loser. We see someone who is born weak and homeless and who
dies naked and friendless. This is hardly a typical idol.

Some Christians, especially in recent times, have questioned this whole
claim about Jesus being God, claiming that it distorts the "humanity" of
Jesus. But early on, the tradition ratified a key piece of Christian doctrine,

maintaining that Jesus is properly fully God and fully human. Not half and half. Not a little bit of God within him. Not a part of God, but fully God. And that is no challenge to seeing him as fully human—except, of course, if you regard humanity and God as in some kind of competition, which is exactly the problem we call idolatry!

One can err here on the other side as well. One can imagine that Jesus' humanity was something like Clark Kent, a disguise concealing Superman's powers. The disciples might get a glimpse or two at the mighty Superman, it might flash on the screen with an occasional miracle, but it's basically hidden under the Clark Kent exterior. This is what the early church called docetism: a Jesus who is God, but at the expense of not being truly human, not really like us. And here again, we see the human-divine competition, resulting in pictures of some sort of Zeus-like Jesus that have absolutely no grounding in the biblical story.

Jesus is God coming and showing that we have nothing to fear from God's love. On the contrary, God's love is boundless and generous and for-giving. God does not seek our harm. God even loves his enemies. By saying that Jesus is fully God, the idols are meant to be put to sleep forever. The true God has been revealed. Not beyond Jesus somewhere, but right there, in Jesus' words and deeds, in Jesus personally. Jesus is the culmination of all of God's calls, for Jesus not only provides us with God's words, but also shows us in the flesh who God is.

By being God coming to meet us, Jesus promises true freedom to those who follow him. This is another tricky plot twist: freedom comes by attach-ing yourself to a person. This only makes sense if we recognize that, when we attach ourselves to idols, we think that we are in control, but in fact what happens is that we become enslaved to the idol. An example might be al-coholism, a sort of idolatry of drinking. The Japanese have a saying, "The man takes a drink, the drink takes a drink, the drink takes the man." At first, it appears that the idol is in our control, serving us to make our lives happy. But in reality the idol takes control of us. Jesus calls us to freedom because his love, God's love, is not competitive or possessive. It is not like the idols. It does not seek to enslave us.

And this is why Christians speak of Jesus as Savior: to be saved is to be rescued from something. Jesus saves us from sin—which, as we saw in the first plotline, is to be saved from our attachment to false gods, whom we try to control and manipulate, whom we fear, and with whom we compete. Salvation from sin does not mean that Jesus is a magic eraser, able to make the little black marks in God's book disappear. Salvation means being released from idolatry, from our false images of God, and receiving the boundless love of the one, true God.

God's Story, Plotline 3: Rejection and Conversion

So why in the world would anyone reject this? Isn't this the god everyone's been waiting for? Turns out, not at all. The biggest plot twist of all is that when God appears, we kill him. We utterly reject this gesture of love. When God is finally fully revealed, we do not rejoice and rush in, but we either try to destroy him or run away in fear. We get to see God's love, but we prefer our idols.

Why? First, because God's love calls us to reorder our lives and we don't want God to interfere. God's love must not be confused with storge. That is, by saying that God is love, the Bible is not saying God is "nice." God is not just standing on a street corner, smiling at everyone and saying, "Have a great day." That's the greeter at the big discount store, not Jesus. No one would kill this God. No doubt some in the history of Christianity will offer this sort of "love" from God. This is another idol, designed to keep God from interfering with our lives.

God's real, radical love, and the call to imitate it, will inevitably disrupt the way we live now, after "the Fall." In the first plotline, we saw that the tendency toward idolatry produces disorder and competition in the world. Therefore, if the world is to be truly oriented to God, the world needs to be reordered. And while the message of God's love may seem initially comforting and attractive, the reordering is not. We reject the good news of love because we cling to the order provided by our idols.

To understand this better we can zoom in on a particular episode from Jesus' ministry, the parable of the prodigal son. This story offers us both a representation of the disordered world and a picture of what that world will look like if it is changed. We know the basics of the story. A father has two sons, and one son asks for his share of the father's inheritance and then goes off and squanders it, while the other son stays at home, serving his father. Each son represents a particular form of idolatry.

Let's focus on the younger son. By asking for his inheritance, the son is basically saying, "Dad, I wish you were dead." The younger son is grasping, trying to take control of his world, even to the extent of pushing his father out of the way. He views his father as a barrier to his happiness in life. So long as his father lives, he cannot find fulfillment. The father, displaying the boundless love of God, the refusal of God to be drawn into our competitive games, grants his request. It would be easy enough to imagine the father becoming angry, saying to his son, "Are you kidding? Behave yourself, or maybe you won't get any inheritance at all." But that would simply reinforce the son's belief that the father is a barrier to him. So the father gives him what he wants.

The son "traveled to a distant country, and there he squandered his property in dissolute living" (Luke 15:13). This is a classic picture of worshipping false gods: seeking pleasure, power, and happiness completely apart from God, living for the moment. God gives us the gifts of life, and we go off thinking that our life is about these idols, these things that will bring us happiness. But as usual, they do not bring the younger son happiness. Instead he finds himself penniless, alone, reduced to feeding pigs. This is where we end up when we truly leave God's house and seek happiness somewhere else. It is fleeting, and it leaves us far less happy than we were before.

But then the son comes to his senses. He thinks to himself, "How many of my father's hired hands have bread enough and to spare, but here I am dying of hunger. I will get up and go to my father, and I will say to him, 'Father, I have sinned against heaven and before you; I am no longer worthy to be called your son; treat me like one of your hired hands'" (Luke 15:17–19). This is not simply a strategic move; note that he doesn't pretend that he can go back to the father and just present himself as the father's son. He has to recognize the truth: he has squandered his status, his sonship.

This is no easy task. How many people, even when confronted with the unhappiness of the life bought from idols, still cannot bear to give them up. They stay in the far country, convinced that somehow they can get back what they've lost. They never have the courage to get up and go back, with all the humiliation that entails. So part of the reason the world rejects God's love is that people simply prefer to stay with their idols in the far country and never come home. They can never say to themselves and others, "I was totally wrong and misguided about my life, and I squandered it."

But Jesus tells the story with "tax collectors and sinners" crowding around to hear (Luke 15:1). He tells them the story because the fate of the younger son, so long as he has the courage to get up and return to his father and confess his mistakes, is a happy one. The father welcomes him with open arms. The father freely gives him back his status as son. He throws a huge party.

Good news, right? Not everyone will think so. This brings us to the other son, the loyal one, the one who has stayed with his father all these years. He was hard at work when he learned of this celebration, and he "became angry and refused to go in" (Luke 15:28). Now it is the younger son who is in the house and the older one outside. The father again shows his love by coming out. The older son airs his grievance, "Listen! For all these years I have been working like a slave for you, and I have never disobeyed your command; yet you have never given me even a young goat so that I might celebrate with my friends. But when this son of yours came back, who has devoured your property with prostitutes, you killed the fattened calf for him" (Luke 15:29–30).

I grew up in a two-child household and I know what the older son is saying: "It's not fair!" He wants nothing to do with the generous love of the father, because it seems to him that, by loving the younger son, the father is somehow cheating the older son. Notice the theme of competition here. The older son, we might infer, enjoys his status as the obedient one. He has a good idea of what the younger son was up to after he left and he congratulates himself on being, in contrast, loyal and obedient. He is the good one. He is loved by the father—as opposed to that despicable black sheep. He is saying to himself exactly the opposite of what the younger son is saying: "I *deserve* to be called your son. I have earned it." We might even detect in his statement a bit of selfishness—he whines that despite his obedience the father has not given him anything.

The tax collectors and sinners were not the only ones listening to Jesus' story—the Pharisees and scribes were there, too, complaining in tones a bit like the older son. The problem with the older son is that he too buys into the competitive world. If the father loves the younger son, then somehow the older son has lost something. The older son can be the older son only if the younger son is the black sheep. His status seems worthless to him, his obedience worthless, if the younger son can be welcomed back. His faithfulness stems not from love for the father, but love for himself and a sense of superiority.

Here, in compact form, we see two sorts of idolatry, two ways in which we remain invested in the order based not on love but on competition. We may cling to false gods and not have the courage to get up and go back home. Or we may claim to cling to God, but follow a self-serving path that does not really represent the generous love of God, much less love for our neighbor. We like the competitive order the way it is, either because we think we are happy worshipping money or power or pleasure, and we won't admit that these things cannot satisfy us, or because we claim to love God, thereby reinforcing our own sense of superiority and respectability. And in either case, Jesus' words and work suggest that we must give up these idols in favor of the generous God who is love.

In the story of the two sons we see why the God of boundless, generous love is not a god that everyone will accept, much less follow. Indeed, we are more likely to reject this God, since we have invested ourselves in the present order, in idols, and built our own status and identity on these idols. In both cases we prefer the idols because they give us the illusion of control and victory in the competition. As we saw from the Cain and Abel episode, competition completely blocks real love. In this story at least the younger son finally realizes that his sense of control is an illusion. But as for the older son, who is trying to control the father's love not by wishing him dead but by fulfilling his every request in hope of reward, it is unclear at story's end whether he is willing to give up control, whether he is willing to allow the father's love to be out of his control, generous, not based on what anyone deserves.

Both sons need conversion. We usually associate conversion with changing churches or religions, but at a much deeper level conversion means a change of heart, a change of god, in the sense of giving up idols and receiving God. As we have already seen, this is not simple, because by worshipping an idol we shape ourselves into the image of the idol. False gods reflect our false selves, our competitive selves. They are images of our false selves: powerful, in control, having others dependent on us. And we have to keep up appearances. We have to think up excuses when we fail so people don't start doubting our power and control. It may not be much control, but at least it gives us some status. These false disguises protect us from others, but they also create fear and anger and greed in us. They are the false self. God's love only wishes that we turn away from this image and see ourselves as we are: hungry, weak, beautiful creatures, God's own beloved creations.

How do we identify the false self in action? There are several telltale signs. First, the false self will always be in competition with others, in a battle where the others need to be defeated—whether in a competitive race for maximum pleasure and social success like the younger son, or the resentful superiority of the older son. In such competition we feel that for us to win, others must be less than us. It is an identity supported by constant comparisons, constant seeking of reassurances that we are winning the game of popularity or love or fashion or wealth or even religious devotion.

The false self is also ultimately afraid. It is afraid of being shown to be less than what is advertised. Remember the classic scene in *The Wizard of Oz*, when Dorothy and her companions finally see "the great and powerful Oz," only to discover that the booming voice and terrifying face are mere projections of a small and ordinary man hiding behind a curtain. So it is in our world: we project an image of togetherness, competence, power, confidence, even perfection, hoping that others will see us in exactly these terms. But always we fear the discovery of our pains, our weaknesses, our ordinariness. The world often demands the false self in jobs, in classrooms, even in friendships and romantic relationships. We are afraid to be ourselves, the broken, needy creatures that we actually are.

The competition and fear of the false self combine to produce a sort of insatiable greed, a constant sense of dissatisfaction and discontentment. The false self can never be truly satisfied with what it has. We may search for greater and novel sensations or products, or we may become dissatisfied with the relationships we have, as if other people aren't good enough for us. Such symptoms manifest the basic emptiness that we feel when we are not rooted in the love of the one who created us.

This may seem a little dark, but it is an essential aspect of the plot. In all four Gospels Jesus predicts his passion and death. The disciples are never receptive to this message—indeed Judas thinks Jesus has gone mad and fallen into self-destructive behavior. The disciples are looking for Israel's messiah, and in Jesus, they believe they have found him. They have witnessed the miracles, the authoritative teaching, even the forgiveness of sins.

So they are expecting him to march into Jerusalem, cleanse the temple, and assume his place on David's throne to rule over Israel—as a messiah should.

Jesus instead tells them what will have to happen to him, and to them as well: "Those who want to save their life will lose it, and those who lose their life for my sake, and for the sake of the gospel, will save it" (Mark 8:35). This odd message means that there is a certain pattern by which God's kingdom succeeds, the pattern of cross and resurrection. Many spiritual writers have spoken of this as the pattern of the paschal mystery, of the great mystery of Good Friday and Easter, where Jesus triumphs as king not by overpowering his enemies, but by loving them to the end.

No Christian can avoid this paschal pattern, this dying of the false self in order to rise in God's love. This is not simply a pattern for martyrs, for those who actually give their lives for the sake of the gospel, but applies equally to us, throughout our lives. We start the Christian journey, more or less, in a fallen world, where our identity is constructed for us in all sorts of false, fear-filled, competitive, non-loving ways. The Christian journey is a journey of recognizing and dying to this false self, of being liberated from it in order to be able to love.

Henri Nouwen describes this transformation as a movement from the house of fear to the house of love (*Lifesigns*, 13–24). Nouwen's use of the term *house* is apt, for we are speaking of the space in which the self dwells and within which it understands itself. To live in the world is to live in the house of fear, a world preoccupied with countless questions of "what if," generated by our uncertainty about the future and our consequent desire to cling to things, people, or images that preserve our sense of identity. Nouwen insists that the Christian life entails a movement into the house of love, whose foundation is built on clinging to nothing but God's free and generous love for us. Since nothing can separate us from the love of God in Christ (Rom. 8:38–39), we no longer have anything to fear. We can live and love.

This invitation to conversion, then, is both attractive and extremely challenging. Attractive, because it is for love that we are made; challenging, because it requires genuine conversion, genuine death of the self-centered self. We might compare it to genuine romantic love, which also bears both attraction and challenge. To fall for someone is, in some way, to be drawn out of ourselves, to become attached to another, to be disrupted and lose control. Can we trust the other person? Should we fear him or her? Will he or she change us? All these calculations help us understand why the love of God in Jesus is rejected despite its boundless quality—or precisely because it is uncalculated and constant.

God's Story, Plotline 4: Reconciliation

We must add one more major plotline to complete our overview. Here we have a strange plot twist: why does this God, whose love is unlimited, constantly pick out special groups? The entire Old Testament is concerned with God's special love for his "chosen people," Israel; Jesus, in the New Testament, picks out particular disciples; these disciples then go on to form communities that we now call the church. This is a big reason why people reject the Christian story these days: God's choosiness, the claim that God has chosen Jesus, and Israel, and the church. But in the biblical text we cannot get away from this dynamic. God is not interested first and foremost in individuals, but in creating communities.

There are two ways to read this plotline. One option, running completely contrary to all three of the other plotlines, says that God chooses people that he thinks are better than others. That is, God's choosing creates a competitive order of winners and losers, good and bad people. Given what we have said about our tendencies to idolatry, it is no surprise that some people would interpret God's choosing in a similarly self-serving and competitive way.

But if the other plotlines are correct, this simply cannot be what God is doing. And the Bible takes great pains to show us that this interpretation is wrong. For example, there is a tendency in the Old Testament for Israel to understand its status as God's people in terms of political superiority: our God is the best, so we are the best. We see this too in the Gospels, when Jesus' disciples argue with one another over who is greatest. They assume that their status as disciples ensures that they will have the most power in the coming kingdom.

But in response to the apostles' claims of power, Jesus washes their feet. He does it himself, thereby setting the example that his status (as Lord) is not meant to place him above others, but to place him fundamentally at the service of others. The act of footwashing was so debasing that only the lowest of slaves were expected to do it. Peter exclaims, "You will never wash my feet," for he, understanding Jesus' lordship as superiority, cannot grasp why Jesus would demean himself this way. But Jesus explains that his status as teacher and master is ordered to lowly service, and that his action is an example of how the disciples should act toward one another. If there is to be competition, it should be competition to serve, not to take first place.

The same theme is echoed in the parable of the final judgment in Matthew's Gospel. This is sometimes read as referring to individuals, but the story says, "All the nations will be gathered before him" (Matt. 25:32). The story is about what it means, in the end, to be a successful nation. Then as now everyone assumed a successful nation was a powerful one, and given that Jesus is presented here as the great emperor over all nations, the nations might assume that their homage to the king will earn them favor. But of course Jesus gives a completely different criterion for judgment. To serve the king is to serve those who are most vulnerable: the sick, the hungry, the exiled, the stranger. Like the footwashing, the judgment involves a completely upside-down standard of judgment, in which status is seen as something to be used for service to others, rather than as a self-serving mark of power over others. The greatest nations will not be those that achieved the most power, but those that best cared for the vulnerable.

The other way—the correct way—to read this plotline is in line with the other three plotlines: God's choosiness is meant for reconciliation, healing, and service, not for furthering competition and power. But why would God use such means? Note that repair—what the Bible calls reconciliation—is not easy. Damage has been done. Patterns have been established. If there is to be real change, and not just nice words, there have to be alternative structures, alternative patterns of behavior, that reshape us toward love of God and neighbor. The alcoholic, for example, needs the Alcoholics Anonymous group, because the group provides a different set of structures and relationships than those in which the alcoholic was trapped before. In God's alternative the hungry are fed, sins are confessed, feet are washed. It is not a world of false, competitive selves. This alternative fellowship gives birth to a new way of living that reconciles what is broken.

When God chooses people he is establishing those real and visible alternatives. Think back to our first plotline: Abraham is called and promised that he will be the father of a great nation. As the story points out, God's purpose is not to show that Abraham is superior, but to "bless" the entire world. Israel is meant to be a distinctive light to the world, evincing God's noncompetitive, nonidolatrous alternative. Yes, God does take special care of Israel, but not because Israel is better or deserves special treatment. Rather, God does this in order that Israel can fulfill its mission of service to the world.

The same is true of Jesus and his disciples. In the Sermon on the Mount he says, "You are the light of the world. A city built on a hill cannot be hid. No one after lighting a lamp puts it under the bushel basket, but on the lampstand, and it gives light to all in the house. In the same way, let your light shine before others, so that they may see your good works and give glory to your Father in heaven" (Matt. 5:14–16). Two things need to be noted here. First, due to a peculiarity of the English language, the passage is often mistakenly applied to individuals. But, in this case, as in most cases in the Gospels, *you* is a plural—"Y'all are the light of the world." Jesus is not asking each individual to let his or her little light shine, but the disciples to shine as a community. Second, their good deeds are not for the purpose of glorifying themselves or earning God's rewards, but so that others might see them and glorify God—or to put it in our terms, that others might see the church and truly see God, as opposed to the idols in their own lives.

This fundamental mission is reinforced and given clarity in one of the most important documents of Vatican II, the constitution on the church. The document is called *Lumen Gentium*—the light to the nations—which already makes the point. The document begins by calling the church a sacrament, the sacrament of Christ to the world. We will talk more about this later, when we discuss the sacrament of marriage, but for now we need to see what this means in terms of the church. A sacrament is something that makes God's love visible and tangible. It is an effective sign of God's love, meaning a sign that actually puts into effect God's love in the world. The sacraments of the Church aren't there to tell us what we already know. Baptism is not just an elaborate welcome for a baby; the Eucharist is not just an odd meal together. Rather, the sacraments are there to show us what we forget, to show us an alternative to our ordinary ways. The church itself is one big sacrament: just as Christ makes God's love visible and makes it effective, so too the church is meant to do this for Christ.

In all these ways, the fourth plotline, that of God's constant electing or choosing particular communities, is God's way of reconciling the world, of working out the alternative to a world of competition and idolatry by offering a community structured around love and service and forgiveness. Now I hardly need to mention that this community regularly gets it wrong. Actually, this is a major element of the story, as we see from the constant failures of Israel and of the disciples. But God remains faithful, and God continues to make the offer of love. For the alternative would be for God to choose a people to carry out his work, watch them fail, and then say to them, "Forget you. I'm going to find someone better." That's exactly the competitive world. That's the father who does *not* welcome back the prodigal son. God never rejects his people. He persists in loving them so that they can become ever clearer on their mission to reconcile and love others.

For Discussion

1. What does *idolatry* mean? To what idols is this generation attached? How do these attachments create competition and possessiveness and conflict?

2. When you hear the words *God's love*, how do you imagine that love? How is that love active in your own life?

3. Where does your life fit in these plotlines? With what characters do you identify? What conversions might you need?

God's Story and Love Stories: Some Preliminary Observations

As we can see, this is not a story about another world. The plotline is not about how to get a heavenly reward for yourself—another idol that makes Christianity like an afterlife competition. It's about *this* world and how it works. It is a master narrative encompassing all of human history. It is a story that makes sense of our "vertical" longings—our individual desire for happiness, for God—and our "horizontal" relationships—the confused promises of love and hostility, of hope and fear, present in our world.

But what does any of this have to do with our sexual and romantic lives? The rest of the book will examine this question, looking at particular issues, actions, and choices, and seeing how they fit into the above storyline. As you probably know, the Bible has some specific things to say about sex, and we will look at those as we go along. But what it says is distorted if we do not have a sense of the overall story within which these teachings occur. Recall our TV show analogy: if you watch one epsiode where two main characters are viciously fighting, you might presume they are enemies, when it turns out that over the course of the series they are actually friends.

However, we are ready to draw some initial conclusions about the relationship of eros to the story of God's love and our idolatry. Specifically, we can identify three ideas that will stay with us throughout our more detailed study of sexual ethics, and we can do so in conversation with Pope Benedict XVI, whose first encyclical is all about love.

As we noted, modern cultural accounts of sexuality view Christianity as a repressive force. Pope Benedict acknowledges that many moderns (including Freud and Foucault) felt Christianity had essentially destroyed our experience of sexual love, of eros. Benedict grants that Christianity has not always been careful and accurate in describing human sexuality within the overall story of the Christian life. Christianity has often denigrated sexual love. In his first letter he set out to explain how the Christian proclamation that God is love deals with the question of eros. In response to the contentions of the moderns he offers a contemporary theological account of how sexual love is integrated into the overall Christian message of love.

Benedict begins by noting that the experience of love we most often associate with men and women "is neither planned nor willed but somehow imposes itself on human beings" (*God Is Love*, no. 3). This sort of love, eros, was celebrated by the ancient Greeks "as a kind of intoxication, the overpowering of reason by a 'divine madness' which tears man away from his finite existence and enables him, in the process of being overwhelmed by divine power, to experience supreme happiness" (*God Is Love*, no. 4). And when we think about it, it is precisely this seeming irresistibility that constitutes the "magic" of love.

However, Benedict argues, both Israel and Christianity—both the Old Testament and the New Testament—oppose such an idea of intoxicating ecstasy as a direct pathway to love. This implicitly opposes the *ars erotica* approach explained earlier by Foucault. Sexual pleasure by itself is not a route to ultimate happiness, and in fact requires significant restraint in order to be pursued well. The Old Testament opposes the orgies and prostitutes so often used to induce the erotic state in pagan religion, and the New Testament entirely omits the term *eros*, preferring *agape* and, occasionally, *philia*. Benedict explains, "An intoxicated and undisciplined eros, then, is not an ascent in 'ecstasy' toward the divine but a fall, a degradation of man. Evidently eros needs to be disciplined and purified if it is to provide not just fleeting pleasure but a certain foretaste of the pinnacle of our existence, of that beatitude for which our whole being yearns" (*God Is Love*, no. 4). As we have suggested, the question of ultimate purpose makes all the difference in discerning what we are to do. We can of course seek the fleeting pleasure of eros, but it will not be a route to the divine happiness we seek. Even at its best, such fleeting and temporary pleasure is not the overall goal of our lives.

Benedict here highlights the first of our three initial implications of the relationship between God's story and eros: we tend to make eros, romantic love, an idol, putting it in the place of God. This can happen with any human thing, but the powerful character of eros makes it especially liable to becoming an idol. This is a problem first because it obviously obscures our relationship to the true God revealed in Jesus. But just as importantly, making eros into an idol disappoints us, because we eventually discover that the false god cannot actually deliver the lasting happiness it promises. We remain unsatisfied, but keep trying: we go from person to person, and undergo medical treatments that will keep us "forever young." Eros as an idol is not just a problem of disappointment from those who play the field. If we overly romanticize marriage, expecting to find the perfect "soul mate" who will make us everlastingly happy, this also is idolatry. It is also inevitably disappointing, which may help explain the high rate of divorce in our culture.

Does this mean that Christianity rejects eros? No, says Benedict. If eros and agape were entirely opposed, "the essence of Christianity would be detached from the vital relations fundamental to human existence and would become a world apart, admirable perhaps, but decisively cut off from the complex fabric of human life" (*God Is Love*, no. 7). Christianity is not a "spirituality," a doctrine about purely spiritual things, but a religion of the incarnation, a love come into the world. Eros is "a primordial human phenomenon"

(*God Is Love*, no. 8), but such love must be purified if it is to fulfill its promise of happiness. This purification comes through its contact with agape, the selfless, "descending" love of God, which must be embodied in our love of neighbor in charity.

Without such purification eros becomes "a commodity, a mere 'thing' to be bought and sold" (*God Is Love*, no. 5). As with any buying and selling, eros becomes a great field of human competition. Instead of giving and receiving love freely, humans compete in the sexual marketplace. In such a setting there are inevitably winners and losers. Here we see a second connection to God's story: our idolatry of eros leads to competitive and destructive human relationships. The implications of this view are enormous. As Benedict notes, "The apparent exaltation of the body [in our culture] can quickly turn into a hatred of bodiliness" (*God Is Love*, no. 5). In order to be sexually competitive, people abuse and manipulate their bodies or invest in expensive surgery, pursuing an impossible body image that makes them hate themselves. Eros, instead of being a source of human peace and communion, becomes a competitive race where there is much psychological destruction. And sometimes the destruction is more than psychological: the losers in the race may fill themselves with pornography and perhaps try to seize by violence what they cannot win competitively.

This happens because such a competitive model of love actually amounts to self-love. For some, every romantic relationship is a new conquest or journey of the self. Others fall in love with people because of what they lack, hoping they will fill some emptiness that they can't fill themselves. But either way, eros doesn't really end up being about the other person; it looks like it is, but in fact it is all about us. And this is exactly the same dynamic that draws people to idols: either wanting to use the god to maintain control, or needing the god because the god has something we don't.

The alternative to such competition consists in placing eros within a larger framework of charity (caritas, agape) in the practice of the Christian life. Real human love is not seen most clearly in sexual (married) love, but in "union with God through sharing in Jesus' self-gift, sharing in his body and blood" (*God Is Love*, no. 13). Thus the Eucharist, and the ways in which Christians "embody" the eucharistic Christ in service to the world, are the real meaning of love. This is not a rejection of sexual love, but it is most certainly a relativization of it and of its importance in our lives. Eros is called to be part of something larger: the eucharistic love of Christ in the life of the church. Hence eros is not rejected, but placed within a larger narrative. This larger narrative is ultimately seen in the fourth plotline, the mission of showing and making Christ's love present in the world, which takes up the second half of Benedict's letter. This is the third connection: eros can be ordered to the overall purpose of serving God's mission in the world.

Much of the twentieth-century debate over sexual love has been a struggle to reposition it, not in the ancient narrative of seeking after the divine, but in some other narrative. Eros freed from the discipline of some kind of narrative becomes quite destructive. Freud especially recognizes this; he is no advocate of free love. He is trying to provide a scientifically compelling narrative for sexual love and desire that can order it, since he presumes that earlier narratives (Judaism and Christianity) are no longer plausible. What Foucault does is alert us to the simple fact that all this narrating is going on, and that in some sense we cannot really authenticate Freud's position or Christianity's position or any position. Rather, we can simply recognize how all these eros-narratives function in the service of powers that dominate our lives and our bodies. Thus, the question is not *whether* eros will be qualified and ordered by a larger story, but *which* story will order it. What power will it serve?

God's story indicates that our sexual lives are meant to serve Christ. Hence the Christian response to Freud and Foucault is Jesus—not simply Jesus' teachings, but Jesus himself as God's supreme act of self-giving love. Benedict notes that the commandment of love of God and neighbor "is not simply a matter of morality—something that could exist apart from and alongside faith in Christ and its sacramental reactualization" (*God Is Love*, no. 14). He means that our ability to follow the God story above, to love God and our neighbor, can come only as a prior gift from God. Even our ability to fall in love is a gift from God. In recognizing this, we can use the gift in service of the Giver.

This sense that love is not something we earn, this joyful receptivity followed by joyful giving, has echoes in our experience of eros itself. For example, one who discovers someone wonderful becomes suddenly eager to shower him or her with gifts. If asked, "What is this gift for?" the lover might respond, "Just for being you." The key here is to recognize all our gifts as ultimately created by God, given to us freely so that we may joyfully pass them on, to God and to others. The euphoric experience of falling in love, then, becomes an opportunity to receive a gift in order that we may give more of ourselves to others.

The theologian Hans Urs von Balthasar explains this further by pointing out how God's love is an overwhelming gift—if we recognize it rightly in Jesus, rather than reducing it to our human experiences of love. He agrees that in eros there can be "the acknowledgement of the pure grace of being loved," which is also intertwined with the lover's fulfillment in loving (*Love Alone Is Credible*, 54). He consistently compares this to our experience of beauty, not just of the opposite sex, but of art or music or nature. Beauty captivates us precisely because it exceeds our expectations, almost compelling our self-giving because of its grace-filled power.

These experiences of love and beauty can give us some idea of God's love, but only in a limited way. Indeed, they reveal to us how mistaken we have been about love and about ourselves. As Balthasar puts it,

> When man encounters the love of God in Christ, not only does he experience what genuine love is, but he is also confronted with the undeniable fact that he, a selfish sinner, does not himself possess true love. He experiences two things at once: the finitude of the creature's love and its sinful frigidity. To be sure, he does possess something of an "anticipation" of what love is; if he did not, he would not be able to make any sense of the sign of Jesus Christ. . . . All the same, man cannot come to a recognition of this sign on the basis of his "anticipation" without a radical conversion—a conversion not only of the heart, which must in the face of this love confess that it has failed to love until now, but also a conversion of thought, which must relearn what love after all really is. (*Love Alone*, 61)

Balthasar's claim recalls what we said about the need for some sort of conversion or movement from false to true self, a move provoked by an experience of the dazzling love seen in Jesus. Encountering God's love causes us to see how poor our love is—not entirely bad, but surely marked with all sorts of selfishness and limitation. We may glimpse God in the experience of falling in love, but we ought not mistake that glimpse for the real thing. As soon as we do, we deceive ourselves by pretending that our love is real love, when it is not. We can only be open to true love when we are open to

God's absolutely infinite and all-forgiving love, when we are responding to an experience of that love as the measure for all other loves.

For Discussion

1. Do the arguments of Benedict and Balthasar make sense? What is the experience that they indicate is found in Jesus? What image of Jesus is required to make sense of their claims?

2. How might we see this love present in our worldly relationships? How might we recognize that our love is distorted by competition and possession?

Conclusion

A look at these Christian theologians' musings on love, therefore, allows us to see some basic parameters for how eros in embedded within God's story. We see that the story depicts God working against our tendencies toward idolatry, and so eros must be recognized as a possible idol. We see that the story depicts a world full of idols as a world of destructive competition, ultimately rooted in competition for the idol's love, and so the idolatry of eros can lead to a destructive sexual competition between human beings. Finally, we see that God's gift of love to us in Jesus is ultimately meant not for ourselves but in order that we may use God's gifts in service to God and to others in love. And this is just as true of the gift of eros as it is of any other worldly good: it should be used for serving others and God, not simply for the self.

Now the three elements of the book's title—love, reason, and God's story—are all on the table. We have used the widest possible lens; next, with the tools and maps provided in these early chapters, we will begin to focus on particular actions and questions. For starters, let's get back to that question Lewis raised in the first chapter: can men and women really be friends?

4 God's Story and Sexuality

Some Initial Controversies

You'll recall in the first chapter C. S. Lewis's intriguing claim that men and woman cannot be friends. Either they remain acquaintances or fall in love. This claim never fails to spark a conversation. It persists in our culture—the classic narrative in recent times is the movie *When Harry Met Sally*.

Best-selling advice books like *Men Are from Mars, Women Are from Venus* talk about how men and women are just different. But of course, not everyone agrees. Aren't we all "free to be you and me," no matter whether we're men or women? These questions suggest that the problem of "men" and "women" needs to be addressed. What are we talking about when we use these words? Are men and women fundamentally different, and does this difference form at least one basic part of any true love story? How do different stories about gender fit within the culture and within God's story, especially when we add the question of sexual orientation to the mix?

Men and Women

In my classes, I always begin this topic by asking my students to break into gender-exclusive groups and create a top ten list of things they can't stand about the opposite sex. Here are some examples, just to get us thinking.

Men complain that women have selective memory and are constantly reminding guys how the guys have screwed up. They complain that women are obsessed with clothing and accessories. They suggest that women are constantly asking one-sided questions—like "How do I look?" or "Do I look fat in this?"—to which they don't want real answers. But some of the best responses are summed up in guy-created pithy phrases: "Guys hate to fight, girls think it's therapy," or, "Women have expectations of ESP," or, "If momma ain't happy, ain't nobody happy."

The women correspondingly complain that guys can't commit to a relationship—or even to specific plans for next Thursday night. Guys never care about how the relationship is going, or if there's a problem, they expect a fixit solution as if the relationship were a car. Guys have total double standards when it comes to appearances (women must look perfect, but it doesn't matter what guys look like). Guys are more enthusiastic about their video games than their relationships. And guys are only interested in sex.

Men and Women: Different or Not?

Obviously, the lists above contain a mixture of truth and exaggeration, of fair observation and unfair stereotyping. But note that students never hesitate to attempt this task, as if the question made no sense. Students don't need a book to tell them that men and women can seem like they are from different planets—it's already part of their stories. Moreover, while everyone finds humor in the exercise, the subsequent discussion shows that there is some truth there as well. The guys usually accept the girls' accusations readily, while the women inevitably protest those of the men—perhaps a little too vociferously. Meanwhile, a few students on both sides become troubled and gradually withdraw from the conversation, either in the single-sex groups or in the larger class debate. They are becoming aware that they don't quite fit the models being constructed by the majority. They realize that the lists reproduce the dynamics of certain men and women, not all men and women. Yet they too will laugh and nod at some of the observations.

These lists point us to the question with which we began our consideration of sexual love: are the supposed differences between men and women biological or natural truths, or just constructions of our society? Historically, the Christian tradition (along with others) has claimed that men and women are naturally different. In a provocative example from the fifth century, St. Augustine analyzed the description of woman as man's "helper" in Genesis. First he considers whether she is to be a fellow-worker, but dismisses that idea on the basis that the woman is weaker and so would not be helpful for shared work. Next he considers whether perhaps "helper" is meant as someone who provides companionship and support and counsel, but again demurs, noting that "for company and conversation, how much more agreeable it is for two male friends to dwell together than for a man and a woman!" Therefore, he concludes, the only thing for which man would need woman's help is for bearing children (*Literal Commentary on Genesis*, quoted in Clark, 28–29).

Of course, we shouldn't be too hard on Augustine, for he merely reflects the cultural assumptions that have dominated most of the history of Western culture. Western culture is patriarchal, meaning that it assumes that men are generally superior to women and therefore have a natural right to rule over women. Patriarchy does not mean that men simply despise women, or that they consider them subhuman or refuse contact with them. It simply means that women (like children or slaves) are a certain sort of human whose natural place in society is to be controlled by other humans.

Before we go on to critique this idea, we should recognize that it is not exactly absurd. Humans are in fact different from one another, and so a notion of radical equality is at first counterintuitive and counter to our experience. Factor in the results of long-term differences in socialization and it's easy to see why Augustine, basing his views on what he saw and heard in his day, might simply assume that some humans are naturally superior to others.

However, we have come to reject that fundamental notion today. The idea is not novel in Western history: Plato, the father of Western philosophy, articulated an ideal republic where men and women were equal. In relatively recent times it has become our dominant view. Even cultural conservatives in America now cite images of non-liberated women under strict Muslim regimes to incite the American people to support a crusade of liberation. Women certainly still experience the effects of sexism, and these should not be minimized, but in a sense, all of us are now feminists. Theologian Lisa Cahill notes that a feminist perspective is "simply a commitment to equal personal respect and equal social power for women and men." Male/female differences may remain, but cannot be used to justify "social systems which grant men in general authority and power over women in general" (*Sex, Gender, and Christian Ethics*, 1–2).

Gender Today

If the superiority of men over women has been rejected, does gender retain any meaning? After all, you can still claim men and women are naturally different without claiming one is naturally better than the other. That is, equality does not necessarily imply sameness. By comparison, the notion that humans can be classified into distinct races (and ranked as "superior" or "inferior") largely based on skin color or other biological attributes has been shown to be completely false, a myth created by modern science's mania to divide and classify. Is the same true of sex and gender?

Let us first clarify terms. *Sex* is often used in contemporary writing on this subject as referring to *biological sex*, the possession of certain genetic or bodily characteristics that identify males and females. *Gender* refers to the psychological and cultural assumptions that overlay these biological markers. Stereotypically, women's affection for shoes or men's affection for sports are marks of gender. Although in practice we know men who like shoes and women who like sports, culturally we construct identities in which certain things are associated with men and others with women. These are gender differences.

The question then becomes whether the markers of biological sex have any real connection to cultural constructions of gender. We can outline three competing views on this question. First, gender essentialists argue that there is a strong connection between biological differences and gender differences. These differences are more far-reaching than simply possessing different organs in certain places. I do not simply possess male sexual characteristics; rather, I *am* a man, and my maleness has meaning and significance beyond the biological. In recent years some strands of feminist thought have sided with gender essentialists by emphasizing the importance of womanhood, suggesting that women's ways of thinking and relating to others are fundamentally different from men's.

Opponents of this view have pointed out that it is notoriously difficult to separate out essential gender differences from culturally formed stereotypes. Assuming, for example, that women are more caring and men more hard-nosed, does this difference arise from biological sexual differences, or from the different ways they've been brought up, the different expectations placed upon them? Moreover, we find that assumed gender differences vary from culture to culture.

The second view, that of the cultural constructionists, maintains that gender is entirely constructed by cultures, usually in a way that serves the people already in power in a given culture. Women and men can only be fully equal if they are seen not to differ in any essential way. That does not mean that the idea of gender is false; it is a real factor in society. However, it is a construction of that society, not a simple description of the nature of men and women.

Curiously, Plato was close to the cultural constructionist position. In his ideal republic he sought the equality of men and women, but he recognized that the only way to achieve this end was to overcome each and every instance of distinction. Thus in his military, men and women were to live together, exercise together, and strip naked and wash together. Children were not to know their biological parents, but only the "parenthood" of the ideal city. A strict equality meant dumping any and all marks of distinction. To use a contemporary example, we would find it repugnant to find bathrooms differentiated by race, seeing such a thing as a sure sign of inequality; so why, Plato might ask, do we persist in differentiating bathrooms by sex?

While it may not be wise to make the question of gender hang on bathroom usage, this example shows that the tension between the essentialists and the cultural constructionists is not easily resolved. In a more pertinent example, a few years ago at a college in St. Paul, Minnesota, a debate began about whether the school policy regarding dorm rooms, which forced men to room with men and women to room with women, constituted discrimination against gay, lesbian, and particularly transsexual students. It was argued that the dorm room policy ran counter to the college's policy of tolerating and embracing a diversity of sexualities and sexual practices.

The debate is even more difficult regarding the more pressing questions we will be considering involving sexual acts, marriage, and children. Essentialists often stress the unique capacity of women to bear and nurse children as an explanation for other female characteristics; for example, that women are more relational and nurturing, and that they are moodier and less rational. Cultural constructionists will reply with fervor that such stereotypes define women by their baby-carrying capacity, without a comparable definition for men, leaving men wide latitude while constricting women. They note that throughout history men have made women responsible for having babies, while taking the rest for themselves. Most women in American society today would not agree that their personhood is essentially defined by their baby-making capacity.

Yet, essentialists will reply, it is still there. Among others, Joseph Ratzinger (before he became pope) argued that feminists' claim that "the idea that 'nature' has something to say is no longer admissible; man is to have the liberty to remodel himself at will. He is to be free from all of the prior givens of his existence. . . . In the end, it is a revolt against our creatureliness. Man is to be his own creator—a modern, new edition of the immemorial attempt to be God, to be like God" (*Salt of the Earth*, 133). Note that cultural constructionists support all sorts of social measures that try to eliminate this difference. Abortion is a key issue for many cultural constructionists not because they like the destruction of fetuses, but because they recognize that without the right to abortion—the right to choose—women are biologically handicapped in their pursuit of equality with men. They must have control over their biology. Similarly, birth control methods now treat menstruation and women's cycles largely as a disease to be cured. Ads for Seasonale, the birth control pill that can now eliminate three-quarters of women's periods, tout the "freedom" it offers. Some critics observe that *freedom* here means making women's bodies work more like men's. The birth control pill as well—so closely tied to women's liberation, particularly in regard to sexual acts—creates a comfortably unisex world by altering women's bodies to become more like men's in that they can engage in sexual acts without potential consequences.

An additional challenge arises from the fact that feminist thought is rather divided on this question. Some feminists have focused on the uniqueness of women's voices and the need for equality and inclusion precisely because of the different gifts and perspectives women bring to the table. The need to use feminine language and images for God, for example, or the objection to an all-male teaching authority are both arguments premised on the fact that something essential is missing if women are not included in the conversation. Later "third-wave" feminists have criticized this position on the grounds of its essentialism—also pointing out that the "women's perspective" claimed in earlier feminism generally meant white, upper-middle-class, college-educated women's perspective. For this group of feminists the equality and full inclusion of women are not needed to add a missing perspective, but simply because all should be equal and included.

Practical Consequences?

But what are the implications of these views? If we move from theory to everyday life, we often carry around both sorts of views in something of a mixture. We have male and female bathrooms, but unisex workplaces. We may oppose abortion, but support birth control. We think women should be able to do and be anything that men can, and yet we read books on relationships that tell us women are from Venus and men are from Mars. We put no restrictions on what people can wear, but our mass media target certain merchandise at women and other items at men. Gender alternately dominates and is rejected, from one moment to the next. Are we moving toward a unisex world or a world where gender is everything?

As we saw in Augustine above, the traditional line of argument attributes a good deal of significance to women as mothers. This is of course a biological point, but it is said to contain much more significance than this. However, this line of argument has been rendered problematic in contemporary culture—not because our culture rejects motherhood, but because it rejects defining a person's whole identity by reference to a single task or function. Note that males are given no corresponding definition, with the result that males can fulfill many different roles, while females are defined by one.

While the Catholic tradition has often been infected by patriarchal views of women's inferiority, recent official teaching has turned to the notion of complementarity, meaning that men and women complement each other in their differences. Thus Catholic teaching affirms the essential difference between men and women while denying that the difference can be formulated in terms of "better" or "worse," or identified with a single act or function. Indeed, complementarity suggests a sort of mutual dependence of each sex on the other. Complementarity has obvious implications for the developing positive view of marriage in the Catholic tradition. Whereas Augustine suggests that marriage, as a relationship, is inferior to friendship between males, supporters of complementarity (particularly Pope John Paul II) argue that the unique and exalted quality of marriage is found in its communion-in-difference, not only on the sexual or reproductive level, but in terms of the whole relationship.

Male-female difference might be described as a mystery—not meaning that it's a puzzle to be solved or a morass that we can't understand, but that there is a depth to the reality, a depth that beckons us to enter into it and participate in it. Christians have long held that God is a mystery. We can't know everything about God, because God is a reality whose depths are impossible to exhaust. We aren't called to figure God out. We are called to live in a relationship with God.

In this sense we can also say that people, all people, are mysteries. They possess a depth, a freedom, which is unique and inexhaustible. Things wear out, but people hold the promise of not wearing out. Loving human relationships are alive in a certain way, growing and developing, allowing us to enter into the unanticipated and unknown. To say something is a mystery is, in one sense, to reverence it, to recognize that we can neither explain it nor eliminate it. Only participation in the mystery can satisfy.

Do the particular relationships of men and women have mystery in this sense, or is something else going on? We can approach this question by asking if we would lose anything if we actually achieved a comfortably unisex world. Such a world might not include sharing bathrooms, but it would include an accessible and convenient control by women over their reproductive capacities, a freedom of sexual interaction where power was equally recognized by each party, an elimination of gender-based institutions and marketing, a casual cooperation in any and all tasks, and a sense of friend-ship that did not differentiate between male and female friends.

And yet, the Catholic tradition suggests, much would indeed be lost. In the relationship of man and woman we have something unique, something different from ordinary human relationships. Surely a part of that mystery has to do with the possibilities this pairing has for generating new life. But could we go further? Would we agree that the meeting of man and woman opens up possibilities for growth and meaning, even before children come on the scene? Would a comfortably unisex world kill the mystery of this relationship?

Wendell Berry goes beyond reproductive biology in his essay, "Sex, Economy, Freedom, and Community," to suggest that the removal of mys-tery and fascination from opposite sex relations results in the loss of our appreciation for the richness of the natural world in all its possibility and complexity. He points to Portia, the main character in Shakespeare's *The Merchant of Venice*; this woman is perhaps stronger and smarter than the male characters of the play, yet even when she disguises herself as a man to accomplish a task, she never ceases to recognize that this is not her real identity. Berry suggests that our fascination with genitalia and midriffs speaks to our sexual functionalism and failure to grasp the mystery. He notes that in Shakespeare the meeting of the sexes occurs through the eyes, which reveal depth and mystery and life.

Developing the promise of this mystery in today's world can be chal-lenging. Like claims about other mysteries, such as Jesus' divinity and the Trinity, most speech is negative: don't say this, or don't say that. God is a mystery not because we can't say anything about God, but because the goal is to participate in it, not to define it and grasp it like an idol we can control. The same goes for gender. On the one side, don't say gender is completely a human construction. On the other, don't harden the differ-ences by mistaking cultural constructions for a precise definition of the mys-tery. Somewhere between these boundaries we have room to acknowledge and learn by experience what it means to share in the mystery of the gifts another can give us.

Thus, when we recognize something real about gender differences we are not thereby required to accept all the ways our culture twists and abuses those differences. Clearly not everything our culture teaches about gender differences should be treated as reverent mystery. On the contrary, some of it should be treated as utter nonsense. Some of the supposed differences—like women's "irrationality" or men's "emotional coldness"—are simply wrong. And, unfortunately, some forms of defining these differences lead not simply to foolishness, but violence. The essential reality of gender difference does not rule out the important critique offered by cultural constructionists. Gender distinctions should be viewed with some suspicion, for they are often used to destroy and oppress. But perhaps we might characterize this critique differently. Instead of eliminating difference, it might be better to distinguish between creative and destructive difference. The problem with a comfortably unisex world, we might say, is that it fails to use all the colors at its disposal in painting the world.

For Discussion

1. Can women and men be essentially different but still be considered equal? Why or why not?

2. How can we identify culturally constructed gender differences versus essential maleness and femaleness?

3. What makes persons of the opposite sex mysterious to you? What is your attitude toward that mystery?

Gender and Sexual Attraction

A further complication of this question today has to do with same-sex sexual attraction. The above discussion, insofar as it refrains from reducing male-female differences to a matter of making babies, would seem to point toward some sort of deep attraction in describing the mystery of this relationship, as suggested in Genesis 2. But some people experience deep attraction for members of the same sex. How does homosexuality fit into a consideration of sex and gender?

The contemporary experience of homosexuality has introduced the issue of sexual orientation. There is much debate about what sexual orientation is and how it comes to be, but more and more people are coming to recognize that people experience their sexual orientation as a deep-seated reality that they discover, rather than as something they choose for themselves.

What Is Sexual Orientation?

Like the notion of sexuality itself, the ideas of homosexuality and sexual orientation are modern constructions. That is not to say that the phenomenon of same-sex attraction and sexual relationships is modern. Homosexual relations are known to have existed in a variety of forms in many, perhaps most, cultures. A well-known example is the common practice of pederasty in ancient Greece, wherein men in their twenties formed quasi-mentoring relationships with young boys. Such relationships were an accepted form of initiation into the adult male world: the older man enjoyed some hero-worship, and the younger gained knowledge and training. However, few societies have practiced what David Greenberg calls egalitarian homosexuality, a socially accepted practice of long-term sexual relationships between adult men of relatively equal social status (*The Construction of Homosexuality*, 66–73).

In European culture, the longstanding rejection of homosexuality has roots in Judaism and Christianity, both of which displayed increasing hostility toward homosexuality as the tradition developed. Though there is some debate on this point, it would appear that homosexuality in the West has been rejected ever since Christianity became the official religion in the fourth century, not least because of the longstanding Christian belief that all sexual activity belongs within marriage and should be for the sake of procreation. That is, Christianity's hostility toward what was called sodomy is of a piece with its rejection of all sexual activity outside marriage.

Greenberg's survey of sixth- through tenth-century penitential literature (manuals that specify penances for specific sins) shows that homosexual acts did not receive excessive attention compared to other sexual sins. However, the existence of such prohibitions proved volatile when combined with the rise of modern medical science.

As noted above, modern science is interested in the careful classification of all phenomena. In the late nineteenth century medical science began to speak about the phenomenon of homosexuality largely in terms of disease. Medicine is, as Greenberg puts it, "of necessity a normative science" (403). It deals with diagnosing health and lack thereof. Just as the nineteenth century offered the label *alcoholism* to what had previously been thought of as drunkenness, so it offered *homosexuality* as a diagnosis of sodomy. By offering such diagnoses, medical science also advanced claims to treat such diseases, extending its authority often at the expense of civil and religious authorities.

Throughout much of the twentieth century, psychologists treated homosexuality as a sort of personality disorder, a maladjusted sexuality. They drew largely on Freud's theories to define normality and deviance, but also cited laws and religious prohibitions. But in 1973 the American Psychology Association voted to withdraw homosexuality from its official list of mental illnesses. Gay liberation movements became prominent in Western societies, demanding not only civil rights but also "a rethinking of human sexuality and its place in society" (Greenberg, 458). The debate over gay marriage is a culmination of such developments.

Yet the debate over classification continues, most notably among advocates of gay rights. A key question remains whether sexual orientation is biological or socially constructed. The discussion generally assumes that homosexuality—same-sex attraction—is natural, meaning that a person is homosexual by nature and not by choice. Common sayings such as "10% of the population is homosexual," or, "God made me this way" reflect this view. The Gallup Poll documents an increase in the number of people who believe that homosexuality is an inborn (versus acquired) tendency, from 13% inborn/56% acquired in 1977 to 38% inborn/44% acquired in 2003.

However, evidence for the biological basis of same-sex attraction is not strong. Law professor and philosopher Edward Stein, in his study *The Mismeasure of Desire*, carefully articulates certain distinctions. First he addresses the distinction between "male" and "female" and the bases on which we are able to classify persons into one or the other category. Roughly, there are three standard ways: by sex chromosomes (XX versus XY), by genitalia, and by secondary sex characteristics (e.g., facial hair, breasts, and menstruation). While these classifications work for most persons, we are aware of cases where any of these three are in some sense mismatched or do not fit the strict classificatory scheme. He further notes (as we have) that psychological and cultural roles for males and females may go far beyond biological differences.

Stein observes that sexual orientation is, however, a different category. While it is largely *related* to the sex/gender of person to whom one is attracted or with whom one has sex, it is obviously not *determined* by sex-gender. He explains three standard ways of classifying sexual orientation: the behaviorist view (classification based simply on the gender of one's sexual partners), the self-identification view (classification based on one's own designation), and the dispositional view (classification based on underlying desires and fantasies, which may or may not be practiced). Sexual orientation, unlike sex-gender, is now ordinarily understood to be about the third—about the sort of persons to whom one is attracted—although Stein cautions that (1) sexual orientation need not be any different than a predilection for certain sorts of sex (e.g., outdoors) or persons (e.g., brunettes versus blondes); (2) sexual orientation is an even trickier category than sex-gender, and likely operates on a continuum rather than as a strict dualism; and (3) the scientific argument for a sexual orientation biologically determined at birth is "deeply flawed." On the final point, he bluntly concludes that "we do not have strong evidence to support the commonly held belief that sexual orientations are natural human kinds" (346).

Stein further cautions that the political use of the biological argument for gay rights could backfire. He argues that the issue of orientation need not be seen as any more important than mixed biological-behavioral factors contributing to certain sleep styles (e.g., on one's back or side) or to certain styles of the opposite sex (e.g., hair color). He asserts, "It is the choices [gays and lesbians] make about how to live their lives, not the origins of their sexual desires, that are most important for lesbian and gay rights. Regardless of whether sexual orientations are directly chosen, indirectly chosen, or not chosen at all . . . , people choose with whom they have sex, people choose whether to be open about their sexual orientations, people choose whether or not to enter romantic relationships, and whether or not to build families" (347). Stein advises a focus on sexual choice, sexual freedom, rather than on biology.

Indeed, the strong biological argument makes strange bedfellows with the general tone of late twentieth-century discourse about sexuality as constructed. While strong arguments about the biological basis of *gender* are being discarded, strong arguments about the biological basis of *sexual orientation* are being championed. Thus many in the academic discourse on homosexuality have turned from biology to argue for the socially constructed character of all sexualities. The academic discourse about homosexuality—sometimes called queer theory—engages the language used to construct sexuality. Writing on lesbian and gay theory is often intentionally obscure, pushing and twisting language in new ways in order to suggest how the recognition and affirmation of homosexual love force us to change our language about sexuality in radical ways.

One example is an essay on lesbian desire written by theorist Elizabeth Grosz. Grosz states that she is not interested in the origins of lesbian desire, as if these mattered or were even possible to find. Rather, she is interested in what lesbian desire can do. She is interested in its creative possibilities, the possibilities of bodily pleasure, relationship, even love, opened up by recognizing and "playing with" lesbian desire.

> Becoming lesbian, if I can put it this way, is thus no longer or not simply a question of being lesbian. . . . The question is not am I—or are you—a lesbian, but what kinds of lesbian connections, what kinds of lesbian-machine, we invest our time, energy, and bodies in, what kinds of sexualities we invest ourselves in, with what other kinds of bodies, with what bodies of our own, and with what effects? What is it that together, in parts and bits and interconnections, we can make that is new, that is exploratory, that opens up further spaces, induces further intensities, speeds up, enervates, and proliferates production (production of the body, production of the world)? ("Refiguring Lesbian Desire," 278)

Grosz's comments illustrate not only the way in which these theorists challenge and bend language, but also the extent to which any sort of sexual "nature"—even a sense of natural desire or orientation—is no longer the important question. The existence of sexual nature is dead; what we have left is sexual energy that we can direct in creative ways. What constitutes good sexual desire is its creativity. It has no inherent purpose other than exploration and intensification of emotions and bodily prowess. Though she does not use the old-fashioned word *pleasure* here, it would seem to be the heart of her argument.

But it is precisely the recognition of how the phenomenon of homosexuality forces radical changes in our speech about sexuality that has led to its strong rejection in some quarters of Christianity, including the official teaching of the Catholic tradition. With the above context in mind, let us turn to the question of homosexuality as considered within the larger narrative of God's story. Specifically, how can a religion based on love be against the love of two (homosexual) people?

The Bible and Homosexuality

Start debating homosexuality among Christians and you are sure to hear two things. Some will say that the Bible condemns homosexuality. Others will assert that the biblical teachings are ambiguous, related to other teachings that we now disregard, and have been taken out of context.

The Bible says almost nothing directly about homosexuality. As noted above, sexuality and sexual orientation are modern constructs; no biblical author could have conceived of a sexual orientation, much less had a view for or against one. The Bible is a complex, historically varied collection of texts by many different authors and often expresses varied or ambiguous views. In this matter we will have an especially difficult time knowing how to apply its brief remarks, which never directly address the issue. As we will see, the Bible has a good deal to say about divorce, but even there it seems to say different things in different places and assumes a different concept of marriage from ours. That certainly does not mean that we should ignore what the Bible has to say about divorce, but it does require some interpretation. On the issue of homosexuality, however, the problem is not interpretation. The problem is that we never get a direct discussion of homosexuality at all.

The Bible does, of course, refer to various acts that we would term homosexual. Israel's priestly code condemns a male lying "with a male as with a woman" as an "abomination" (Lev. 18:22). It seems that God's destruction of the city of Sodom was understood, both by the Israelites and by early Christians (Jude 7), to be due at least partly to its homosexual practices. Paul almost casually cites the sexual desire of men for other men as evidence of the fallen condition of the world (Rom. 1:26–27). In addition, the writings of Paul and his disciples contain lists of people who will not "inherit" the kingdom of God, and these lists include various terms that seem to refer to homosexuals.

Now there is *something* here. But let's recognize the limited use of these biblical texts. For one thing, the biblical authors certainly had no idea of long-term, committed, same-sex relationships. Whenever they saw homosexual acts being performed, it was always in some problematic context. The Israelites were surrounded by cultures in which homosexual acts were part of ceremonies worshipping pagan gods. Paul's remarks were addressed to Greek culture, where homosexual acts usually occurred either in the context of promiscuous orgies or were a matter of older men taking advantage of young boys. Such acts quite understandably seemed to Paul to demonstrate the fallen state of the world. I think we can see why the biblical authors might view homosexual acts negatively.

Moreover, lacking the concept of sexual orientation, the biblical authors undoubtedly assumed that the people who performed these acts were acting completely contrary to their basic human impulses. That is to say, the biblical authors looked at homosexual acts the way we might look at people who are bulimic or anorexic. We know these people have a problem because they are acting against their basic human desire to feed and nourish themselves. Similarly Paul and others most likely assumed that those they saw performing same-sex sexual acts were acting contrary to their own natural passions, and so must be sick in some way. Their seeming abnormality was taken as a sign of a twisted world, just as anorexics are a sign of the unrealistic body images so prevalent in our culture.

However, the discussion increasingly turns not to these texts condemning homosexuality per se, but to fundamental texts indicating the importance of male-female marriage. The Genesis creation narratives, as we have seen, attribute a significance to male-female difference that they do not indicate about other forms of human difference. Throughout God's story, this male-female union is central. The Bible is not simply a history of war heroes or prophets. It is the history of a people, and its key movements are all bound up in the male-female relationship. Homosexual actions are rejected in scripture (Rom. 1:26–27 in particular) for the same reason we would reject proposals to create a world where it is always night or where it is always day.

This would reflect a disorder, an intervention in God's design, which would inevitably create disharmony. It would be a sort of idolatry.

Homosexuality and the Christian Tradition Today

Recent discussion has questioned this assessment of the natural order, particularly in light of the potential that sexual orientation is an inborn characteristic. *The Church and the Homosexual*, published in 1976 by John J. McNeill (a Jesuit priest and psychologist), crystallized a debate already arising within Catholic and broader Christian circles about both the morality of homosexuality and the pastoral character of the ministry of the church to homosexuals. McNeill's highly readable book argued for a reevaluation of homosexuality based on two factors: (1) the detrimental effects of the church's condemnation on homosexuals' self-image and sense of dignity and (2) change in Catholic sexual ethics highlighting the interpersonal value of sexual relationships over the traditional emphasis on procreation. McNeill did not see his relatively modest arguments as disruptive of the tradition as a whole. He suggested that movements in the tradition itself (the recognition of the dignity of all people and the recognition of the interpersonal value of sexual relationships) allow for an expansion of what counts as good sexual action. He was less concerned with fundamental issues of gender, and more with the pastoral care of homosexual Christians in loving and committed relationships.

More recent work on homosexuality, however, has focused on the question of gender. Such work—based on New Testament arguments about ways that the coming of Jesus destabilizes gender—has proposed that gay and lesbian relationships offer a distinctive witness within the Christian community to the overcoming of the separation imposed by male and female differences. British theologian Elizabeth Stuart follows the Foucaultian path by arguing that neither gender nor desire are innate, but come about through performing scripts society hands to us. The nonnatural character of desire is exposed precisely by gender-bending images such as drag queens and butch lesbians. The immediate connection to theology is not evident to most, but Stuart reminds us that Christianity itself has a long tradition of gender-bending scripts, such as giving nuns male names or assigning the title *father* to a figure who performs fundamentally maternal tasks (such as washing and feeding) for the community. Stuart also cites the tradition of mystical literature, as well as the overall gendering of the church as female, for both women and men are destined to be "the bride of Christ."

Conservative theologians and the magisterial teaching authority have taken a different view. In 1976, in the context of a larger discussion of sexual ethics, the Congregation for the Doctrine of the Faith stated simply, "Sexual relations between persons of the same sex are necessarily and essentially disordered according to the objective moral order" (*Declaration on Certain Questions of Sexual Ethics*, no. 8). Even in light of orientation, which provides a perspective for the *subjective* culpability of homosexual acts, the acts remain *objectively* disordered—put simply, contrary to the basic order of creation in which males and females are made for each other sexually. Then, in 1986, the Congregation (headed by the future Pope Benedict XVI) issued a specific document addressing the question. It is worthwhile to include an extended quotation from this document.

> Providing a basic plan for understanding this entire discussion of homosexuality is the theology of creation we find in Genesis. God, in his infinite wisdom and love, brings into existence all of reality as a reflection of his goodness. He fashions mankind, male and female, in his own image and likeness. Human beings, therefore, are nothing less than the work of God himself; and in the complementarity of the sexes, they are called to reflect the inner unity of the Creator. They do this in a striking way in their cooperation with him in the transmission of life by a mutual donation of the self to the other. To choose someone of the same sex for one's sexual activity is to annul the rich symbolism and meaning, not to mention the goals, of the Creator's sexual design. Homosexual activity is not a complementary union, able to transmit life; and so it thwarts the call to a life of that form of self-giving which the Gospel says is the essence of Christian living. This does not mean that homosexual persons are not often generous and giving of themselves; but when they engage in homosexual activity they confirm within themselves a disordered sexual inclination which is essentially self-indulgent. (nos. 6–7)

The argument here disputes the claim about Christianity disrupting standard scripts. What is wrong with homosexual acts, the Congregation argues, is precisely that it disrupts "the rich symbolism . . . of the Creator's sexual design." The script offered in Genesis and reinforced by natural law reasoning, about men and women as fundamentally complementary, cannot tolerate the practice of homosexual sex. Note that the Congregation does not deny the generosity and self-giving that is present between homosexual partners. Rather, it denies that homosexual sex acts express the self-giving that heterosexual sex can express. They cannot express the essence of sexual love because they are not directed to the proper object of sexual love, a member of the other sex. Thus homosexual acts, even within a loving relationship, are "essentially self-indulgent."

For many, the teachings seem incoherent, as if the CDF wants it both ways. Understanding the position of these and other documents hinges on the distinction made between homosexual orientation and homosexual acts. The orientation itself is not sinful, although it is "objectively disordered." This mysterious phrase has recently gained even greater prominence because of its seeming amplification in the 2005 letter on gays in the priesthood, and therefore needs to be explained further. In technical terms, "objectively disordered" means that, considered in the abstract rather than subjectively, same-sex attraction is a desire incapable of being ordered to the purposes of human sexuality and to the purposes of human happiness generally. This is so because men and women, by nature, are created for one another. "Objectively disordered" is not a medical term but a moral one, in the sense just described. Yet no such condition could be "objectively sinful" unless it is *chosen*. As noted in the first chapter, ethics is concerned with human actions that are chosen or intended, and the existence of such desires or such attraction is rarely, if ever, chosen. Hence it cannot be wrong (or right). It can only be described in the abstract terminology "objectively disordered," indicating that such attraction cannot aim at the purposes sexual attraction is supposed to pursue.

However, the church continues to reject absolutely all same-sex sexual acts, which presumably are freely chosen, just as heterosexual acts are freely chosen by heterosexuals. The church's position in this regard has been questioned in a number of ways. First, if homosexual acts are to be rejected because they are not procreative, what about infertile couples or couples past childbearing age? Should such couples not marry or not engage in sexual acts, since they know that such acts cannot be procreative? Since the church marries infertile couples and older couples, it seems inconsistent to claim that homosexual couples cannot present themselves to the church for marriage because they aren't capable of bearing children. The church is thus forced to claim that even the sexual acts of infertile couples are "objectively" open to procreation, even if there are particular concrete factors that prevent procreation. The Bible offers many examples of pregnancies in couples thought to be sterile or past childbearing age. However, since homosexual couples do not *choose* that their sexual acts be nonprocreative, they may still fit the analogy of infertile or elderly couples.

The traditional position seems in fact to hang on the question, previously discussed in this chapter, of whether there is a unique maleness and femaleness, such that the partners in a marriage must be of the opposite sex. The entire argument rests on the claim of "objective disorder," which itself rests on the further claim about the essential character of humanity as sexually ordered according to gender. If maleness and femaleness are not part of the essential order of creation, there can be little objection to homosexual acts per se.

Reflection for Debate on Sexual Orientation

This debate, probably more than any other we address in this book, is deeply unresolved. Outside Catholicism, this issue is literally tearing apart a number of Protestant churches. Why is the debate so heated? The other issues we will come across mostly involve particular *acts*, and they are important, but they do not cross into *personal identity* the way this issue does. Because the teaching verges on criticism of personal identity, it is often perceived as deeply at odds with a compassionate, loving Jesus who welcomes the outcast. Even classroom discussions of this issue have proved difficult, for disagreements often turn personal. Some find it is like trying to have a debate between white supremacists and civil rights advocates. For others the whole subject is distasteful. It is difficult to get to the actual arguments, as I have tried to do in this text. But it is necessary to offer some evaluation, however tentative, so take this as a starting point for further discussion, not a conclusion.

Some have argued that we ought to understand homosexual orientation as analogous to alcoholism. Alcoholism is a genetic disposition to certain actions. It is of course not a good disposition, because the actions to which it leads are destructive to self and others. Hence, alcoholics have to avoid certain actions that are all right for others.

The analogy has proved popular for a number of reasons. First, it supports that idea that just because we have genetic predispositions to certain behaviors does not automatically make it good to pursue those inclinations. Second, it deals with a behavior—drinking—that has often been treated as analogous to our inclinations toward sex. Third, it provides an analogy for telling homosexuals not to engage in a behavior that is permissible for others—one may legitimately urge alcoholics not to drink while maintaining that drinking alcohol is fine for most people.

However, the analogy has been vigorously challenged, and rightly so. For one thing, alcoholics who drink produce destructive consequences, while it is not at all clear that homosexuals who engage in homosexual acts and relationships produce destructive consequences—in fact, they seem to produce some benefits. The question of whether certain predispositions should be acted upon or not should be resolved by observing their consequences; judge behaviors by their fruits.

Personally, I am not a fan of resting ethical evaluation on consequences, due to the difficulty of knowing how to specify and weigh them. Therefore I would like to propose a different way in which the alcoholism analogy fails. The predisposition towards alcoholism means that alcoholics are not able to drink responsibly. They tend to drink to excess and are prone to becoming dependent on drinking. It is an addiction problem. It is known that different people have different predispositions toward alcohol or a powerful drug like nicotine. While usage levels and cultural formation affect the question of whether one is "addicted" to alcohol or cigarettes, it also seems to be the case that some people have genetic predispositions to certain addictions. Some people can drink large amounts and not be alcoholics, while others may not drink much, but fall into the cycle of addiction.

If the analogy with homosexuality worked, we would expect homosexuals to be "sexually addicted." We would have to say that they have an appetite which, when exercised, cannot be exercised in appropriate moderation, but is always tending toward an excess that is destructive to self and others. Some people try to argue that this is the case and associate homosexuality with promiscuity. But this claim is untenable: homosexuals are not necessarily promiscuous. It may be the case that a certain cultural usage leads easily to excess, but now that homosexuals can live in the mainstream of society, it simply cannot be held that homosexuality and promiscuity go together. Homosexuals can practice chastity and engage in reasonable control of their sexual desires; if they could not, there would be no long-term, stable, monogamous homosexual relationships. But there clearly are.

If the alcoholism analogy fails, are we left with a neutral stance about sexual orientation? As we have seen, one author compares sexual orientation to sleep orientation: we are genetically disposed to sleep in certain positions and for certain lengths of time, all different, but no one attaches normative significance to one's sleep orientation. However, it seems to me that such analogies are also weak, regardless of which side of the issue you embrace, because sexual orientation is so much more important than such matters. How then to understand it?

The sleep orientation analogy points us back to an earlier issue in this chapter: the mystery of God's creating humans as male and female. The Bible does not give any weight to skin color, sleep orientation, right- or left-handedness, or any other natural characteristic. But it does to man and woman. It does to the extent that the man, on seeing the woman, cries out, "This at last is bone of my bones and flesh of my flesh" (Gen. 2:23). Can we still see this mystery if maleness and femaleness are no longer in the story?

For Discussion

1. What is your take on these analogies? Consider both sides: what weaknesses can you see in these arguments?

2. Regardless of the Catholic teaching against homosexual acts, the tradition teaches that homosexual *persons* are to be given all the respect and love deserved by all people. How do you think this could be done? *Can* it be done?

Conclusion and Transition

This chapter fills out conceptions of men and women necessary to understanding how love stories work, both in the culture at large and within the Christian story. Now—finally—we can get to actions. Most actions we take in society are parts of practices. According to philosopher Alasdair MacIntyre, *practices* are "any coherent and complex form of socially established cooperative human activity through which goods internal to that form of activity are realized in the course of trying to achieve those standards of excellence which are appropriate to, and partially definitive of, that form of activity" (*After Virtue*, 187). He goes on to observe, "Throwing a football with skill" is not a practice, "but the game of football is. . . . Planting turnips is not a practice; farming is." But of course the actions described (throwing a football, planting turnips) are understandable in the context of overall aims (what MacIntyre calls goods) internal to the overall practice. Individual choices and actions (e.g., "Should I have sex with my boyfriend?" "Should I marry him?") take place within practices (e.g., the practice of being boyfriend/girlfriend, the practice of marriage), and so our exploration of individual actions will have to explore the larger question of practices, and in particular the aims and purposes of engaging in these practices.

Thus, in the second part of this text, we will finally get around to asking and answering the basic ethical question, "What are you doing?" when it comes to sex and relationships. Hopefully we can now do so with a richer language and a greater awareness of how our sexual actions, choices, and relationships fit into our overall lives and especially God's story.

Part 2

Sexuality and Catholicism
Exploring the Practices

5
Practices of Sexuality
The Purposes of Dating

Do you have a significant other? Do you want one? Why? And what does it mean when you have one? What's that relationship about? Where is it going? How do other people perceive it?

Welcome to the sexual world of most college students—involved in and seeking sexual relationships, but not engaged or married. For want of a better term we call this social practice dating—although, as we'll see, the term covers a number of different possible social practices. In this chapter, we'll try to describe the practice in general, try to figure out what it might have to do with love and God's story, and try to figure out what's reasonable to do and not do if you're dating someone.

To date is to be in some sort of ongoing relationship with a purpose—all actions have purposes, remember? *Dating* is the catch-all term that refers to the various ways we in our culture organize and practice sexual or romantic relationships prior to marriage. We could also say *having a boyfriend/girlfriend* or *having a significant other* or (if we are old-fashioned) *going steady*. But we also might mean just sort of hanging out a lot (if there's "interest") or meeting someone for a formal date. Note that dating is not a type of love, but a social practice, a cultural way of organizing human relationships with some particular purpose in mind. *Practice* means what we meant in the first chapter by *action*, but it's a complicated sort of action, since it involves coordinating with other people. It is a shared action.

Dating relationships are by definition premarital. Once married, it is generally understood in our culture that one no longer has these types of relationships. By contrast, we continue to have friendships after we marry, even friendships with members of the opposite sex. But a dating relationship is prior to marriage. A defining characteristic is that dating relationships involve sex. *Sex* here should be broadly construed, as covering everything from kissing and holding hands to actual intercourse. Some sort of physical activity is going on here that is not going on between friends.

Dating in Historical Context

What is the purpose of dating? Is it to find a marriage partner? Are these relationships mini-marriages, or are they just a matter of having some fun and getting some experience before marriage? Purpose is, as always, our first concern in ethics.

All social practices have histories, and histories indicate that practices change over time. Recognizing these changes can help us understand what we are doing right now. For example, the Catholic mass looked quite a bit different fifty years ago: it was in Latin, the priest faced away from the congregation, and many of the people present were busy saying rosaries or their own prayers while the priest was leading. What changed (at Vatican II) was a desire to allow everyone to participate in the prayer. Hence, prayer was to be in the native language of the people, so they could understand and participate. The priest today faces the people, so that the focus of the celebration is the whole gathering.

Dating represents a new innovation in what we might call more generally premarital relationships. All cultures have marriage in some form and so all cultures also develop some way of moving toward marriage. We will talk more about marriage in later chapters; here suffice it to say that older cultures ordinarily set up straightforward forms of premarital relationships as simple steps that led directly to marriage.

In older cultures, marriages were often arranged by parents, relatives, or close community friends. Most matches were formed by families, or at least approved by family members, for everyone belonged to some form of family unit. Colonial New England actually had laws that made living alone a crime. All people were attached to a household, whether their own, or their parents' or relatives', or their masters.'

The purpose of the couplings thus arranged was simple: children. Earlier historical periods had relatively high infant mortality rates and shorter life expectancies, and so tended to encourage the bearing of children. More importantly, the household was the center of production, and children provided labor for the farm or workshop or home industry. Everyone agreed that children required a family, and therefore required marriage.

Of course this does not mean that there were no sexual relationships outside of marriage. Historians John D'Emilio and Estelle Freedman relate the story of "Merry Mount," an early New England settlement founded by Thomas Morton where people engaged in "profane and dissolute living," including free sex. Needless to say, Morton was deported, and when he returned, placed in irons. There were prostitution, affairs, and even some buggery (what we would now call bestiality). All of these were, to various degrees, crimes: society was concerned that such behavior outside of marriage would lead to illegitimate children, children where the father was not known and whose care would become the responsibility of the community. Bestiality was punished severely because it was feared that such action would give birth to half-human, half-animal monsters.

So throughout most historical periods there simply was no time or social space for romantic relationships that were not directly aimed at marriage. But in the eighteenth and nineteenth centuries, Europe and North America saw an increased sense of personal and individual freedom coupled with a new emphasis on romantic love in marriage. The notion of personal freedom as central to a good life is especially important. The person was no longer absolutely defined by family ties or social class. Rather, individuals were to determine their lives for themselves, setting out in a world among other selves with "life, liberty, and the pursuit of happiness."

The elevation of personal freedom over preexisting social ties had major effects on how men and women met and related prior to marriage. Choosing one's own partner became paramount. But how to go about it? Jane Austen's novels are prime examples of the transition, where family opinion and responsibility are sometimes pitted against a good match in a relationship. Austen, however, has not entirely given way to romantic love. Austen's heroines, exemplified by Elizabeth in *Pride and Prejudice*, are independent-minded in their choosing of a mate, but nevertheless choose for "sensible" reasons, reasons of character, not of romantic feeling. The handsome Mr. Darcy only becomes a suitable match when his true character is revealed; before that, Elizabeth despises him, despite his allure. However, as Austen's novels also display, there is no dating going on. People meet and mingle at community social occasions, and occasionally pay visits to one another's houses. But there is no "going out."

Eventually, the system of visiting houses of prospective marriage partners evolved into "calling." In contrast to rural and small-town life, the life of the urban middle class was increasingly compartmentalized, often by gender, so general public opportunities to meet and mingle became fewer. How then to get sons and daughters together? Often young men would indicate their desire to call on a young woman at her house; she might or might not accept, and if she did, some conversation might ensue. Couples would meet in the parlor, first with family, and then by themselves. The ritual was highly formalized, and often tinged with what we would now see as sappy but sincere declarations of love. While there was some expectation that the couple should "fall in love" before they marry, there was little of the drama and questioning we associate with romantic love. The visits either went well or badly and, usually in a relatively short time, the woman indicated whether she was interested in marriage.

Dating gradually came into being in the first quarter of the twentieth century, replacing the system of calling. It spread among both upper and lower classes. The shift from calling to dating involved a number of underlying shifts that changed the nature of the premarital relationship. First, dating ordinarily took place away from the family in an anonymous public setting, and so was no longer bound to the home. Second, it shifted power from women to men. The system of calling meant the man had to go into the woman's sphere, whereas dating meant the woman had to go out into the man's sphere, where he had command of the itinerary and the pocketbook. Moreover, women issued the invitation for a suitor to call, whereas dating was understood as being initiated by the man. Third, the relationship was far less defined. Beth Bailey points out that calling provided "measured steps," which were "a test of suitability, breeding, and background" (*From Front Porch to Back Seat*, 16). Dating offered a far greater degree of freedom and flexibility, without clearly defined steps.

This freedom and flexibility made for a looser connection to the goal of marriage than was the case in prior systems—no one went calling just for fun. Dating relationships were not aimed narrowly at marriage but could have purposes in and of themselves. They might offer the opportunity for companionship, or sex, or intimacy and care apart from one's home and one's family. Thus, dating marks a decisive shift not only because it moves premarital sexual relationships out of the sphere of the home, but also because it suddenly allows these relationships to stand on their own, as distinct entities from marriage, with purposes that may not involve getting married.

As close-knit urban and rural neighborhoods and family systems broke down after World War II, dating became entirely normal, though at first the practice remained circumscribed and limited by social norms. Obviously the opportunity for sexual activity was higher in dating because it was more private and the man was not circumscribed by external custom. Add this to the increasing availability of effective birth control, and sexual conventions began to give way. The so-called sexual revolution of the 1960s finally detached sexual activity from the question of marriage.

Coupled with the independence of sex from marriage and the new equality of men and women, our culture saw a steadily rising marriage age and delayed entrance into the adult world of work. Going to college became the norm rather than the exception. In the 1950s, perhaps the heyday of traditional dating, average marriage age hovered around twenty-two for men and twenty for women. As one study of a Midwestern city indicated, fully 50% of women married by age twenty, many of them by age eighteen. (The authors of the study noted that lower-class girls were much more likely to marry early, as were ones that were unsuccessful academically or socially in the high school setting.) In the United States the average marriage age has risen dramatically. High school students typically have no thoughts of marriage when bringing their date to the prom, and even college students are less likely to view the campus as a place to meet their mate.

Is the contemporary system a good one? As you now know, an action can be judged "good" only in reference to its purpose. So, what is the modern system good for? Having fun? Sexual pleasure? Selection of mates? Arranging suitable marriages? Developing healthy, whole persons?

Explaining the Contemporary Scene

As we noted in chapter 1, we must begin with accurate description—so we examine the contemporary situation. Due to our standardized educational system and to career expectations, we can roughly divide the dating period into three eras: high school, college, and emerging adulthood. Sociologist Jeffrey Arnett nicely sums up the entire dating period:

> The expectation for emerging adults today is that they will have a number of love partners in their late teens and early twenties before settling on someone to marry. . . . Finding a love partner in your teens and continuing in a relationship with that person through your early twenties, culminating in marriage, is now viewed as unhealthy, a mistake, a path likely to lead to disaster. . . . Those who do not experiment with different partners are warned that they are limiting their options too narrowly by staying with one person and that they will eventually wonder what they are missing, to the detriment of their marriage. (*Emerging Adulthood*, 73)

In the high school era there are already many variations in dating practices. One study divides people into four groups: those looking for a romantic fusion of sex and love, those who play the field recreationally, those who are more focused on schoolwork and activities than any sort of relationship, and those who hold a strong connection between sex, marriage, and procreation. As with most behaviors among high schoolers, dating behavior tends to be influenced by the person's peer group of friends and the expectations and behaviors of the parents. While many high schoolers do engage in sexual intercourse, recent studies have seen an increase in those who abstain: they now constitute a majority.

Similar patterns persist in college, though with more intensity and with more opportunity for individuals to choose their own patterns rather than reflect the patterns of peers or parents. Those who play the field now have unrestricted access to what is known as the hook-up culture. People who are looking for a fusion of sex and love can now be "joined at the hip," because of the self-contained atmosphere of college where people work, play, eat, and live together. Of course, others find these options too stark and develop their own patterns for meeting and relating to people, though many complain that the near absence of any traditional dating makes it difficult to know exactly how to meet and develop relationships. Everything becomes guesswork.

College is also the period where questions about commitment start to become more important—and more confusing. Students today tend both to desire and fear commitment, possibly because of the widespread presence of divorce among their parents. Others suggest that the ambiguity comes from the need to juggle romantic commitments with future career and educational paths, which may or may not take precedence. The ambiguity also has to do with contrasting expectations of men and women: women tend to be more interested in relationships involving commitment, men less so, with the result that each side tries to work out compromises with the other's expectations. For example, women may participate in the hook-up culture, hoping that sex might turn into "something more," and men may make gestures of commitment and care, thinking they will leave when they find something better.

The post-collegiate period of emerging adulthood tends to intensify the ambiguities of the college patterns. The desire for and fear of commitment both increase as marriage becomes more thinkable. Women and men continue to have contrasting expectations: one study finds that around 70% of women seek relationships for the purposes of intimacy, companionship, and emotional bonding, whereas only 30% of men aim at these ends. As the possibility of marriage increases, the ruses for disguising intentions have to become more elaborate. But because there is no settled expectation for when or whom to marry, the drama of deciding this question becomes, again, a matter of guesswork and improvisation. The absence of a clear cultural road map has given birth to an explosion of advice books, movies, novels, and TV series concerned with charting the romantic territory of this period. There is no consensus. The average age at marriage is rising, and although the United States continues to hold marriage as a usual life expectation for everyone, some indicators suggest that the number of people living together is starting to match the level of European cultures, where many people simply do not marry.

There are many exceptions to the above patterns, both among individuals and cultural subgroups. But the combination of recreation, love, prioritizing work, and strongly advocating marriage has proven to be a resilient menu of patterns for these years. In each case, relationships are seen as having a purpose, but one has to look more closely to understand which purpose is being pursued.

Getting Theological: The Christian Dating Debate

Now we have to turn to the question of how such purposes do or do not fit into larger stories. The question of a larger story has two levels here: first, the obvious question of marriage and family and, second, the more specifically Christian question of God's story. The Christian story obviously assumes some things about the marriage story, but not vice versa. We will want to pay attention to both, but we will begin where the two stories overlap: where does dating fit into the marriage part of God's story?

While the tradition has always had a good deal to say about the place of marriage in Christian life, it has not paid the same attention to premarital relationships. Informally, Christian societies oversaw the marriages of their young, but since earlier systems were generally brief preludes to marriage there was little reason to theologize about them. Today, however, many Christians spend fifteen years in this sea of relationships, often personally formative years, and so it is about time we pay attention. Recently two basic positions on Christians and dating have emerged, which will help us understand the argument over the purposes of dating and how they do or do not fit in the Christian life.

On one side of the debate are the anti-daters, typified by Josh Harris and his book *I Kissed Dating Goodbye*. Harris criticizes the practice of dating for a variety of reasons. Perhaps the most important is the claim that serial dating is essentially practice for divorce. People get involved in serious emotional and physical commitments with one another, then conflict arises, and the relationship breaks up. This is poor training for marriage but excellent training for divorce. The inherently temporary nature of dating constitutes its major problem.

Moreover, the ambiguities of the situation described earlier in the chapter make for enormous potential for harm. Put in terms of our earlier chapter on eros and the Christian story, dating has become highly competitive, a matter of extended test-drives and competing demands, like negotiating and completing a sale. As with any major purchase, both sides try to get the best deal, often concealing information, presenting things as better than they are, and making false promises—all of which can happen because there are no rules for working out the deal. Much harm results.

The anti-daters propose a return to a more formal system of dating aimed at determining suitability for marriage. While not rejecting the whole idea of going out and being together, they suggest that the purpose of being together is not a matter of either thrills or intimacy, but a much more practical focus on learning who the other person is with the purpose of identifying a good marriage partner. Most anti-daters assume that God plays the central role in finding them a marriage partner, and so they are not concerned that staying out of the dating marketplace will harm their chances of finding a partner.

Needless to say, anti-daters also place strict limits on the sexual intimacy of such premarital relationships. This is not simply because they are against premarital sex. Rather, as Harris puts it, "the longer your 'no big deal' list is before marriage, the shorter your 'special' list will be after marriage" (*Boy Meets Girl*, 157–59). Postponing physical intimacy now will pay big dividends later, it is said. Actions are chosen with the overall purpose of a good marriage firmly in mind.

Against this position, Donna Freitas and Jason King claim in *Save the Date* that we learn a great deal from those whom we date, even if the relationship eventually breaks up. It is not training for divorce. In dating, they maintain, we see the values we find in all human relationships: "Relationships—whether they be with friends, family, spouses, or dates—provide us with some of the best experiences for developing our understanding of who God calls us to be, because they call us outside of ourselves toward the concerns and needs of another person. . . . Thus, when we have relationships, when we turn toward others, we open ourselves up to new possibilities. We can grow and change as individuals, try new things, become better people, and even find God in and through our interactions" (p. 67).

Freitas and King criticize the anti-daters on two grounds. First, they claim that anti-daters resist even non-dating relationships because their position is grounded in fear, implying "a basic mistrust of others" (p. 57). Anti-daters are prone to view members of the opposite sex as a threat or temptation, and advise their readers to stay away from such relationships—even friend-ships—lest they become opportunities to date. Freitas and King deride this attitude by wondering how having as few relationships as possible with the opposite sex can be the best preparation for marriage. Second, Freitas and King suggest that anti-daters tacitly agree with the culture in equating dat-ing with sex. What anti-daters oppose is non-marital sex: they assume that dating is all about sex, and so they reject dating. But is dating just about sex?

Quite the contrary, Freitas and King reply. Dating and romance are par-ticularly important because they involve caring for another person "in a way that is often deeper than friendship" (p. 70). They point out that the need for romantic gestures and coordination teaches us how to attend in detailed ways to the needs of others.

Even more importantly, dating seems to offer possibilities for personal transformation not found in other relationships. They relate a story—one that many of us have seen repeated—of a guy who started dating a woman and "suddenly began to like different things" (p. 81). He even became more responsible and aware of others. "New possibilities for self-understanding sometimes come from the embrace of someone else or from an opening up and merging of another's perspective with one's own" (p. 81). Dating rela-tionships become occasions not only to love others, but to expand the self.

Freitas and King thus suggest that dating relationships that aren't aimed directly at marriage can nevertheless be consistent with God's story of love. The anti-daters seem to imply that every dating relationship is simply a mat-ter of people using one another, but Freitas and King argue that this sort of competition and commodification, while it may occur, is not intrinsic to dat-ing. Indeed, such relationships can rightly aim at God: "Falling in love makes people appear to us as gifts. . . . We are thus called to love like this: seeing people as good, as gifts, and as potentially opening us to God and to new spiritual horizons" (p. 83).

For Discussion

1. What valid points does each of these positions make about dating? What assumptions are questionable?

2. Do you see dating as mostly a source of heartbreak, harm, and competition or as mostly a source of love, care, and growth in personal intimacy?

Dating and Ethics: Reason and God's Story

The two positions outlined above serve as a useful frame for formulating the ethics of dating. Notice that neither position says that dating is wrong per se. Sometimes in making choices there are actions we simply should not take, actions that are flat-out and always contrary to the ultimate purposes of our lives, and especially of others' lives. But even anti-daters accept a certain, limited form of dating—they don't, for example, suggest we go back to arranged marriages. But the two positions disagree about two things: (1) valid purposes for entering a dating relationship, and (2) what to do when you're dating. This makes for an interesting parallel with another common ethical question in the Catholic tradition: the ethics of war. The "just war" ethic of Catholicism has rejected two positions: (1) never enter a war, and (2) enter a war whenever you want, for whatever purpose you choose. Rather, the tradition develops a set of purposes indicating when it is acceptable to go to war (*jus ad bellum* norms), as well as a set of rules for how to act during the war (*jus in bello* norms). These limitations on the purposes of going to war and of actions within the war nicely parallel the disagreement above about dating. Thus, for the rest of the chapter, we will look first at the purposes for dating, and then appropriate actions within dating relationships.

Purposes for Dating: Only Marriage or Also Intimacy?

The question of the aims for dating divides the two positions above. But before exploring that division, we should notice where they agree. Both sides agree in rejecting recreational, competitive dating—dating for fun, for sexual pleasure, for social status. Why this rejection?

The anti-daters—in keeping with our outline of God's story above—assert that this sort of dating does great harm to everyone involved. Basically such dating uses other human beings to pursue one's own happiness. Whether you are the "user" or the "usee" in such relationships, you learn habits that are precisely the opposite of love. Your own dignity and the dignity of the other person are sacrificed.

Put positively, both the anti-daters and the pro-daters agree that the purpose of dating relationships is to learn how to give. According to anti-daters, you learn how to give yourself in the gift of marriage; according to pro-daters, you learn how to focus on someone else's needs. But recreational dating is always about "getting," not about giving, and that purpose runs contrary to God's story—and contrary to love stories like *High Fidelity*. Even friendships do not involve people using one another to get what they want, but sharing with one another, looking out for the other person.

Put in the most straightforward terms, recreational dating is part of a different master narrative, a way of thinking about your actions and desires in life that presumes happiness is a matter of getting everything you want, from whomever, in whatever way necessary. It is not all that different from dictators who make war whenever they want to, using their citizens as instruments to achieve their personal power. Those who live this way are living a story at odds with God's story and at odds with any story in which love and respect for others is a part of happiness. This is exactly the sort of competition that God's story views as the fruit of our fallenness and fear. The "false self" competes to try to manipulate someone else into loving him or her.

While the two camps agree on rejecting recreational dating, they disagree on dating when marriage is not on the table. The anti-daters say that you should date only if potential marriage is the explicit purpose of both parties. The other side maintains that even when marriage is not clearly the goal, dating can have good purposes—specifically, growth in intimacy and giving.

How can we choose who's right here? What arguments can be made? Whenever we meet a question like this, where there is no immediately obvious answer, it is advisable to define why there is such a disagreement, in hopes of moving beyond it to more clarity about good and bad choices. Here there is no obvious answer from the master narrative. Both authors are arguing in terms consistent with love of God and neighbor.

A major reason for this disagreement stems from the different ways the two sides characterize dating. One thinks of it as practice for divorce, filled with breaking of commitments and mistrust and deception. The other thinks of it as practice for marriage, filled with making commitments and building trust and love. One wonders whether the two camps are looking at the same action.

Certainly dating as a whole contains both these elements, and it would seem reasonable to consider how dating might build trust and love, not break them down. The anti-daters have a point: if you get used to the experience of getting together and breaking up with various people, you will enter marriage with the same expectations, and that will make divorce much easier.

Lauren Winner, arguing against the anti-daters here, suggests that the issue is not so much dating per se as dating in isolation from a community, particularly a Christian community. She argues that many of the problems associated with contemporary dating happen because the couple is an isolated unit, particularly emotionally.

Winner argues strenuously that the Christian tradition rejects this privatization of sexual relationships. In our culture, we tend to believe "one person's sexual behavior is not anyone else's concern" (*Real Sex*, 48). Winner denies this; the community can and should intrude on sexual matters, though she also notes that "the first step in speaking to my friends about sex was making sure that we enjoyed relationships built on top of hundreds of ordinary shared experiences" (p. 59).

The acceptance of this privatized and individualistic perspective on dating relationships leads anti-daters to construct elaborate rules for courtship, all the while denying that they are being legalists. It leads to obsessive boundary-drawing between the parties. Winner worries that anti-dater rejection of kissing leads straight to a sort of body-denying gnosticism, in which we are uncomfortable with the idea that we inhabit bodies that experience sexual desire. Instead of attempting to appreciate and order that desire, anti-daters too often simply try to turn it off.

Winner reminds us that each relationship is different; what matters is not a set of inflexible physical boundaries but that one's Christian community is involved with the relationship. "The point is to discern, with your community, what behaviors can protect the body and God's created sexual intent" (p. 107). She denies that parents are the sole arbiters of such issues, noting that in a mobile, late-marrying society such as ours parents are often out of touch with their children.

We will consider Winner's "rotunda rule" later, but we should mention another aspect to Winner's argument for communal dating: the desirability of such relationships going on in public. This is not meant to be a ringing endorsement of "public displays of affection." Instead, it emphasizes how much it matters to conduct relationships in the living context of other people. As has long been explained in the Christian tradition, sin always desires to hide itself from scrutiny. Dating relationships that we'd rather keep under wraps, away from trusted friends, parents, and others in our lives, are likely to be dysfunctional. They tend to be the relationships where the "spark" is misleading and overwhelming our reason. We love stories of star-crossed lovers, but such relationships are fertile ground for our dysfunctions to play out, often to the injury of ourselves and the other person. A relationship in which the couple is connected to a community will be far less likely to engage in outright deception, more likely to confront and deal with problems constructively early on, and will have a community of support and care if the couple breaks up. Ideally Winner assumes a common, shared community, not his friends and her friends. As we will see repeatedly, one way the church can be a true light to the world is by offering a space in which healthy dating relationships—true training grounds in love and intimacy—can be pursued.

Ethicist Karen Lebacqz considers terms we might apply to good dating, words like "caring," "tender," "supportive," "eye-opening," and "healing." She points out that, in focusing exclusively on marriage and children, the tradition has failed to appreciate another good involved in our sexuality, that of vulnerability. She invokes the "original nakedness" of Adam and Eve to indicate that our sexual relationships aim at this state of vulnerability. Indeed, the goods above are all products of relationships where vulnerability is involved. Lebacqz warns that the traditional Christian preference for marriage is right insofar as it recognizes that vulnerability requires safeguards. Therefore, the more vulnerability that is to be shown, the more protection and trust is needed. Singleness, she says, "is an unsafe environment for the expression of vulnerability" ("Appropriate Vulnerability," 260). Vulnerability exposes us, and when we are exposed we can be hurt and rejection will affect us most. Thus placing the relationship in a community of support and aid provides some protection for couples to risk being vulnerable.

Reflecting on the importance of trust, intimacy, vulnerability, and the like as purposes for a dating relationship, it is worthwhile to raise the question again: but why not friendship? One would hope that friendships also contain trust, sharing, even vulnerability, so what makes dating different? Freitas and King explain why the positives of dating could not also be found in friendships, and they use themselves as an example. They are both religion PhDs, writing a book together, but they are not and never have been involved romantically. Why didn't they even risk trying a relationship? They write, "We have never had that 'spark' between us" (p. 71).

The "spark," they argue, is not merely sexual, but "makes one individual attentive to another individual in a new way" (p. 70). So it would appear that, as Lewis argued earlier, eros (the spark) is not simply about the body, but about attention to the whole, unique person. But they immediately add, "The friendship is now transformed into a focus primarily on each other with an added physical dimension" (p. 70). What happened to the spark being "more than sexual"?

We can see that more detailed thought needs to be given to the friendship/dating question. Even today, just "hanging out" has become a standard way to initiate both friendships and romantic relationships, albeit an ambiguous one. If the "spark" is not to be purely sexual—pure venus, in Lewis's terms—then we might turn to other issues. We might want to recall our discussion of the mystery of male-female relationships in the last chapter. How might this be particularly fostered in romantic relationships? Moreover, even if such dating relationships are open-ended they involve some notion that the person is a potential marriage partner, and this adds weight beyond friendship.

For Discussion

1. Are casual, recreational relationships truly a matter of two people using each other for selfish purposes? Are there other descriptions? What's going on there? And is there any way to place those relationships within a larger story of love?

2. Think of the reasons why you or your close friends are seeking or are involved in serious relationships. Are these qualities also found in your friendships? Why or why not?

3. What examples could you give of "appropriate vulnerability," times when you opened yourself up to someone and found care and support? What are examples of "inappropriate vulnerability"? Can you explain the differences?

4. How do you figure out whether the person you're dating is someone you might consider marrying? Do you do it right away, or does it take time? What factors do you consider? What does that tell you about your idea of marriage?

Practicing Dating: Latitude, Anarchy, or Chastity?

The second issue to address is the question raised above about the *jus in bello* rules for dating, the balance between latitude and anarchy in practicing the relationship. Jeramy and Jerusha Clark, Christian pro-dating writers, sum up their perspective on dating by saying, "You cannot date well without a plan" ("The Purposeful Path," 178). Such plans address the obvious issue of physical boundaries, but they also outline boundaries for emotional intimacy—communication and the like.

But such plans may strike you as involving a lot of defensive detail, all of which ought to be discerned before you date. It may seem a rigid approach that precludes the kind of building of trust the relationship is supposed to offer. The problem here, as Lauren Winner obliquely points out, is that a lot of this emphasis on planning is placed there for the purpose of minimizing risk and pain. But if building or learning love is the true purpose of dating, she argues, love necessarily involves risk and pain ("The Countercultural Path," 36–37). Extensive planning and rule-setting is always, in all areas of life, a hedge against risk and pain. Our society often reacts to situations of potential risk by creating extensive and detailed rules. One of my favorite examples is the presence of red left-turn arrows, those pesky traffic signals that prevent you from making a left turn even when there is no oncoming traffic. Such arrows used to be present only at the most dangerous and busy intersections, in order to prevent people from making their own, potentially risky judgments about whether they had enough room to turn. But now they seem to be everywhere. True, they minimize risk, but at the cost of forward movement. These traffic signals are only a small sign of a society where we, in the name of safety, often set up ridiculous and elaborate rules that interrupt the flow of life.

Perhaps a better example might be taking a road trip: planning the last detail, with reservations made and every turn mapped by MapQuest, may minimize the possibility of going wrong. However, it may also squelch enjoyment, preventing spontaneous choices that could end up being the most memorable parts of the trip.

One root of this increase in rule-based planning is a basic fear of others, a basic lack of trust where, in less rule-bound situations, others may endanger us. We do not trust others to be wise or to make the right decisions, so we make decisions for them, in advance, so that their behavior can be predictable. In intimate relationships between single people, we do in fact need certain protections and boundaries in order have appropriate vulnerability. However, as Winner argues, this is a tricky business.

The second root is a failure to develop the virtues of prudence and temperance. We haven't discussed virtues much, though we mentioned them briefly at the end of the first chapter. Virtues are the dispositions that grow in us and allow us to make decisions habitually that order our desires and actions toward their goal. In any area of life, individual variation dictates that many decisions cannot be anticipated by a hard and fast rule. The virtue of prudence allows us to determine what to do in such situations. For example, much of what goes on among friends is determined by prudence. Your friend just came to the rescue when you were in a tough situation—now what do you do for him or her? There is no rule here; rather, a wise decision comes from knowing your friend and knowing your particular relationship. It's like determining when it is appropriate to make a left turn. We can't set up exact rules, because the speed limit, the road conditions, the condition of your car, the clarity of your vision of oncoming traffic all affect this decision. You end up learning from experience—not by failing a lot, but by being careful at the beginning and then getting used to making the fitting decision given the circumstances.

Some will argue that we need clear boundaries because people's judgments fail a lot. This may be debatable in terms of red left-turn arrows, but not so much in terms of sexual relationships. However, just as good driving requires sobriety and attention and decent reflexes, good sexual relationships require a virtue called temperance, in which we are able to exercise appropriate control over ourselves so that we can control the vehicle. Temperance (or its offspring, chastity) is the virtue that moderates our natural desires for food, sex, conversation, and any other pleasures we might enjoy. Without temperance we simply follow our desires—with results no less problematic for sexual relationships than for traffic. While we will discuss chastity further below, here we simply observe that obsession with rules and boundaries indicates a lack of attention to the virtues.

These two basic roots have a lot to tell us about how to conduct dating relationships. First, if we are in a situation where we fear someone as a threat to us, we should probably question what exactly we are doing. Second, we should anticipate that in a good relationship we will be exercising prudence regularly in making decisions about what to do, where to go, what to talk about, and who does what. We should also expect that both partners are reasonably moderate in their sexual desires.

With regard to rule-setting in dating, it is interesting to note that, were we to suggest the same set of heavily-scripted rules for friendships, everyone would laugh. We all know that friendships evolve and that it would be ridiculous to say, "You cannot do friendships well without a plan." That's not to say we don't make tons of mistakes in friendships, but somehow those mistakes do not inflame the same fears as do dating relationships. But surely Winner is right that any significant human relationship—friendship or otherwise—evolves into genuine love because there is a willingness to take risks, be vulnerable, experience pain, and the like. So sets of rules and plans are likely to result in artificial relationships, which may be safe but which also may prevent us from both giving and receiving genuine love.

Given this comparison, why do dating relationships need all these rules? Why can't they just evolve, as friendships do? And yet friendships need virtues, too. This intuition may be the reason it seems best to allow romantic relationships to grow out of friendships. In establishing friendships, we all seem a bit more prudent. But why is that?

Perhaps the introduction of another term of description will be helpful here. Dating relationships seem to be put in danger by promiscuity. Promiscuity, a prominent category in the history of moral theology, involves inappropriately excessive activity, activity that exceeds good judgment. It most often refers to sexual issues. But promiscuity takes various forms. Numerous writers speak of "emotional promiscuity," where excessive intimate sharing of feelings and hopes burdens a relationship, much as excessive and premature sex might. Promiscuity might be seen in many other areas of our lives. People who cannot control their credit card debt might be said to be financially promiscuous, for example.

The importance of avoiding promiscuity lies in the fact that promiscuity almost always reveals a compulsive and excessive need that comes from inside of us. Take the financial promiscuity issue. The person may be buying fine apparel, it may make them happy, but an inability to control our spending most often indicates a lack inside of ourselves that we are constantly trying to fill through buying things. Promiscuity might be seen as the opposite of prudence, or signifying a lack of prudence, in the sense that our actions are not able to be ordered well to our ultimate happiness.

Promiscuity in relationships is the same way. It is driven neither by love for the other person nor by rationality, but by our own needs. These needs may be sexual, emotional, or crassly instrumental. But in all cases, intimacy is built up not out of love and respect for the other person, gradually, but in instant ways, which may give some gratification in the short run but involve the feeding of needs in the long run.

Interestingly, promiscuity seems far less a problem in our friendships. Of course there are needy people out there, but we rarely worry about setting lots of boundaries in friendships, because it would seem as though most friendships evolve naturally and organically, such that we are alert to levels of appropriateness. Or we may simply experience neediness and hunger over dating relationships far more than over friendships, perhaps because finding and getting "the one" is such a preoccupation in our culture.

On the flip side, many people who are blatantly physically promiscuous in romantic relationships actually have solid and strong friendships. In one context they are willing to use another person to gratify their need, but in the context of friendship they would never do such a thing. These people are not running the danger of emotional promiscuity; rather, they are clearly subject to their physical desires for sex at any cost. They don't appear insecure to us because we are used to defining insecurity in terms of emotional desires, but in fact they are insecure in the sense that an alcoholic or a shopaholic is insecure in his or her need for a fix.

We can tie this back to the larger God story by saying that promiscuity in any area of our lives is a telltale sign of idolatry. The excessive desire and focus on something should indicate to us that we are risking making a thing or a person into a god, making it too important, and therefore opening us to actions that point us away from genuine love and toward possession, away from giving and toward getting.

The words that are usually set in opposition to promiscuity are not always inviting: "purity," "chastity," "modesty," "restraint." One writer comments that Christianity has a problem because it has no middle term between promiscuity and chastity. But this is because *chastity* is the middle term! The opposite of promiscuity should be something like frigidity or coldness or distance. Chastity is the sexual version of the virtue of temperance, a habitual disposition within us that aims our desires properly and moderately at our happiness, rather than allowing the desires to be excessive or deficient. The word is usually associated with sexual restraint, but writers have, as above, extended its meaning. It can apply to being sexually chaste—not the same thing as celibacy! But it can also be emotional chastity, a restraint involving intimacy of conversation and feeling. In either case, chastity names a self-control appropriate to human relationships, an ability to allow genuine love to be the aim and purpose of the relationship.

The spiritual writer Ronald Rolheiser suggests *reverence* as an alternate term: "Ultimately, chastity is reverence—and sin, all sin, is irreverence. To be chaste is to experience people, things, places, entertainment, the phases of our lives, and sex in a way that does not violate them or ourselves. To be chaste is to experience things reverently, in such a way that the experience leaves both them and ourselves more, not less, integrated" (*The Holy Longing*, 202).

Reverence is not worship here. It may mean something more like respect, but it's a bit stronger than that. Respect is something that may govern our treatment of things or of anonymous strangers, but it is insufficient for actual relationships with other people. Remember, as we discussed much earlier, people are not isolated and separate entities—we respect things that are separate, but to be in relationship with another person is to enter into the mystery and freedom of our unity and uniqueness. This sort of communion requires reverence, not simply respect.

Reverence most fundamentally involves a sense of awe and care. It says to the person, "You are something infinitely more valuable than anything I could make myself." It involves being in the presence of something greater than one's self. At a fundamental level, it is a decentering of the self away from the self, a recognition of something greater. In older and other cultures, this sense of reverence was much more easily identifiable. One might feel it in the presence of a national monument, or a holy man or woman, or a sacred space. One might feel it anywhere you might properly recognize someone being irreverent, someone behaving in a way that showed him or her to be ignorant of the mystery you've sensed. For example, it is the feeling many people have when enjoying natural grandeur, and then encountering a clear-cut mountainside: we are left wondering how anyone could do such a thing.

Reverence is undercut by many things, but fundamentally we invade the sacred because we want something for ourselves. We do this with other people as well. Restraint, both emotionally and sexually, is not a matter of thinking sex or intimacy is bad, but simply a matter of not taking it lightly. Restraint is not so much self-protection as protecting the other, of truly loving the other. It is a way of giving space to the other and not allowing the other to become captive to my desires.

For Discussion

1. All people have some line for themselves between what is chaste and what is promiscuous. Where is your line? Compare it to others. Where do these strong evaluations come from?

2. What would it mean to show reverence for your significant other? For a friend?

Conclusion

In this chapter, we have sought to name, clarify, and begin to evaluate the various non-marital sexual relationships that we call dating. We have looked at the cultural context—some would say confusion—of these relationships and explored how these relationships might fit into the Christian master narrative. In particular, we have developed some language of strong evaluation—promiscuity and chastity—which helps us get a handle on the characteristics of such relationships. We have not yet looked at the question of specific sexual acts within such relationships. To that task we now turn.

6

Rules of the Practice

Sexual Activity in Dating

Every practice in human life requires rules. Having a practice without any rules would be like playing a sport that didn't have a rule book. It would be like a baseball game where, upon hitting the ball, the batter sometimes decided to run to third base and sometimes run to first and sometimes not run at all. It would be like a football game with no sidelines. It would be like driving with no signs, no rules of the road, not even lane markings. As a shared activity, any practice relies on certain agreements and parameters that allow for the practice to achieve its purposes, rather than break down into chaos.

The same holds true for sexual relationships: if the relationships are not to break down into chaos, there have to be shared rules governing the activity, guiding it towards its purpose. In this chapter, we will explore and debate the arguments surrounding such rules—what the Catholic tradition calls absolute norms.

Absolute Norms: A Primer

Recall that in the last chapter we compared the ethical question of dating to that of war in the sense that there is no absolute norm against these actions, but there are parameters that shape when and what and how. In the Christian theology of war, there are certain absolutes: no taking of vengeance on the enemy (killing is to be for the purpose of defense, not showing hatred) and no killing of innocent civilians. Similarly, sexual ethics has many areas that involve prudential judgment, but also has absolutes—a controversial one being "no premarital sex." While dating may be a wonderful school for intimacy, one of the traditional rules is still supposed to apply: no sex.

Clearly there is a lot of disagreement about this issue. This chapter is meant to explore the question of sexual acts outside of marriage. In order for us to understand what is meant by an absolute norm, though, we need to set out certain issues. It will be helpful to do so in terms of a particular form of extra-marital sex: prostitution.

The first point to recall, from chapter 1, is that when we talk about an absolute norm we are talking about an action, not simply a set of physical movements. That is, we are evaluating purpose. Judas kissing Jesus, for example, is a kiss, but it's not a sexual action at all. It has an entirely different purpose. If your significant other hugs someone of the opposite sex, is that cheating? If it is the conventional hug we give friends and acquaintances in our culture, it is not cheating. The point is that in order to evaluate an action, we have to consider its purpose.

Absolute norms deal with actions that are always wrong. That means the purpose of these actions is never compatible with the pursuit of genuine happiness, our ultimate purpose for ourselves and others. Absolute norms are, as John Finnis puts it, "few but strategic" (*Moral Absolutes*, 1). They head off flat-out mistakes that will take us in precisely the opposite direction of our ultimate end. The formal way to put this is that "rules protect goods."

A complementary way of thinking about absolute rules is that they perform the function of rejecting actions that would result in the breakdown of the "game"—in this case, society. Murder can be thought of either as an act that cuts off someone's pursuit of happiness, or as an act that must be prohibited in order to build relationships in community. We can't go through life in constant fear of getting murdered. This is a community in a state of breakdown.

In either case, such rules are not a simple matter of an authority saying "no" to us. The "no" has a purpose, which is to protect something else positive, such as our life and the lives of others, as in the rule against murder. If there is no positive good protected, we call the rule a taboo. "Don't walk under a ladder" is a taboo, because we know that it is mere superstition and thus does not really promote a good.

What we have said so far is uncontroversial. Anyone who tells you "there are no rules" is lying—it's simply impossible. But controversies over rules do erupt, for two reasons. A rule becomes controversial when it changes (or is perceived to have changed) or when it has exceptions.

Rules can change. Two hundred years ago people didn't think slavery was absolutely wrong; now we do. Don't boundaries change over time? Don't different cultures have different moral absolutes?

This is a key question, and so it is important to respond carefully. To some extent, this is true. Things do change. As one document from the Vatican's Congregation for the Doctrine of the Faith said, discussing sexuality, "In the course of history civilization has taken many forms, [and] the requirements for human living have changed considerably and . . . many changes are still to come" (*Declaration Concerning Certain Questions of Sexual Ethics*, no. 3). As we have already noted, plenty of moral decisions do not involve absolutes, but judgments. For Catholics, "do not date" is not a moral absolute any more than "do not drink alcohol." It is also true that what is acceptable and not acceptable in a given culture—what is customary—does change over time. That's fine. Indeed, too many moral absolutes can be bad, as we have already noted in the discussion about dating.

However, the room for cultural change is limited by broader boundaries that are universally applicable to all times and cultures. The Congregation goes on: "But limits must be set to the evolution of mores and lifestyles, limits set by the unchangeable principles based on the elements that go to make up the human person and on his essential relationships. Such things transcend historical circumstances" (*Certain Questions*, no. 3). As we have already seen in regard to rape, nearly everyone agrees with this. Almost everyone recognizes that there are universals. The question is rather, what are they?

And what about exceptions? Many people hold what I call the "speed limit model" regarding rules: like speed limits, rules are necessary to slow us down, but we don't have to follow them exactly. We all drive over the speed limit sometimes, right? A speed limit is a sort of approximation. That means driving fifteen miles per hour over might be wrong, but five miles per hour is no big deal. A lot of choices we make in life are like this: they have approximate guidelines, but no hard and fast rules. A lot of morality—for example, the whole preceding section on the dynamics of intimacy in a dating relationship—involves guidelines. And most positive moral rules (e.g., love your neighbor, or honor your parents) are also guidelines, in the sense that we are always trying to size up how to do these things. There are many ways this works.

Negative moral rules include exceptionless absolutes like "do not murder." They don't mean, "Do not murder, except in these circumstances." Such actions are always wrong because they are logically incompatible with the pursuit of the good, of happiness. The purpose of the action points in one direction (death), and the pursuit of happiness points in the other (life).

What about killing in war? What about self-defense? Aren't these exceptions? No! This is a crucial point. Self-defense is not an exception to "do not murder" because the term "murder" does not apply to the action of killing in self-defense. This is, as we discussed in chapter 1, a matter of description of purpose. It is something like the hugging we discussed above. The physical movements and results of self-defense may look the same as murder, but the purpose of the action is different. The purpose of murder is to take someone else's life. The purpose of self-defense is, obviously, to defend your own life against an attacker. Your defense may result in the attacker's death, but that's not your purpose. Or if it is your purpose, then the action is accurately described as murder. Thus the question is not, "Is murder ever justified?" Rather, it is, "Is this action murder?"

Now let's consider the example of prostitution. The practice of prostitution has always been considered wrong by Jews and Christians, and still is. Here we have an absolute rule: do not go to prostitutes and do not prostitute yourself. Why this rule? Recalling what we said above, we need to ask two things: what goods are protected by this rule, and what counts as prostitution? For example, if you go to an R-rated film specifically because a certain actress in it turns you on, are you essentially paying for her sexual services? If that sounds ridiculous, why is that?

Clearly we have to formulate an accurate description of prostitution. An initial and common way to describe it might be "paying for sex." But we pay for lots of things in life, right? And it doesn't seem like a problem. Thus we see that the issue is not really about payment, but payment *for sex*. There must be something different about sex.

Prostitution turns sex into a commodity, a thing, and somehow this must contradict the real meaning of sexual actions. We saw in the last chapter that recreational dating involved using another person selfishly, rather than loving him or her, and this nicely explains the problem with prostitution. It turns sex into something we can use for our own pleasure, for recreation—we are using another person, and thus aiming in the opposite direction of sex for the purpose of fostering love, intimacy, and trust. It is logically contradictory to say that sometimes sex can be about giving and loving, and sometimes it can be about recreation. That would be like going to a prostitute on Wednesday and then having sex with your spouse on Friday, and claiming there was nothing contradictory in it because the two actions were unrelated. No spouse will buy that.

Thus, the moral problem with prostitution is using sex like a thing, a commodity, for your own pleasure and recreation. But what then counts as prostitution? One important skill in ethics is recognizing analogies in description; in this instance we have to wonder, isn't this really the same purpose as going out on a Friday night and "hooking up"? This type of recreational sex has been around a long time, but traditionally men have had to pay women to get it. Now they don't. It is hard to identify a difference between prostitution and hooking up, other than the fact that no payment is made and there is a bit more artfulness and drama in getting the deal done. Perhaps someone with a head for business will form a union of college women and start demanding that guys pay for what they get.

Does that sound unduly harsh? If there's a difference between hooking up and prostitution it can only be that, however weakly, there are a relationship, feelings, and meaning involved. You feel loved, needed, affirmed, and powerful because you've hooked up. But there, too, you've got a problem, because you want sex to be meaningful between two people, but you're doing it in a way that robs it of its meaning. This is of course what people are doing when they participate in hookups because they are lonely and yearning for a relationship, vaguely hoping that the feeling of intimacy will last. This is like using drugs to make you happy about your life: it's an artificial substitute for what you really need. It never lasts, and you feel worse in the morning.

All of this presumes that sex has real purpose, real meaning, and that certain acts flatly contradict these purposes. We might argue over whether this or that action constitutes prostitution, but we agree that what counts is the purpose of the action. If we are against prostitution we are against its purpose, the use of sex as a thing, a recreational commodity. This is how an absolute norm functions: it names an action whose purpose always contradicts the good.

For Discussion

1. A classic way to do ethics is to raise objections. What objections can be raised to the above argument against prostitution? What story about the overall purposes of sex and of life do the objections reflect?

2. Can the purpose of hook-up sex be described in any other way than it is above?

3. Is there a difference between an occasional hookup and the regular habit of hooking up? Do you think it's true that hooking up makes it harder to have more intimate and meaningful sexual relationships later? Why or why not?

Evaluating Sexual Actions: Relationship Sex

The Christian tradition does not simply oppose prostitution or hook-up sex. It opposes premarital sex. So we have to investigate the more difficult case of sex within some sort of relationship context, where sex is not simply recreational.

In order to evaluate this issue we have to place sexual actions within the overall context of relationships discussed in the last chapter. First, some relationships are in fact all about sex. What bonds the partners together is sexual chemistry, literally. Their conversation consists of sexual innuendo and repartee, and their time together consists of either sexual activity or activities that make for good foreplay. These relationships tend to look a lot better than they are.

Second, there are relationships that at first mean a lot of things, connecting on a lot of levels, but eventually become mostly about sex. There may be some shared goods and some shared sense of personal care and intimacy. But these relationships can be endangered all the more because they seem better than mere chemistry. Actual personal intimacy may lead the couple to stronger desires for sexual intimacy—which then rolls forward all too quickly—because the intimacy is good. But the sex can end up undermining the relationship, because the partners start devoting more of themselves to the sex than to each other. There is a sense of intimacy, but it is stalled. As in the relationship above, the bodily intimacy serves as an effective mask of other problems. Sexual actions form intimacy. We feel closer to people in a relationship when we have sex with them. But it is much easier to foster sexual intimacy than to build a relationship of personal intimacy and trust. In particular, when the couple encounters challenges in the emotional or personal intimacy part of the relationship, it is tempting to substitute the artificial sweetener of sex.

The problem in both these relationships is that the bodily sharing ends up speaking more intimacy than is actually there. Sex is not really all that challenging, especially with the right person. It is easy for sex to charge ahead of the relationship, but eventually the couple will be caught with their pants down (pun intended).

In past eras, instead of indulging sexual desires, cultures actually found it sexy to restrain them. And this is of course what is called for in the above situations. Unfulfilled sexual desire, especially when not suppressed but entertainingly engaged, can actually help a relationship. It shows the partners to be chaste. Being chaste conjures up images of depressingly dull people stripped of their sexual energy and desire—cold, stuffy, or just plain repressed. But the real meaning of chastity is not having a low sexual desire, but having a handle on your sexual desire. You know when and how to let it go and when and how to pull back on the reins. Chastity is both about restraint and about indulgence, about recognizing and acting in appropriate contexts.

In our culture, by contrast, the mere idea of restraint is repressive. And not just about sex. Our culture loves instant gratification. We develop endless technologies so that when a desire hits us, we can fulfill it instantly. In a sense, we've lost a lot of our creativity. Sexual chemistry in a relationship can be fanned by restraint. More importantly, restraint allows the relationship to develop on other grounds. So a first step might be a little practice in the virtue of restraint.

We're being cagey here. Restraint is one thing; "no premarital sex" is another. The big question is, how do you determine what the appropriate level of commitment is? When is it OK to have intercourse? When is it OK to have oral sex? Some argue in favor of some premarital sex from a Christian perspective, ordinarily taking one of two routes. First, some authors distinguish premarital sex from "preceremonial" sex. "Preceremonial" sex is sex between a couple who is committed to marriage in the future, but for various reasons (economic, educational, etc.) cannot get married at the present time. In essence, these authors argue, the marital commitment is already there, even if the ceremony has not yet happened. It is wrong for a couple who does not have a shared commitment to marry to have sex, but it is not wrong for a couple that has that commitment to do so.

This position does not reject the traditional purpose of sex as expressing committed love, nor does it deny the orientation toward marriage. Rather, the authors introduce fluidity into the question of timing in various ways. Some argue that modern marriages are difficult to plan and execute; others that marriage is a process in any case. But while the set of exceptions is large, the basic criterion is clear-cut: the couple must have a mutually stated and solid intention to marry in the future. All that's left is setting the date.

A somewhat more daring argument is made by other authors, most notably Gareth Moore. In *The Body in Context,* he argues that there are no actions without intentions (what we have called purposes), and so all bodily acts express meaning and purpose in context. Hugging, for example, may always include the physical act of throwing one's arms around another person, but that action has different meanings in different contexts because the purpose differs. When a spouse hugs his sister-in-law it does not mean he is being unfaithful—unless the hug has that purpose.

Moore then wonders why we do not think the same thing about more intense sexual actions. He is not saying, of course, that a husband can say with any seriousness, "Oh, I had sex with your sister, but it was meaningless." The range of possible meanings is not infinite. However, he does argue that sexual intercourse need not mean the total and complete commitment of love made in marriage. It has a range of purposes, most of which can be good in the right context. Thus it is incoherent of the tradition to take this one action and say, essentially, it can only have a single meaning, regardless of our intentions and regardless of context. Moreover, hugging other people does not ruin the special meaning of hugging one's spouse, so the tradition has no grounds for saying that if one has sex in committed relationships, then one is ruining the meaning and purpose of sex with one's spouse.

Moore's argument suggests that the meaning of bodily actions is not "just there," but is taken from the context, and it is not obvious why sexual actions cannot be valid outside of the single context of marriage. One theologian, outlining a position somewhat like Moore's, made a distinction between "regressive" and "progressive" premarital relationships (Marciano Vidal, "*Moral de las relaciones sexuales prematrimonales*," 517–32). Regressive relationships do not aim at all toward the ends of marriage. They include relationships of exploitation, pleasure, and mere play. Progressive relationships tend toward the purposes found ultimately in marriage. This tendency is effective, he argues, in the sense that progressive premarital relationships do in fact form and shape us to be good married people by offering us the chance to practice the associated virtues (fidelity, care, etc.). The author avoids endorsing premarital sex in progressive relationships but suggests that such actions can be accepted insofar as their tendencies to mimic the aims of sex in marriage are actualized.

Notice that these authors do not argue in terms of sexual self-fulfillment but follow a similar logic to the one we used in the last section about dating. Recall that dating relationships that function as training for the sort of love, care, and trust desired in marriage—that aim in the same direction as marriage—were seen as good. Here these authors similarly argue that so long as the relationship aims at ends compatible with those of marriage, and in particular self-giving love, sex can be good and reasonable.

Official Catholic teaching, however, states that premarital sex is never good, that it is always wrong, in any circumstances, whether as a one-night stand or a week before your wedding. Why does the tradition say this? Many writers argue that premarital sex is always a lie. They don't mean by this that it is always the result of an intentional deception. Rather, they argue that sexual intercourse is an act of total self-giving, so if our overall commitment is not total (i.e., marriage), then our act of total physical self-giving is a false expression of unity.

The Catholic position is strengthened by the fact that it is so difficult to know where to place the line indicating "we're ready." As many know from experience, that sort of a conversation is hard to have in the absence of a total commitment. It is all too easy for persons who want sex to say they are committed or to say the right things about marriage but not mean them.

Moral theologian Richard McCormick, in surveying some of these arguments, offers two further practical objections. He notes that "the intention to marry, however sincere and intense . . . can be, often is, and not infrequently should be revoked" (*Notes on Moral Theology 1965–1980*, 458). Especially for Catholic couples going through various programs of marriage preparation, the period of engagement ought to be a period of the most intense discernment, especially concerning one's partner. Introducing sex at this time is unlikely to help such reflection. McCormick also notes that "the process leading to marriage cannot be converted that easily to read marriage-as-process" (p. 458). McCormick agrees that marriage is a process, but where the process most naturally begins is with the vows and the celebration; there is a prior process, but it should not be named marriage.

As for the argument from context, Lauren Winner turns Moore's argument on its head. Winner argues that premarital sex is "fake sex" because it lacks the reality of the context of lifelong commitment.

> Indeed, one can say that in Christianity's vocabulary the only real sex is the sex that happens in a marriage; the faux sex that goes on outside marriage is not really sex at all. The physical coming together that happens between two people who are not married is only a distorted imitation of sex, as Walt Disney's Wilderness Lodge Resort is only a simulation of real wilderness. The danger is that when we spend too much time in the simulations, we lose the capacity to distinguish between the ersatz and the real. (*Real Sex*, 38)

The context really does matter, and that's why it's essential for sex to happen within marriage, within the day-to-day life of a household to which both partners are committed for a lifetime. Winner forthrightly acknowledges that premarital sex can feel good, but that feeling does not validate the goodness of the action. "Good sex" before marriage often mimics marriage. That mimicking is the problem. Imitations can often produce all sorts of problems.

David McCarthy's analysis of the day-to-day life of marriage makes a similar move. He essentially argues that no married couple will tell you that the meaning of every one of their sexual actions is "total self-giving." Indeed, the "transcendent meaning" of sex may be found in those peak experiences people often feel outside of marriage. Instead, McCarthy suggests, sex should be in marriage specifically because it can mean so many different things, but only insofar as it is connected to the whole of a common, shared life together. Premarital sex, by contrast, can only mean one of two things: it is either about mutual sexual pleasure or it is about a transcendent thrill detached from the everyday tasks of real love (*Sex and Love in the Home*, 46–48).

For Discussion

1. What's the difference between the commitment in a "committed" relationship and the commitment in marriage? How does this difference affect the meaning of sex in either relationship?

2. Can the total giving of the body in sex logically precede the total giving of the whole person in marriage? How would you justify either side of this argument?

3. Explain how you might be able to tell whether a particular relationship is progressive or regressive. What are the criteria for differentiation?

Evaluating Sexual Actions: Sex and Procreation

McCarthy's analysis in particular points us toward something we have hitherto ignored in analyzing sexual intercourse: its baby-making purpose, usually called procreation. Whenever my class is divided up between the one-night-standers and the committed-relationship-sex advocates, the latter group will almost always pull out the "what if you have a one-night stand and get pregnant?" card. Sex can be procreative, whether we want it to or not.

This adds an extra criterion to "committed relationship" sex. Not only must the partners be truly committed to one another, but they also must be prepared to deal with the possibility of getting pregnant. You shouldn't have sex with someone without having a plan for that possibility, they say. To do so is to open the door to abortion.

Thus the classic basis for the rule against all premarital sex is that such an action involves an injustice to the baby that might be conceived. Thomas Aquinas argues exactly this in asserting that premarital sex (which he calls fornication) is not only a sin, but a mortal sin. "Every sin committed directly against human life is a mortal sin. Now simple fornication implies an inordinateness that tends to injure the life of the offspring to be born of this union" (*Summa Theologica*, II–II, 154, 2). That is, the lack of order in this action is its failure to recognize that it is not only the couple who has an interest in the action, but also any possible offspring. This possible baby requires care and upbringing, not simply in terms of basic nourishment but also in terms of education, formation, and the like. In the case where the couple has formed what Aquinas calls an "indeterminate union" the offspring is likely to be deprived of the care it justly deserves. The critical failure of love in premarital sex may not be between the man and woman, but of both parties to the possible baby. Aquinas thinks it is particularly likely, in such cases, that males will neglect their role in raising the child.

For Aquinas, this line of argument is far more important than any question of lust or incomplete love. It is pointed out as a counterargument that "inordinate use of food is not always a mortal sin" (obj. 6), so perhaps inordinate use of sex is not always a mortal sin. Aquinas replies that the parallel fails because fornication does not simply involve excessive sexual desires. If it did, it might not be a mortal sin. But fornication hinders the good of the possible child, whereas "one meal does not hinder the good of a man's whole life." Thus Aquinas makes clear that sexual action involves something more than just sexual appetite specifically because it results in conception.

What are possible responses? First, the couple might maintain that they are ready to take care of a possible baby. They would not resort to abortion. But would they marry? This raises a further question: is an accidental pregnancy a good reason to get married? Marriage, as we will see in the next chapter, is meant to be a free choice, a vow made by each partner to the other, not because of any external pressure, but simply out of love. Obviously, if an unintended pregnancy is the trigger for deciding to get married, it is not clear that such a choice is free. Hence there is potential harm not only for the child, but also for the couple.

The reader may respond that I have moved too quickly to assume that "taking care of the baby" means the couple getting married. Aren't there other options, such as putting the child up for adoption or raising the child as a single mother? One must consider whether these options involve an injustice to the child—which is a delicate question these days!

Let us first consider the option of single motherhood. It is certainly the case that our society has seen a rapid and dramatic increase in single-parent families. One survey showed that in 1960, 17% of children under age eighteen lived apart from their biological fathers whereas that number increased to 35% by the late 1990s (National Marriage Project, "The State of Our Unions"). These numbers are not likely to decrease, as 33% of all births in 1999, and 38% in 2005, were to unwed mothers, versus about 5% in 1960. Moreover, from a Catholic perspective, these numbers must be considered "after abortion"—if abortion is not an option, these numbers would certainly be much higher (approximately 25% of all pregnancies are aborted).

However, public opinion about single motherhood has certainly shifted along with these trends. Some 51% of high school senior boys, and 56% of girls, said that having a child without being married is worthwhile and not harmful to anyone. These numbers show a particularly rapid increase over the years among women. A clear majority of young people today see no problem with the possibility of single parenthood. Yet these views run counter to nearly all the sociological evidence, which suggests that single parenthood adversely affects not only the child but also the single parent. This is particularly true in cases where the parent is poor or working-class and in cases where large numbers of children in a given community or sub-culture are being parented by single parents—for example, 69% of all African-American births in 1999 were to single mothers. And research by the National Marriage Project shows that stepfamilies are no improvement for children over single-parent households.

This is a particularly delicate issue because, without doubt, there are single parents who raise children well, even heroically, and arguments against single parenthood seem to imply otherwise. But it is one thing to accept and heroically take on single parenthood because of adverse and unintended circumstances; it is quite another to intend single parenthood or act in ways that make it likely to happen. It is unrealistic to presume that single parenthood does not impose many strains on both parent and children—it does. It is a difficult thing that few people would directly desire. And clearly people do not desire it, as evinced by the use of contraceptions in premarital sex, and the fear of getting pregnant that many women have in such relationships.

Adoption is a somewhat different issue. Our society has an extensive and well-regulated system of adoption, and there is a particularly long waiting list for healthy white infants. The emotional issues involved in adoption are more complicated. Obviously the woman must carry a child for nine months and then deliver it, only to give it up and never see it again. This is not generally something one would desire as a good, though it may be a good act in certain circumstances—compared with other options, it may indeed be the best one. But the question we are considering here is whether one is reasonable in choosing the risk of carrying a child and putting it up for adoption when choosing to have sex outside a marital relationship.

There's an obvious objection at this point: most acts of premarital sex do not result in children, especially since the advent of effective and widely available contraception—not an option when Aquinas was writing. The increasing acceptability of premarital sex relies on the presence of effective contraceptive methods.

Of course, Catholic teaching regards the use of contraception as immoral in all circumstances, marital or extramarital. We will not explore that issue here, other than to note that Aquinas's argument is considerably weakened if reliable contraception is available and deemed morally acceptable. But how effective is contraception? By far the most popular forms today are condoms and birth-control pills. Condoms are notoriously prone to failure, due to various mechanical problems. Further, despite concerted efforts by condom manufacturers and safe-sex advocates, condoms aren't considered sexy. The popularity of birth-control pills testifies to their greater rate of effectiveness (claims range as high as 99%) and the advantage of "invisibility." However, pills do not protect against sexually transmitted diseases, and there are concerns about the possible long-term effects of regular pill usage on women's bodies. While some in the health community would more or less like to see every woman of childbearing age on the pill, others have suggested that, as with earlier versions of the pill, its use is like one long-term extended experiment with the female population, ultimately for the sake of making women's bodies work more like men's.

More importantly, the effectiveness of contraception is perceived to be much higher than it actually is. A recent study by an abortion-rights group states that half of all abortions were performed on women who were using contraceptives. The same study gives an actual failure rate for the pill at 8% and barrier methods at 15%. The odds of getting pregnant while using the pill are approximately the same as the odds of a regular cigarette smoker getting lung cancer. Notice that our perspective on the effectiveness of birth control is skewed. Most people would affirm, "Pills effectively prevent pregnancy," but would not affirm, "Cigarette smoking does not cause lung cancer"—but the statistical evidence for both statements is the same!

A further moral consideration is that spontaneous abortions are one way that modern birth control pills prevent pregnancy. The early birth control pills had high doses of hormones that effectively prevented conception but had serious side effects on women's health. As manufacturers reduced levels of hormones, the possibility of conception increased. Thus modern, low-dose birth control pills have several lines of defense against pregnancy, one of which is weakening the mother's placenta, so that even if conception does occur, the fetus will fail to implant in the womb. If one believes that life begins at conception, such an event is an abortion.

None of these arguments clinches the moral case for or against contraception: there are contraceptive methods that do not pose the abortion problem, use of multiple methods can increase effectiveness, and the vast majority of occurrences of premarital sex do not result in children. The important point is that specific moral issues are not isolated from one another. One's attitude toward premarital sex is related to one's evaluation of both abortion, contraception, and single-parent households. All these issues are interrelated.

Not-Quite-Sex Actions

So maybe you're persuaded by the above arguments, or maybe you just think sex is a special act that it is fitting and beautiful to give only to one's spouse. That's a good argument, too. But obviously there are plenty of other sexual actions besides intercourse. What about these? Or, as a student once asked in the title of an excellent paper, "Is Oral Moral?"

Let's start by considering Aquinas's argument against premarital sex based on the injustice done to the child that is thus conceived. When considering the question of the sinfulness of "touches and kisses" (*Summa Theologica*, II-II, 154, 4), naturally someone raises the objection that these do not result in any future child, so perhaps they are not sinful, or at least not mortally sinful. Aquinas responds by noting first that intention must be considered. Obviously, we hug and kiss and touch friends and family, in joy or comfort or affection. There is no sin in this. But, he says, when we hug and kiss and touch with the specific intention of experiencing "lustful pleasure," we sin mortally. Aquinas cites the passage where Jesus says, "Everyone who looks at a woman with lust has already committed adultery with her in his heart" (Matt. 5:28). Aquinas adds that the source of premarital sex and these other "lesser" acts is the same, so to encourage the source is ultimately to hurt possible future offspring.

It may seem that Aquinas is arguing that sexual pleasure is bad, but that is not the case. He argues that married couples may enjoy sex, so long as their specific intention for having sex is not exclusively pleasure. What he means here is pleasure outside of due order (i.e., marriage) is wrong. At this point, critics maintain that the entire Christian tradition is flawed because of its fear of sexual pleasure. And we may concede that Aquinas shares his predecessors' suspicions about sexual pleasure. The argument about sexual actions other than intercourse largely hangs on the background argument about the place of sexual pleasure in the Christian life. Is sexual pleasure contrary to the love of neighbor? Is it compatible with it?

We need to note here that Aquinas is thinking on an extremely broad scale. He includes "soft speeches" and "jocularity" in his definition, actions we might consider flirting or arousing conversation. He is consistent here, for what is at issue in all of these is the question of the use of sexual pleasure.

Catholic teaching has come to see sexual pleasure as a good thing. Indeed, even in the nineteenth century one archbishop advised husbands to learn how to have sex with their wives in ways that encourage their pleasure and orgasm. John Paul II spoke of the almost transcendent quality of mutual orgasm, where this pleasure is completely shared. We have come a long way from Augustine, who suggested that even marital sex was somewhat sinful since there was absolutely no way to avoid experiencing pleasure!

The official teaching remains that all not-quite-sex acts are wrong, but the arguments now used are different from Aquinas's—and somewhat tortured. One group of authors admit, "There is always some difficulty in teaching these matters in balanced ways to young people" (Ronald Lawler, Joseph Boyle, and William E. May, *Catholic Sexual Ethics*, 185). Denying that the teaching is "excessively prudish," and rather defending its "inner consistency," they maintain that acceptance of not-quite-sex actions will inevitably lead to the acceptance of premarital sex and masturbation. That is, they make a slippery slope argument: once you accept making out for pleasure, then you can't stop the slide down the slope until other sexual actions, including intercourse, look reasonable on the same grounds.

The question for all slippery slope arguments is: how slippery is the slope? That is to say, how closely connected are the supposed analogies of action? On the one hand, the authors are right in saying that such actions often lead to intercourse. There is a reason why the analogy of "first base" or "second base" is sometimes used in referring to stages of sexual intimacy: they do lead from one to another. Biologically, one need only look at male arousal. It is also true that if pleasure is accepted as a good reason for trivial sexual acts, more serious sexual acts can be justified on the same basis.

On the other hand, the slope seems to have some quite clear footholds. Couples can recognize that sexual intercourse can result in pregnancy, while other sexual acts cannot. For some that will be reason enough not to slide down the slope. Moreover, masturbation is fundamentally different from all these acts. It aims at pleasure but is unable to express love because it is solitary, not relational. Not-quite-sex acts performed by a couple, in contrast, express love and mutual enjoyment, at whatever level.

Jason Evert may be taken as a representative defender of the traditional attitude. He suggests that any action you wouldn't do if Jesus were sitting next to you on the couch can't be loving. He notes that people can and do get sexual diseases from oral sex. He argues that such acts endanger the soul of the other person by drawing him or her into lust, and so cannot be loving. He suggests that one should think about what one's future spouse is doing right now: if she is giving some other guy head, are you OK with that? He says that French kissing is "penetrative" and therefore "tells a man's body that it should prepare for intercourse, and when a man is aroused, generally he is not satisfied until he is relieved" (*If You Really Loved Me*, 101). He says, "If a guy needs to place his genitals into the mouth of his girlfriend in order to show her what she means to him, then it shows exactly what she means to him" (p. 104).

This is clever rhetoric—but clever only goes so far. Evert fails to differentiate between rhetorical flourishes and actual arguments here. For one thing, sexual acts are naturally intimate—I wouldn't want Jesus physically sitting next to me on the couch, but I don't want him sitting next to me on my marriage bed either, because the act is intimate. Moreover, a man who cannot control his arousal "until he is relieved" may have more troubles in life than French kissing. And a future spouse's sexual history might be susceptible to forgiveness, as are many things in our lives, and so the purity image fails in terms of the gospel.

It's not that Evert's conclusions are indefensible. The question is whether they are mandatory for everyone. The issue is purpose, as both Aquinas and Evert recognize. Evert wisely notes that when he was young he couldn't differentiate between desiring pleasure and loving someone. It all got mixed together. Unless you are truly able to make this distinction, he urges, you ought not to engage in sexual acts. Any action in which we use the other person's body simply for our own pleasure is instrumentalization and is incompatible with the command to love others. But surely, at least with some degree of maturity, we ought to be able to hug and kiss and touch out of genuine love for the other person.

Aquinas's argument remains critical, although we may suggest that some actions will be acceptable even if sexual, even if pleasure is experienced, as long as we are not specifically seeking the pleasure. Concretely, what does this look like? I suspect we know when physical acts of affection are truly a matter of love, a sort of equivalence to the elegance of dancing as an activity of physical affection. We might say that appropriate sexual acts *accompany* shared activity, rather than *constitute* the main activity. In some sense, this is very much what marital sexuality will also look like, albeit at a much deeper and more constant level. Sexual acts accompany the shared life of the couple. This consistency between premarital and marital sexual action is often lost, even by defenders of the tradition. They sometimes sound as though marriage is a license for pleasure, like a license to drive: before you've got it, you can't go anywhere, but after you've got it, you can go anywhere you want. Those of us who grew up in old-fashioned city neighborhoods know that going places doesn't always require a car: we walked, we took the bus, we biked, and slowly but surely the range of places we could go on our own expanded over time. This helped us understand ourselves, and so too does a gradual expansion of our sexual actions, so long as those actions are consistently aimed at the good of the other person rather than our own pleasure.

By now some of you are exhausted and frustrated with all this, all your stereotypes about moral theology confirmed. What's the big deal, you say? Can't Catholics just be normal? Why not just leave it at no premarital sex? Actually, you wouldn't be frustrated with all this reflection if it weren't a big deal to you as well. If somebody tells you not to eat insects, you might rightly respond, "No big deal," because you don't want to eat insects. But when somebody tells you not to do something you really want to do, then it's a big deal. All we're doing here is trying to understand and evaluate an action, just as one might evaluate any other action.

For those of you who want more concrete guidance, the best I've found comes from Lauren Winner. She reports that her pastor proposed the "rotunda rule" for her and her boyfriend. At the center of the University of Virginia campus there is a large rotunda where she and he would often take walks and stop and talk. As a guideline the pastor suggested that they not do anything they wouldn't mind doing on the steps of the rotunda. The pastor moved the issue away from concerns about "how far" and toward concerns about context. Essentially, the pastor offered them a relatively quiet place, but still a public one. By thinking in terms of public places, even quiet ones, the couple might naturally engage in physical actions that were affectionate but limited.

Winner observes that one can kiss for a long time on the steps of the rotunda, but one is unlikely to start stripping. Partly, the rotunda rule reflects the underlying key that a couple's dating relationship, because not publicly vowed, should remain a relationship *in public*, even as it becomes intimate. This is not out of fear, but out of respect—respect for the lack of commitment, respect for the proper limits of emotional sharing and attachment. It is a form of reverence. But Winner notes that the rotunda rule is also an example of using one's community for discernment about these issues. In her case, she was "experienced" sexually, whereas her boyfriend had not really had any sexual experience. The rule provided a reasonable balance for them. Winner suggests that different couples, with different backgrounds and different histories, might set up somewhat different limits.

Essentially, these "rules" point back to the importance of finding the right basis for a dating relationship in the first place and having a real community within which you share the relationship. Get these right, fulfill these purposes, and all this hair-splitting sex stuff might not seem so complicated.

For Discussion

1. Which of the above proposals makes the most sense to you, and why?

2. How do these rules avoid becoming merely legalistic? That is, how are they meant to contribute to the overall purpose of the practice of dating relationships?

Masturbation

As already mentioned, Catholicism has consistently held an absolute norm against masturbation, again with the idea that the purpose of our actions is to learn how to control and give ourselves sexually, not how to use sex to fulfill personal needs. This argument is not easy to process, because masturbation is quite common. According to one study of adults, over 60% of men and 40% of women report masturbating in the past year, with almost 30%

of men reporting that they did so once a week or more. The numbers, especially among women, show a decrease with older generations, and so it is reasonable to assume that, as it is discussed more freely, it will be practiced more regularly. The survey also suggests that the theory that masturbation is an outlet or substitute for the sexually deprived is false; instead, "it is an activity that stimulates and is stimulated by other sexual behavior" (Robert T. Michael et al., *Sex in America*, 165).

The traditional condemnation of masturbation by Christians sometimes relied on a faulty biological view of reproduction. Specifically, it was thought that the male semen contained the entire active element for a new human life, while the female simply provided a place for this life to develop. Hence, masturbation to orgasm ("spilling one's seed") was seen as something like murder, or at the least a wasting of life, which had negative effects for the human race as a whole. Certainly classic writers also suggested that the purely pleasure-seeking character of masturbation also suggested problems, but the reproductive concern remained paramount.

Contemporary Catholic debate over masturbation has shifted towards regarding the morality of masturbation along more psychological grounds—that is—in terms of purposes—with the recognition that not all acts of masturbation are subject to the same moral description. Thus, the debate has centered on whether or not certain sorts of masturbation should still be considered wrong. The official position has maintained that all such acts must be regarded as wrong, since no act of masturbation can be ordered properly to the actual good of human sexuality. However, levels of personal responsibility for the wrongness of the act are understood to vary considerably. That is to say, there is a great difference between an adolescent engaging in some, perhaps quite indescribable, experimentation and the adult who jerks off several times a day.

Other moral theologians have sought a more fine-grained analysis, acknowledging that masturbation is best viewed not as a moral problem in itself, but as a symptom that might indicate different things in different contexts. Perhaps most importantly such theologians have differentiated between three broad types of masturbation: adolescent masturbation, compensatory masturbation, and hedonistic masturbation.

Following psychological research, adolescent masturbation may simply be a normal phenomenon of sexual development, minimally problematic unless the activity becomes habitual or is not gradually integrated with relationships. Such acts may indeed be "objectively wrong," in the sense that they do not achieve the real purposes of human sexuality, but involve little if any hostility toward these purposes. Indeed, focusing on the condemnation of these acts may serve to hinder development.

Compensatory masturbation refers to acts of masturbation that are driven by a sense of loneliness, isolation, separation, or frustration, whether due to hostile family life, separation from one's spouse, or some other factor. It is evident that the problem in these situations is not the masturbation itself, but the underlying sense of isolation. This is not to say that the masturbation is acceptable or good (although some moralists argue this), but it does suggest that simple willpower is not the solution here. Such occasional acts can lead to a dependence on masturbation that would be problematic. This sort of masturbation is "pathetic" in the sense of denoting something sad: it deserves a sort of pity. From the point of view of the purposes of human sexuality, it would appear that such masturbation is an unfortunately twisted attempt at communion, a way of expressing a longing that is frustrated.

Catholic moralists, on the other hand, are united in condemning hedonistic masturbation, which surely involves a significant misunderstanding of purpose. One author asserts, "Masturbation simply for the sake of the pleasure involved, without any effort at control or integration, can be indicative of self-centeredness, isolation, and evasion of relational responsibility. . . . Exploitation of one's sexuality freely, deliberately, and consistently in this manner . . . constitutes the substantial inversion of the sexual order" (Kosnik, *Human Sexuality*, 228). Such masturbation is freely chosen and not subjected to any sort of control. This "inversion of the sexual order" involves a fundamental understanding of sexuality and sexual acts as focused on self-gratification, which is basically all that masturbation can provide. Sexual acts focused on the self cannot be ordered toward the love of another. In an objective sense, such masturbation is a symptom of exactly this misunderstanding of sexuality, with the result that it is a serious matter, perhaps more serious than the other, relational issues we have discussed in this chapter.

This will seem a harsh conclusion to many, since habitual masturbation for pleasure is not at all uncommon in the adult population. Traditionally, Catholic moral theologians have been priests; their major experience with problems of masturbation occurred in the context of being trained for and living out vows of celibacy. Hence there was a sense that masturbation was most commonly of the second kind above, a compensatory strategy that would pass with growth and the support of community. However, the findings cited in the survey above, as well as the common experience of college students and young adults, suggest that much masturbation is basically hedonistic rather than compensatory. If so, a serious problem with our fundamental understanding of sexuality may be at issue.

Some may object that masturbation seems to involve little if any harm, and masturbation is largely practiced not as a substitute for ordinary sexual relations, but as a supplement to them, thus calling into question the claim that hedonistic masturbation constitutes an inversion of the sexual order.

In response to the first problem, one should note that if one attempts to construe sexual morality purely in terms of "harm"—presumably visible and tangible harm—many actions will seem acceptable, including hooking up, consensual adultery, and even well-regulated prostitution. This position fails not simply because "harm" is inadequate as a moral norm, but more importantly because harm in these activities is hard to construe, particularly in terms of harming the self or harming the psychological and moral aim of the self and others. Now to be sure these activities are not socially harmless, but the personal harm involved is often great and difficult to measure. In the issue under discussion, masturbators are unlikely to be persons capable of carrying on a well-ordered, truly loving relationship. They have made sexuality into something different.

If that claim is true, then what of the second problem? Why does the hedonistic masturbator seek relationships at all? The point is that the masturbator has made sexuality into something different—has more or less ruined the meaning of sex—in such a way that what he or she seeks from all sexual acts is self-gratification. That is, the masturbator is unable to allow sexual acts to mean what they are supposed to mean. The problem is not that masturbation will act as a substitute for sexual acts with others; indeed, the indication is that it may make one more eager to have sex with others. But to what end? That is the problem. The masturbator has ultimately made all sexual acts, not just masturbation, about the self, and so is ultimately unable to experience the vulnerability and relationality appropriate to sexual actions.

For Discussion

1. What common explanations do you hear used to justify masturbation? What do these explanations implicitly say about the purpose of sexuality?

2. In terms of purpose, is masturbation morally different from the use of drugs? Explain possible similarities and differences.

Conclusion

What was applied to the hedonistic masturbator might be used as a summary for this entire section. Ultimately our desires to perform all these sexual acts apart from the commitment of marriage indicates that we have begun to see sex as something of a personal right, something we deserve and need for ourselves. It is not for the sake of the other, and certainly not simply for the sake of procreation. Exercising our sexuality is exercising our personal rights, rights to self-expression and pleasure. If indeed we view our sexuality like this, then it is no wonder that someone telling us not to do these things sounds downright oppressive to us. The problem is not that most people have no sexual morality: the problem is the view that any actions involving consenting bodies should not be objectionable. Our bodies are ours to do with as we please. That's our right.

To recognize that our bodies do not belong to us like a piece of property is to see these bodies as gifts, both to us and others. Seeing bodies as gifts, we can then use them as gifts to others. This gift-based view of our bodies fundamentally undergirds traditional Catholic opposition to many of these non-marital sexual acts. Our bodies are gifts of love, to another and to the future generation. This notion of the gift character and potential of our bodies is the strongest of the "strong evaluations" that underlie our evaluation of particular sexual acts.

Of course, it is not as simple as some people make it out to be. Reading the above description, you'd think our society was divided into selfish hedonists and generous lovers. Actually we see a mixture of both. As we noted earlier, American society is deeply divided on this point, opening itself to hedonism and freedom while steadfastly maintaining an overwhelming sentimentality and attachment to happy, romantic endings about true love. So we exist with both narratives, and often enough, we try to practice both simultaneously. Perhaps we engage the hedonist, hoping to convert him or her to true love. Perhaps we find innocence attractive, introducing it to a sexier life. There are many scripts, but all walk the edge of trying to balance these two ultimately incompatible stories. And these two scripts live within most of us.

Which script do we follow, really? Living out two incompatible scripts in any area of our life is bound to produce confusion. It can be exciting. If we're lucky it might even result in happiness. But it also leaves us subject to catastrophe, living both scripts incompletely and ending up with no clear sense of an end at all. Ethical reflection on the particular sexual actions of our lives ought to turn us back to this deeper question, of what sort of sexual people we are aiming to be, what we really want, and what stories do and do not aim us at that end of true happiness.

7

Practices of Sexuality
The Purposes of Marriage

All of the chapters in this book have been leading up to this one. The central action in Catholic sexual ethics is the complex practice we call marriage. Marriage is not just the wedding-day act of getting married. Marriage, in the Catholic tradition, names the purpose of our being sexual creatures—to make this commitment and carry it out, with all the actions that entails.

Marriage is not simply a Catholic thing: it is both a natural reality and a sacrament. It is not a result of the Catholic God-story that our sexuality focuses ultimately on marriage: the practice is shared with nearly every other human culture and story, albeit with different details. A sacrament is not just something special or something celebrated in church. Many Protestant churches celebrate marriages in church, but do not regard marriage as a sacrament. Perhaps the most vivid Catholic definition of sacrament is found in the Vatican II document, *Lumen Gentium*, on the mystery of the church. The document proclaims that the church is "the sacrament of Christ to the world." The church is the community that takes up the things of God's creation and transforms them into visible signs that not only point to but actually make Christ present to the world. The same document calls Christ "the sacrament of God," for Jesus is the one who points to and embodies God's presence in the world.

Sacraments, in terms of God's story, involve plotlines in which we as Christians—our individual and communal actions—are ways of shining the light of God's love into the wider world. A sacrament "acts" by taking up ordinary things and transforming them to show a different reality, a new creation, God's kingdom. The Eucharist is a meal: the preparation and sharing of the meal unify the church with Christ, and the community with one another. It is also a sacrifice, Christ's sacrifice of himself, giving up his life for the sake of the world.

Marriage, to put it bluntly, is weird. It is the one sacrament where the "human reality" involved is not merely symbolic, but the actual reality. The Eucharist is a *symbolic* meal and baptism is a *symbolic* bath, but marriage is *actually* marriage. It is the fullness of the natural human reality, but it is also that reality transformed into a sign of Christ, a place where Christ is made visible and present to the world.

In his *Summa Theologica*, Thomas Aquinas divides the purposes of marriage between those that belong to marriage "as an office of nature" and those that belong to it "as a sacrament of the Church." The Catholic tradition has long struggled to relate and understand these two overlapping realities of marriage. We will divide our treatment of marriage into two sections: the natural human reality, and the sacramental transformation of that reality taken up in service of the kingdom of God. These are certainly connected, both in theory and in practice; yet the distinction is vital for understanding what Christians are doing when they marry.

Marriage and Contemporary American Society

Let's start with a question: who do you want to marry? Most people will not be hard pressed to come up with an answer. Even if you don't have a specific person in mind, you can imagine the sort of person you'd want to marry. Perhaps a list of qualities will come to mind. You want to marry your best friend. You want to marry someone with a sense of humor. You want to share certain interests, so you can do activities together. You want to marry someone who is a good sexual partner. You want to marry someone who will be there for you when you are hurting or suffering, or who will come to your defense in time of trial. You probably want someone who looks a certain way and who will be a good parent. The list can go on. While each of us may have different specifications on the list, the general categories will probably be consistent.

In a recent survey, 94% of young Americans indicated they wanted to marry someone who was their soul mate (Popenoe, "The State of Our Unions"). This indicates how much we really want marriage, how marriage is the ultimate aim of our sexual lives. Notice that I did not ask, "Do you want to get married?" For most of us it is almost a given that marriage constitutes one of our most important ends in life. And yet it's not inevitable that people choose to get married. In today's society, where it is possible to get a lot of the benefits of marriage without marrying, some question whether people should marry at all. Why not just have relationships? When one goes bad, move on to the next. Isn't that what happens with divorce anyway?

The answer to the question, *who* do you want to marry? can tell us a lot about *why* we marry. As we've seen from the first chapter, *why?* is a question about purpose. Just as we discussed the practice of dating in terms of purposes, we need to explore our aim when choosing to marry. Is the purpose of marriage to satisfy all your desires? Or would that be idolatry?

In terms of ethics, it's not easy to define what, exactly, people are doing when they get married in our society. Are two people who fly to Vegas to get married doing the same action as two conservative Christians who get married? Complicating the picture even further is the fact that when our parents or grandparents got married it involved a partnership where gender roles and tasks were well defined. Becoming a wife or husband meant something different to our grandparents than it does to most of us.

The diversity of our cultural attitudes makes it challenging to generalize about marriage in today's culture. However, there are certain trends that can be highlighted as generally true.

Most people plan to marry. Surveys indicate that over 90% of teens and young adults say that they intend to marry someday. For most, marriage constitutes an important life project. Only a small percentage utterly reject marriage. In some northern European countries, more than half of cohabitating couples are in quasi-permanent relationships but have not married, but such couples form a small minority in American society. The choice to marry remains a central one for defining our lives.

People are marrying at a later age. The average marriage age in American in 1950 was twenty-two for males and twenty for females. The most recent numbers indicate an average age of twenty-seven and twenty-five for men and women, respectively (Census Bureau Current Population Survey 2003, "Not Married Yet?" 3A). Reasons for postponing marriage vary widely, although practical considerations (job training, education, career, and housing) remain important. Just as important is a trend toward "identity exploration"—a sense that the twenties are a time when the self is engaged in the project of discovering who one is through experimentation with a wide variety of experiences, including experiences with various romantic partners.

People are participating in quasi-marital long-term relationships, usually involving sexual activity and living together. For many the intention to delay marriage is paired with involvement in relationships that look a lot like marriage. Such quasi-marital relationships, even when they don't involve living together, often involve intimacy and shared activity that are similar to that of a married couple. It is hard to know whether to categorize them as dating or marriage.

The fear of divorce is prominent. It is not news anymore that half of American marriages end in divorce—although to be fair, the statistics rightly understood would now peg the number at more like 40%. That high percentage makes people feel vulnerable. The current generation is the first with parents that had such a high divorce rate. The experience of their parents' divorce strongly colors the view of many. Even so, most couples do not think it will happen to them: in one recent survey, 86% of couples marrying today said that they could never imagine their marriage falling apart (Alan Wolfe, *Moral Freedom*, 41).

People are looking for a soul mate. If anything unites people with different views of marriage, it is that their ideal is marriage with a soul mate: 94% of Americans in their twenties agreed with the statement, "When you marry you want your spouse to be your soul mate, first and foremost." Even more extraordinary, 88% believed that the perfect person was indeed out there and would turn up in their lives. The soul mate ideal encompasses many different aspects of one's identity, including leisure interests, political views, personal habits, personality style, sexual chemistry, and beliefs and values—though not explicit religious affiliation. Only 42% of survey respondents thought it was "important" to find someone who shared their religious faith. The authors note, "The popular soul-mate ideal may be a substitute for more traditional religious understandings of marriage. In a secular society, . . . young people may be attracted to the soul-mate ideal because it endows intimate relationships with a higher spiritual, though not explicitly religious, significance" (Popenoe, "Unions," 4).

As you read these trends, did you think, "This is a good thing," or, "Oh, no, this is moving in the wrong direction"? Marriage is a social practice, and while social trends are important for accurate description, they do not tell us if this or that trend is good. Evaluation of trends depends on some sort of "standard story" of the purpose or purposes of marriage: are we moving closer to that ideal, or further from it? Part of the difficulty in discussing marriage in today's society is a lack of clarity about what is essential to marriage in the standard story. Historian Stephanie Coontz, writing in response to the many authors who claim marriage is in crisis, suggests that we often fall into a nostalgia trap involving a vision of a mythical ideal of marriage and the family. In fact, there is no single model of a traditional family. Even when we focus on a specific past model that we think is good, we may forget the conditions that made such a model possible. For example, do we want to give up on women's equality? Coontz points out that models of marriage and family do not exist in isolation from other social choices and trends in a society. In adopting a mythic model as our standard, we may be engaging in wishful thinking.

In our focus on various debates about ideal *forms* of marriage, we are sometimes distracted from the *essentials*. There are plenty of accidental features of marriage, rather like optional equipment on a car. One might like this or that option, but it is not essential to the vehicle. Are there essential elements, features that must be present for something to be called a good marriage? Are there purposes for this practice that are essential to it? These *purposes*, and not any particular *form*, are our concern as we evaluate the decision to marry.

For Discussion

1. How do you react to the trends in contemporary marriage cited above? Do you see a crisis or a new, liberating flexibility? Why? Notice how your response says something about the purposes you see as essential to marriage.

2. In your experience, how would you say your parents' marriage or your grandparents' marriage differs from the marriage to which you aspire?

The Two Purposes of Marriage

At least since the fifth century the Catholic tradition has recognized two purposes for natural marriage: the bearing and raising of children (procreation) and companionship and fidelity between the spouses (communion). These two purposes continue to form the backbone of Catholic reflection on the meaning and practice of marriage. Christians obviously did not invent these purposes but recognized them as a part of God's created order, visible to and (potentially) known by all. Marriage predates Christianity as something natural and common to all. These are, as Aquinas noted, the characteristics of marriage "as an office of nature." Just as the Catholic tradition teaches that it is wrong to kill and that it is right to help the poor, not for religious reasons, but for human ones that apply regardless of your faith, so too Catholicism has reflected on marriage as a human reality, a created reality that affects everyone's lives. These two purposes for marriage are also found outside the Catholic tradition, for they can be discovered either through revelation (reflection on God's self-communication to us through scripture and tradition) or through reason. We will draw on both sources as we explore the twin purposes of marriage.

Marriage in History: The Primacy of Procreation

So God created humankind in his image, in the image of God he created them; male and female he created them. God blessed them, and God said to them, "Be fruitful and multiply, and fill the earth and subdue it." (Gen. 1:27–28)

Every human being is part of the human race, and human nature is a social reality and possesses a great and natural good, the power of friendship. . . . The first natural union of human society is the husband and wife. God did not create even these as separate individuals and join them together as if they were alien to each other, but he created the one from the other. . . . The result is the bonding of society in children, who are the one honorable fruit, not of the union of male and female, but of sexual intercourse. (Augustine, *On the Good of Marriage*, 1.1)

In earlier times, finding a soul mate was not usually the purpose of marriage. Marriage, in all its variety, served a single underlying concern: having and raising children. Whether in service to their family name and property or the larger state or even God, men entered into this relationship with women in order to have children by them and be assured of the legitimate paternity of the children. As Aquinas writes, "The law of marriage was instituted to prohibit promiscuous copulation, which would prevent ascertaining the father of offspring. This is so because if any man could indiscriminately have intercourse with any woman, and no woman were to be limited to intercourse with him, ascertaining the father of offspring would be impossible, and so the care of fathers in rearing their children would be removed. And this is contrary to what befits human nature" (*On Evil*, Q. 15, a. 1). The purpose of marriage is to ensure that children will be born and raised, and in particular that men will take proper responsibility for them.

The first creation myth in Genesis describes God's desired order for the world he has created. In this story, humans are created male and female specifically so that they can "be fruitful and multiply." Like everything else God has created in this story, God finds maleness and femaleness "good"—indeed, it was "very good" (Gen. 1:31). This procreative purpose is accompanied by a blessing from God indicating its goodness and importance.

As the story of Israel unfolds in the Old Testament, this procreative purpose stands at the center of the story. Abraham, the father of the nation of Israel, and his wife Sarah receive a promise from God, a covenant, which is the foundation of God's special relationship with Israel. This promise is explicitly about descendents, and yet Abraham and Sarah have no children. After an episode in which the couple tries to produce an heir by having Abraham sleep with Sarah's maidservant (a not uncommon practice at the time), God reaffirms that the promise will be fulfilled through Abraham and Sarah—and it is. The importance of the child is dramatically highlighted in the story where God calls on Abraham to sacrifice this child as a test of faith. This is not a sentimental tale; the whole fate of Abraham's people hangs on the child.

Dramatic stories surrounding the miraculous birth or miraculous survival of Israelite children continue throughout the history of the people, and all suggest that children are a supreme blessing from God. After all, it is through the family unit that God's promise to Israel, God's covenant, is maintained.

Other stories in Israel's history reinforce the need to marry for the purpose of offspring. The levirate marriage law (Deut. 25:5–10) requires the late husband's brother to marry the widow, in order that the deceased should have heirs and the family line should continue. In Numbers 36:1–9, a dispute arises about intermarriage between different tribes in Israel, and Moses proclaims that each woman with an inheritance should marry within her own ancestral tribe "so that all Israelites may continue to possess their ancestral inheritance." Again, the concern is producing offspring in the right way, for the good of the tribe.

In all these cases, the aim of procreating was connected to the God story. God's care for Israel is an ongoing care, from generation to generation, for God has ordained Israel to a particular and special destiny. Having and rearing children is the way the story proceeds. The New Testament offers something of a twist on this theme, which we will discuss later.

Israel attached a spiritual significance to its children that Greco-Roman culture did not, but Roman society similarly saw marriage as a relationship contracted between a man and woman for the purposes of raising children—or more precisely, raising good citizens for the society. Laws were passed mandating the duty of bearing children. Philosophers often extolled the importance of sex for procreation.

Some have suggested this means that ancient marriages were loveless, but the evidence quite clearly points in a different direction. Examples of ancient marriage from Israel, Greece, and Rome indicate real affection between husband and wife. However, this affection was neither the foundation nor the purpose of the relationship, but a natural consequence as husband and wife ran a household and raised children together. Such tasks promote a kind of companionship, a shared life in which affection will grow.

How did pagan cultures deal with sexual desire? Most research indicates that in the Roman Empire men married in their late twenties, after they had established a career. This was particularly true for men of high rank, who needed to establish their reputations before settling down. Prior to marriage, several well-established options were open: prostitution was common; some men used female slaves as quasi-prostitutes; and the practice of concubinage (living with a woman in order to have sex with her, but without the intention of marrying her) was widespread. Saint Augustine, before his conversion, lived with a concubine for over a decade and developed a great deal of affection for her.

All of these institutions separated relationships designed for sexual passion from relationships designed for childrearing. Sexual relationships were almost always with a lower-class woman, without the sort of breeding and family that made for a suitable wife.

Jewish tradition officially discouraged these pagan practices. While it would be naïve to suggest that there was no prostitution in Israel, Jewish society does seem to have developed a different set of practices for marriage and sexual desire. Even during the time of the Roman Empire, young Jewish men married considerably younger than Gentiles (usually by age twenty) and were strongly discouraged from the alternative sexual practices discussed above.

For Discussion

1. What makes marriage a suitable practice for having and rearing children?

2. What is strange to you about the stories of ancient cultures cited in this section?

Love (Communion) in Ancient Marriage

Then the Lord God said, "It is not good that the man should be alone. I will make him a helper as his partner." . . . Therefore a man leaves his father and his mother and clings to his wife, and they become one flesh. And the man and his wife were both naked, and were not ashamed. (Gen. 2:18, 24–25)

[St. Paul] does not say, "And he will live with his wife," but he will be joined to her, in order to show a complete union and an intense love. (St. John Chrysostom, *Homily 20 on Ephesians*)

There is love in these ancient stories. For example, the story of Jacob (Gen. 29–31) shows him working an extra seven years in order to marry the sister, Rachel, that he preferred, and Rachel continued to be the preferred wife, even as his other wife, Leah, produced more offspring. In Israel the sense of love was indeed transferred to marriage. We might illustrate this by the famous story of David and Bathsheba. King David of Israel spies a beautiful woman bathing, finds out she is married to a poor man in his army, Uriah, but sleeps with her anyway. When she conceives, David sends Uriah out to the front lines of battle, giving orders that Uriah be left without support so that he will be killed. Uriah dies, Bathsheba weeps, then she and David get married. God, to say the least, is not pleased (2 Sam. 11:1–12:25). But it is clear that David was in love.

The moral of such stories might be that falling in love is not a good idea. In all of these contexts, falling in love does not seem to be related to any personality match or shared interest, but is based on the woman's beauty—note that we are not told that the woman falls in love with the man. The sexual attraction then leads the man, often enough, into misdeeds.

Some stories from later in Israel's history depict love a bit differently. The book of Tobit describes a marriage in detail. Tobias, a faithful man, is told by an angel, "We must stay this night in the home of Raguel. He is your relative, and he has a daughter named Sarah. He has no male heir and no daughter except Sarah only, and you, as next of kin to her, have before all other men a hereditary claim on her. Also it is right for you to inherit her father's possessions. Moreover, the girl is sensible, brave, and very beautiful, and her father is a good man" (Tob. 6:11–12). We see here what might constitute good purposes for pursuing a marriage. As one scholar remarks, "The property must be kept in the family. If the woman was beautiful, that was a bonus" (John J. Collins, "Marriage in the Old Testament," 15). We hear later that Tobias, upon learning that other suitors had died of a curse so as to preserve Sarah for him because she was his kinswoman, "loved her very much, and his heart was drawn to her" (Tob. 6:18).

In Israel's Wisdom literature a famous passage extols the virtues of a good wife, the wife who is "capable." The wife depicted is an asset to her husband because of her amazing householding skills. However, these skills should not be confused with those of a modern housewife: this woman makes business deals for land, plants crops, does good deeds for the poor, speaks with wisdom, and courageously "laughs at the time to come" (Prov. 31:25). The moral of the story? "Charm is deceitful, and beauty is vain, but a woman who fears the Lord is to be praised" (Prov. 31:30). The Wisdom literature is filled with such advice to young Israelite men to choose wives for reasons other than their charm and beauty—other than love.

We cannot leave out the Song of Songs, a group of marriage poems that are part of the biblical canon. Without a single reference to God—though many read them as a metaphor for God's love—the poems extol mutual love in explicitly erotic terms. Without reference to procreation, the lovers describe their delight in each other's presence, particularly in each other's bodies, which are described again and again with a plethora of sensual metaphors. These poems were probably common in marriage ceremonies, and served to encourage the young couple to attach the same sentiments to each other. The poems conclude with a marriage pledge: "Set me as a seal upon your heart, as a seal upon your arm; for love is strong as death, passion fierce as the grave. Its flashes are flashes of fire, a raging flame. Many waters cannot quench love, neither can floods drown it. If one offered for love all the wealth of his house, it would be utterly scorned" (Song of Sol. 8:6–7). Certainly we might recognize this as the sort of married love we are more likely to have in mind. However, such feelings were not regarded as a reasonable foundation for the choice to marry.

Similar sorts of advice to marry based on reason, not sexual attraction, can be found in Greco-Roman culture. Men are encouraged to marry "sensibly," and marriage based on eros is depicted as dangerous, even foolish.

Early Christian writers are not terribly interested in this issue, but we find glimpses of the sort of affection they feel is proper to marriage. Tertullian, one of the few married church fathers, writes to his spouse urging her not to remarry if he should die. He emphasizes the goodness of marriage, but suggests that God intends people to marry just once, and that God was more lax in earlier times specifically for the purpose of producing more offspring. However, marriage's purpose is to unite one man and one woman in complete faithfulness. If she is to remarry, he urges her strongly to marry "in the Lord." "Side by side in the Church of God and at the banquet of God, side by side in difficulties in times of persecution, and in times of consolation. Neither hides anything from the other, neither shuns the other, neither is a burden to the other" (cited by David Hunter in *Marriage in the Early Church*, 38). Mutual affection was present in the early church.

Augustine defines this purpose of marriage as "the natural association (*societas*) between the sexes." Even in couples past childbearing age, "the order of charity between husband and wife still thrives" (in Hunter, 104). He calls this purpose "fidelity," since its main force seems to be "fidelity in rendering the duty of the flesh" (in Hunter, 114). That is to say, the purpose of marriage is to keep spouses from having indiscriminate sex with others by remaining available to their spouse for sex. This may seem a meager good, but for Augustine (and for many others later in the tradition) it is quite an important service. It is a form of charity, of bodily self-giving, of putting one's body at the service of another for his or her good.

For Discussion

1. Does love arise out of married life or does it have to precede married life? If the latter, how do you react to the above stories?

2. Are certain members of the opposite sex more "sensible" marriage choices than others? What qualities do you think make for a "sensible" choice?

Contemporary Reflection and Discussion on the Purposes of Marriage

From the time of Augustine (fifth century) to the twentieth century, this basic view of the two purposes of marriage was the standard of the Catholic tradition. Thomas Aquinas, in the Middle Ages, affirmed that marriage "as an office of nature" has two purposes: "offspring" and "faith," the latter of which means fidelity in sexual intercourse, but also the unity of the one man and one woman. The modern Code of Canon Law (1917) stated, "The primary end of marriage is the procreation and education of children; its secondary end is mutual help and the allaying of concupiscence" (canon 1013, 1). *Concupiscence* here means sexual desire. Crucial to the definition, as we will see, is the classification of the two purposes as primary and secondary.

At this point in history, two important developments for the Catholic theology of marriage occur. First, in 1930, Pope Pius XI issued the encyclical *Casti Connubi* (*On Chaste Marriage*), which provided the first extensive treatment of marriage by a modern pope. The occasion of *Casti Connubi* was almost certainly the acceptance of the use of contraception by the Church of England and its affiliates, including the Episcopal Church in the United States. *Casti Connubi* retained the traditional opposition to contraception. However, *Casti Connubi* is significant because Pius XI attempts to integrate a notion of "mutual love" or "conjugal love" into the purposes of marriage.

The second development occurred among theologians known as "Catholic personalists." The personalists not only sought to integrate marital love into the purposes of marriage, but also sought to overturn the language of "primary" and "secondary" that had become attached to these purposes. The name of this group reflected the basis for their arguments: whatever legal, biological, or social purposes marriage might have, the primary meaning or essence of marriage is a relationship of persons. Regarding procreation, while personalist writers did not want to deny procreation as an intrinsic purpose of marriage, they did want to suggest that marriage is not simply an instrument. Marriage and sex are biological, but they are also human and personal. Personalists were divided on how to define this meaning clearly. Dietrich von Hildebrand spoke of total mutual self-giving, while Herbert Doms preferred the language of "a community of life embracing the whole human being." But the underlying point was clear: to shift the Catholic understanding of marriage from a primarily juridical focus on contract or marriage bond to a personal focus on the relationship itself. Personalists claimed to be following Pius XI, though their position was called into question by a Vatican document in 1944 that insisted that Catholic writers could not deny the language of "primary" and "secondary," nor suggest that the ends of marriage "are equally principal and independent."

A resolution occurred in the documents of the Second Vatican Council, which included a hotly debated section on marriage in the modern world. This document constitutes the most authoritative description of marriage offered by the Catholic tradition. The final version seemed something of a vindication for personalists: the document takes great pains to avoid the language of primary and secondary ends. Children are termed the "supreme gift" of marriage, the "ultimate crown" of marriage, the "aim" of conjugal love and life, but the phrase "while not making the other purposes of matrimony of less account" qualifies the procreative purpose. The document, rather than reinforcing the hierarchy of ends, instead treats marriage as a single reality. It is an "intimate partnership of married life and love" that is "rooted in the conjugal covenant of irrevocable personal consent." Here, the Council carefully ties together both the juridical and personal sides of marriage, connecting the partnership of persons with the consent that makes such a partnership possible. This single reality, both juridical and personal, is then explained in terms of "conjugal love," which is "an affection of the will" (i.e., a choice) and "the begetting and educating of children." Rather than stress the hierarchy of the ends, the Council insists on their harmonization in ways that "preserve the full sense of mutual self-giving and human procreation in the context of true love." The Council intentionally avoided the question of birth control, at the request of Pope Paul VI, who had appointed a special commission to study the issue. The resultant document represents a careful integration of traditional teaching with new insight from the personalist perspective.

A final "crown" of this development occurred within the work of Pope John Paul II, who married personalist philosophy with biblical narrative to produce a comprehensive theology of marriage and sexuality now known as "the theology of the body." In a series of talks in his first five years as pope, John Paul II produced the most extensive description of sex and marriage ever given by the hierarchical authority. He insists that self-giving love is the sum of the Christian story. It is the essence of God ("God is love"), who is a Triune communion of persons. It dominates the story of salvation history, in which God creates all from nothing out of love, so loves humanity that he becomes incarnate in Jesus Christ, and invites humanity to "share in the divine nature" in the communion of saints. Love, seen most obviously in the great commandment, is also the way of discipleship, the way of beginning to participate in that divine nature, even in this life.

But this is no spiritualized love; the meaning of life is "written on our very bodies." As John Paul II claims in *Theology of the Body*, "awareness of the meaning of the human body . . . in particular its nuptial meaning—is the fundamental element of human existence in the world" (21). What is the nuptial meaning of the body? This original phrase of John Paul II refers to the human body's "capacity of expressing love, that love in which a person becomes a gift and—by means of that gift—fulfills the meaning of his being and existence" (9). It is the body's "capacity of living the fact that the other—the woman for the man and the man for the woman—is, by means of the body, someone willed by the Creator for his or her own sake" (33). John Paul grounds this entire theology in a careful reading of the creation stories in Genesis.

Something like the theology of the body would have been unthinkable from any bishop fifty years before; here the pope himself praised marriage and sexuality as potentially the closest analogy we have to understanding the love of God, not simply for us, but within the Godhead, as Father, Son, and Spirit.

Debating the Purposes of Marriage

The purposes of marriage—love and children—do not tell us much about what truly counts as a good marriage. At the most basic level, these could mean simply not sleeping with anyone else and having children.

Married Love

We can start our discussion of married love by reflecting on the soul mate ideal of our culture. Married love is supposed to be a feeling that never goes away, a feeling not only of happiness, but of comfort and security. Many of us have felt something like this in relationships: every day is filled with eagerness to see the other person, all the time spent together is filled with excitement and joy and tenderness, each person's whole world seems to revolve in perfect harmony around the other.

This romantic script defines married love in one sentence: "And they lived happily ever after." We know this script, but it does not fit reality. Reflect on your relationship with your significant other. How would you tell the story of your relationship to another person? Eva Illouz reports on a study in which people were given three different scripts. The first story describes a whirlwind romance leading to marriage upon a chance meeting. The second is an arranged match where two people are set up and eventually decide their relationship is good enough to marry. In the third, two people work together, date sporadically, decide they "work well together," and marry when one of them receives a promotion. Most people surveyed identified the first script as illusory infatuation found in movie scripts, and responded more favorably to the rational exploration and measured decision-making of the second and third. However, when asked to write a script of their own personal love stories, people invariably used the pattern of the first script. The survey illustrates the split personality we have about genuine romantic love: in theory we recognize the need for rational choice and measured behavior, but we want the rush of passion that the soul mate ideal gives us.

The split personality is evident if we actually look at how people come to choose marriage today. Jeffrey Arnett explores the new phase of life he calls "emerging adulthood," a time of life in the twenties and early thirties that, for most, culminates in marriage. He describes the difficulties young adults have in determining when and whom to marry. They "meander" toward marriage, he says, caught between common advice not to marry "too young" and a vague "deadline" past which their chances of marrying drop. The deadline presses particularly hard on women, partially because of the biological clock and partially because it is much more common for a man to marry a younger woman.

Arnett's study confirms the challenges involved in seeking the soul mate ideal. Because there are no clear cultural guidelines for when and whom to marry, and because there is a lingering fear of making the wrong choice in a culture where divorce is common, young adults are left guessing whether a particular relationship is in fact "the One." Often arbitrary deadlines are set after a few years in a relationship, or sometimes couples decide to cohabit in order to be sure—despite clear evidence that cohabitation is correlated to higher, not lower, divorce rates. In short, the criterion by which we measure the ideal partner is so vague that we are never sure whether we have found true love, and consequently fall back on other factors in deciding whether it is the right time to marry.

Given the enormous pressure the soul mate ideal puts on both partners, we might want to look for alternatives when offering a strong evaluation of married love. It may be helpful to look more closely at married love. Far from a magic feeling, married love can be seen in three dimensions: as something intended or chosen by both partners in the vows taken in the wedding (*vowed* love); as something built by the partners in the course of the relationship (*built* love); and as something oriented to larger common aims beyond the couple itself (*shared* love). In exploring these three dimensions, we will draw on a variety of sources, both theological and sociological, in our attempt to get a sense of this married love that most of us see as a crucial aim in marriage.

Vowed Love: Permanence and Exclusivity

If there is one clear difference between the meaning of love in dating and in marriage, the vows are that difference. The wedding vows highlight several things. First, married love is unconditional. Most agreements we make in our lives have conditions: if I do my job, you pay me my salary; or I will pay rent on this apartment until the end of the lease. These agreements have conditions. Marriage does not. Marriage vows, by indicating that the love will be present "for better or worse, for richer for poorer," mean that our commitment does not depend on the spouse's job, health, or anything else.

The fact that married love is unconditional leads to a second characteristic: it is promised, and therefore has permanence. Married love is a love that makes a promise.

Promise-making (and -keeping) is one of the most distinctive things that humans do. Many have argued that the whole society rests on the fact that, in general, we can expect people to keep their promises. Certainly God's story in the Bible has to do with whether God will keep God's promises, even in the face of denial and abandonment by God's people. In everyday matters we make promises to one another because we need to cooperate with one another and to depend on others to do what they say they are going to do. In order to teach, I have to count on people taking care of the facilities at my college and people maintaining the computers and people plowing the snowy roads in January. If they do not follow through on their commitments, I can't follow through on mine. We make promises because we need each other, so we can depend on one another.

Married couples need to depend on one another's love. They are engaged in "a partnership of the whole of life" (*Catechism*, 1601), sharing a household and eventually raising children. Perhaps the biggest difference that one should experience between love in a relationship and married love is exactly this sort of unquestioned dependability.

In both of these ways, married love is a promise to give not just something, but to give oneself to the other person, to place one's life in the other's hands. Such a promise has to be mutual, and that's why each partner makes vows to the other.

Because married love is an unconditional promise, it looks a great deal like God's love. Pope John Paul II compares married love to the "ever faithful love of God," which is faithful to the covenant with Israel even when Israel is not faithful (*Familiaris Consortio*, no. 12). The God encountered in the Jewish and Christian scriptures is interested in promise-making and promise-keeping. The entire Old Testament records Israel's history as the drama of the covenant and of the struggles of each side to remain faithful to it. The vindication toward which the story points is always the hope that God's love is in fact unconditional and total, that God will never revoke his covenant with Israel. God has committed his fate in the world to the people of Israel, permanently.

The pope further describes this covenant in married love as total mutual self-giving. It is "the love by which a man and a woman commit themselves totally to one another until death" (*Familiaris Consortio*, no. 11). The "total" character of the commitment is its crucial element. It is a giving on all levels:

body, mind, and spirit. And it is a giving that includes "the temporal dimension." The pope states, "If the person were to withhold something or reserve the possibility of deciding otherwise in the future, by this very fact he or she would not be giving totally" (*Familiaris Consortio*, no. 11). Marriage is an exchange of gifts, but the gifts given and received are not some aspect of ourselves (e.g., sex, property, the rights to children), but our whole selves. This is what it means when the story of creation says that the man and woman become "one flesh."

Married couples promise not only permanence, but exclusivity. The love promised to the other cannot and will not be promised to anyone else. In an episode of the TV series *Mad About You*, a series about a young married couple, Paul and Jamie, Jamie's scatterbrained sister Lisa takes their dog Murray for a walk, only to lose him when she lets him off the leash. Luckily she finds him and brings him back home, but something is wrong. Murray is a dumb, un-obedient dog, but this dog—who looks exactly like Murray—responds to all sorts of commands, even at one point responding to a request to get a pad of paper to write on. Who would want Murray when you could have a dog that looks exactly like Murray, but who is obviously better? The occasion allows Paul and Jamie to get into a conversation about each other. Jamie asks Paul, "What if someone came home who was exactly like you, but . . . better in certain ways?" Eventually, Paul saves the day by saying that Murray just has a "Murrayness," and so does Jamie. Even if this other dog seems better, he is still not Murray, and Paul wants Murray.

The point of the story is that marriage is about irreplaceability. The person you marry is not just a set of qualities and characteristics that you love; rather, you love the whole person. That is why, in the wedding vows, you say each other's name. You do not marry a package but a person. You call that person by name. Confessing irreplaceability to each other is one of the most profound things we can do to affirm the inherent and total dignity of another—and to have such dignity affirmed about ourselves. As the philosopher Jules Toner puts it, "It is because of you . . . the last word is you. I love you because you are you" (*The Experience of Love*, 198).

Building Love: Mutuality, Intimacy, Companionship, and Conversion

We know that the vows of love in a wedding are no guarantee that either spouse will feel or act in loving ways every day of the entire marriage. A promise to do something does not guarantee that one will do it. So perhaps the most crucial component of understanding married love is knowing how to *build* it. The vows are designed to create a space in which the challenges and bumps involved in the journey to unity can be survived and trust can continue even through failure.

Put another way, total mutual self-giving is not a practical idea, but a formal one. It does not give us much of an idea of how to act on a day-to-day basis. A formal idea is something that gives a definitive form to the rest of your life. Total self-giving to your spouse makes possible a space in which the practical task of actually loving the spouse can be undertaken.

Judith Wallerstein and Sandra Blakeslee, while researching good marriages in our society, found that all the couples studied "had early on created a firm basis for their relationship and had continued to build it together" (*The Good Marriage*, 330–31). Note the active verbs they use here: the couples had committed themselves to creating and building a relationship, rather than simply letting it happen. Wallerstein, who has also studied divorced couples, notes that failed marriages do not lay this foundation. When the inevitable glow wears off or when challenges make life difficult, the marriage is suddenly exposed as fragile.

How exactly does one build married love? In his book, *A Daring Promise*, theologian Richard Gaillardetz describes three aspects of marital communion: mutuality, intimacy, and companionship. Gaillardetz also warns that the real test of a marriage is in recognizing the moments when conversion and self-renunciation are needed for the sake of the other.

Mutuality, Gaillardetz says, is not to be confused with equality or simple justice. Rather, it involves the logic of "gift," "whereby we both receive gifts from our spouses and receive our spouses as gifts" (p. 46). Mutuality crucially involves asymmetrical giving and taking. Giving and receiving gifts is not a matter of demands or of equality, but a matter of exchange. Married couples must establish a relationship where there is giving and receiving.

Underlying the dynamic of giving and receiving is a more fundamental sense of the other person as a gift, as in the appreciation of "Murrayness" noted above. Wallerstein notes that all the people she studied consistently felt "respected and cherished" by their spouses, recognized and appreciated for who they were (Wallerstein and Blakeslee, *The Good Marriage*, 329). Being around a person you respect and admire naturally leads you into acts of mutuality, even outside of a marriage relationship. Conversely, divorcing couples almost always speak of losing respect for their spouses, with a consequent loss of desire to give and receive.

Intimacy is perhaps the most novel and cherished aspect of contemporary marriage. It is the emotional closeness and connection we expect to find in our marriages. Gaillardetz describes intimacy as going "beyond a desire for closeness to a genuine vulnerability before one another" (p. 53). Personal dreams, personal failures, all are shared. We could call intimacy revealing your own incompleteness to another.

Pope John Paul II identified intimacy in the Genesis creation myth in the reference to the "original nakedness" of the man and the woman, which he calls "precisely the key" for understanding God's intention for human sexuality. The nakedness is not merely physical; the body itself symbolizes the natural, unguarded quality of their personal communication. The pope says they "see and know each other . . . with all the peace of the interior gaze" (*Theology of the Body*, 57). We might reflect upon what it would feel like to have someone "gaze" on our entire interior life, our heart fully exposed to the other person, with no editing, no sprucing up, no spin. The pope points out the connection between physical and personal nakedness. Physical nakedness may feel intimate in certain ways, but it is not intimacy unless the sharing of bodies is accompanied by the sharing of hearts. In fact, physical nakedness without personal nakedness is a sort of fake version of intimacy, an imitation, counterfeit intimacy.

Finally, married love is characterized by companionship. Companionship may be the characteristic of married love that is least distinctive to today's context. *Companion* comes from Latin words meaning someone with whom you share bread; companionship involves the daily participation in a shared life of activities, in which love is nurtured by cooperation. In sharing activities, Gaillardetz writes, "we are invited to identify the needs of our spouses and, where necessary, to respond to them."

Companionship can be seen in the traditional description of the "rights" of marriage as "bed and board." Few things are more essential to human life than a place to eat and a place to sleep. In these most fundamental places the marriage relationship is shared. Robert Farrar Capon describes bed and board as the "geography of matrimony," the basic outline of the home (in whatever form) that the married couple make (*Bed and Board*, 67). They are the fundamental spaces of sharing. Think of how difficult it is to endure a meal or to lie down to sleep beside a person with whom you feel upset, angry, or distanced. You can endure days of shopping or TV-watching or yard chores, but come face-to-face over a meal and watch the distractions come out: TV, reading material, distracted glances around the restaurant—anything to avoid face-to-face conversation over the meal. Sharing a bed in such circumstances is even harder. It may be painful to sleep alone, but it is even more painful to sleep alone when you are not alone.

In spite of the hard work involved, we desire mutuality, intimacy, and companionship. It is not always easy and its most difficult moments may be the times when the marriage hangs in the balance.

Gaillardetz remarks that his wife is his way to salvation, and vice versa. The word *salvation* comes from the word save—to need salvation is to need rescuing from some sort of trouble. The trouble, as we saw in God's story, is a matter of selfishness, competition, and idolatry. To be saved from this is to be loved out of this stance into the true purposes of our lives—to give ourselves.

Mutuality, intimacy, and companionship are fine for perfect people, but real marriages are built by imperfect people. As theologian Stanley Hauerwas quips, "The fundamental axiom of marriage is: you always marry the wrong person." The friction produced by your mutual "wrongness" can either be your destruction or your salvation. It can convince you that you are right or it can lead you to change and reach out. This may sound a bit brutal, but it is a waking up to reality.

Jean Vanier is perhaps the greatest contemporary commentator on community because of his amazing experience with mentally handicapped persons. He writes that in community we are always tempted to identify the "enemy without," and enter into a cycle of blame, separation, division, and eventually violence against that enemy. People who appear to be our enemies in community should offer us an opportunity to discover "the enemy within" (*Community and Growth*, 29). People resist community precisely because they know that community will expose them to the brokenness, frustration, and conflict of dealing with others, and when so confronted, they will be left with a choice: make them your enemy, or discover why *you* are feeling frustration. Only by recognizing the enemy within will we feel safe enough to seek the greatest of all gifts: forgiveness. We will forsake victory over our enemies in favor of receiving forgiveness and finding reconciliation with them.

Sharing Love: Moving beyond Each Other

Perfect love, the kind we associate with the soul mate ideal, is assumed to be whole. It is supposed to be a completion, a "fit," which brings perpetual satisfaction. Real love is something more challenging and less complete. Ronald Rolheiser compares it to a symphony that will never be finished in this life. We long to hear the whole tune, but we will live with "a lifelong unfinished symphony" (*The Holy Longing*, 204).

That lack of finish, though, is not a flaw. Genuinely perfect love would "kill" us, in a sense; it would deaden the fire and restlessness inside that enlivens us into action. In a marriage, the unfinished quality of our love can keep our lives open to others. The incompletion of married love contains a promise, the promise of expanding ourselves to include others in an ever-greater symphony. Beyond the love promised and built between the couple, then, married love is designed to be shared.

While such sharing might seem to take away attention from the couple's love for each other, it actually can support and enhance that love. The old cliché is true: you get love by giving it away. We are so dominated by the economic idea of scarcity that we even think of love in its cruel terms. We think if we give love to others, we will take it away from our spouse. Married love is fundamentally productive and functions by the principle of abundance, not scarcity. Regardless of how strong it is, it will not be able to sustain itself without being shared beyond the couple. Love is like a fire that needs to burn and spread if it is to keep going. It is, in fact, the Holy Spirit, which proceeds from the overflowing love between the Father and the Son.

Evelyn and James Whitehead speak of this need to share by explaining that married love must make a transition from "we are" to "we care." They pose the typical questions of scarcity: "Are the resources of support and challenge that we generate in our family to be spent solely within our family? Or is there 'enough' of us so that we can take the risk of sharing some of our resources (of love or concern or time or goods) with the world beyond?" (*Marrying Well*, 109–10). They point out that the failure to move beyond the love of the couple imperils love itself. While "a stage of mutual absorption" is natural and to be expected early in a relationship, the couple needs to move beyond it in order for the love to mature. They note that psychologists urge this outward movement, for a "pseudo-intimacy" can develop unless love is shared more widely, which results ironically not in "an intimacy more protected and complete, but stagnation" (p. 111).

This "moving beyond" will occupy the rest of our discussion. The most obvious version of moving beyond comes when the couple welcomes children into the world, bestowing on them the gift of the love husband and wife have found with one another.

For Discussion

1. Consider your experience of loving relationships. Do they display these characteristics? How?

2. Who do you see as an ideal of married love? Why?

3. How do these aspects of love fit marriage into God's overall story? How does a marriage that displays these characteristics contribute a subplot to that story?

Why Have and Raise Children?

In our culture, choosing marriage and choosing to have children have become separated. That is a novel development, and so in this section we need to understand the connection. While most people who want to marry also express a desire to have children, the actual statistics do not match our

aspirations. Yet the tradition still wants to connect the choice of marriage with the choice to have children.

This insistence is not well received by many. Having children constitutes a far greater threat to some of our culture's core values—individualism, autonomy, and freedom—than even self-giving marital love. There are fundamental ways in which children compromise an individualistic lifestyle.

Even if we take this concern as extreme, it is honest. Theologian Julie Hanlon Rubio notes how parents almost universally say that "family comes first" in our society, and yet their actual practices do not indicate a priority put on parenting (*A Christian Theology of Marriage and Family*, 90–92). Rubio recognizes that a major part of this problem has to do with the genuine "dual vocation"—to family and to work in the world—that most parents have. There is an explicitly Christian aspect to this dilemma, which affects all couples in today's society. The teaching of Vatican II says, "While not making the other purposes of matrimony of less account, the true practice of conjugal love, and its whole meaning of the family life which results from it, have this aim: that the couple be ready with stout hearts to cooperate with the love of the Creator and the Savior, who through them will enlarge and enrich His own family day by day" (*Pastoral Constitution on the Church in the Modern World*, no. 50).

The responsibilities of childrearing seem endless and fraught with peril. There seems no way to do it exactly right. Moreover, we feel the task has become more difficult. In a recent survey, 88% of adults agreed with the statement, "It has become much harder to raise children in our society" (Alan Wolfe, *One Nation, After All*, 116–17).

The fear exists because the task is perhaps the most special that we can have as human beings. One of my friends from high school commented to me six months after having his first child that nothing has ever made him realize more that the world doesn't revolve around him. Another friend, Christopher Ruddy, writes of his transformation by discovering a devotion to the Sacred Heart:

> On a particular difficult afternoon last summer, I took Peter [his one-year-old son] for a walk. We wound up at a church in our neighborhood, and . . . almost accidently, I stopped in front of a woodcarving of the Sacred Heart. Caught somewhere between rage and tears, I looked up at the heart and, for the first time, saw beyond the barbed-wire crown

of thorns encircling it, into its gentleness. A prayer rose up in me: Jesus, give me a bigger heart. I looked at Peter in shame and in hope, and I went out into the day. (*Awake, My Soul*, 6)

These stories of people so different display the struggle and the grace in childrearing, the way that raising children forces us to give up some of our most cherished individualism and self-centeredness. These descriptions point to ways that marriage, by having children, can become properly oriented to the master narrative of loving God and neighbor, rather than focusing life on the self.

Are children essential to marriage, rather than an optional add-on? The traditional way of thinking here faces serious challenges. As we saw above, procreation has traditionally been sanctioned as the primary purpose of marriage. It is hard to deny that the tradition now rejects some of the arguments that have been used to support that conclusion. Such a stance relied in part on the assumption of women's inferiority. It relied on the further biological assumption that the act of ejaculation contained the whole person, and therefore ejaculating semen without intending pregnancy was destructive. Even more, it relied on a squeamishness about the good of sex itself. Many Christian writers in the tradition suggest more or less that the dangers of sin and lust involved in having sex are offset only by the "noble" purpose of having children. Thankfully, the tradition has almost completely reversed this negative view of sex. Yet the tradition continues to insist that having children is of the essence of marriage, not optional. There are a variety of explanations for this.

The theological account. Pope John Paul II calls it *fecundity*, "the fruit and sign of conjugal love, the living testimony of the full reciprocal self-giving of the spouses" (*Familiaris Consortio*, no. 28). To say that marital love is truly like God's love, we have to say that it is creative, not of things or of feelings, but of actual persons. This love needs "living testimony." While the pope indicates that the fruits of marriage for the life of the world are many, only the generation of new life is unique. If we hold that God's love is in fact a model for married love, we have to keep that love connected to the transmission of life—not the improvement of life, but life itself. God's love generates this new life. So the connection between the character of married love and the raising of children is not accidental.

The biological account. At the most basic level, married love and children are connected because sex is essential to marriage. Almost no one will suggest that married love should be asexual; therefore, we have to contend with the intrinsic connection between the prime expression of married love and the fact that this act has the possibility of producing children.

Some ethicists argue that you cannot derive an "ought" from an "is." That is to say, you can't look at the world as it *is*, and conclude necessarily that it *ought* to be that way. However, sometimes the "is-ought" point is taken too far. While biology can't dictate ethics, ethics cannot ignore biology. While "is" does not make "ought," "ought" needs to account for "is." For the sake of argument, imagine that someone suggests we redesign our mouths in a way that makes them better for kissing, but that design happens to making eating impossible. We might say that we *ought* not redesign the mouth in such a fashion. Analogously, while sexual biology can't dictate ethics, ethics needs to take biological facts into account. And a key fact is that sex acts result in babies.

The therapeutic account. As noted above, psychologists find that married love tends to stagnate and cave in on itself if its energy is not directed outward. While having children is certainly not the only way this happens, it does promote the expansion of love's boundaries. Moreover, it does so in a unique way, since the child is actually conceived in the midst of the love, and then nurtured in the environment of that love. Children require someone to love them unconditionally and are capable of unconditional love toward their parents. The context of unconditional married love seems to fit the characteristics needed for raising children.

The social account. The most obvious reason for the connection is still the oldest: without children society has no future. Few of us have this in mind when thinking about connecting our married love with having children. If one couple decides they can just be married and not have children, society is barely affected; but if most couples make that decision, the society suffers.

We can mention—all too briefly—some examples of this social impact. In many northern European countries the birth rate is far, far below what demographers call "replacement level." The connection between married love and children is far weaker than in American society, and the consequence has been an inability to replace the population. A persistent birthrate of this sort will result in the collapse of the society; it will be burdened with institutions that it can no longer support, and people will be forced to leave. Conversely, we find in many impoverished American inner cities a disconnection between marriage and childbirth that has led to social breakdown, not because there are too many couples with too few births, but too many births and too few married couples. The numbers are staggering: fully a third of all births in the United States were to unmarried women in 1999, but the number jumps to around two-thirds for poor and oppressed populations in some areas (Popenoe, "Unions"). While it is primarily an economic problem, it certainly does result in societal breakdown when the connection between marriage and children is lost.

We could summarize these examples by saying that society needs children, and that some sort of stable, long-term context is necessary in which to raise, nurture, and teach them. The absence of children eventually decimates a society, as does the absence of a context in which to raise them.

None of this is meant as a moral judgment on anyone. The point here is to show that social facts dictate a connection between married love and having children. The absence of such a connection at a society-wide level produces serious negative social effects.

For Discussion

1. Are having children and marriage separate actions, or are they inseparably intertwined, like college and classes? Give reasons for your view.

2. Which of the four accounts of why children are necessary for marriage is most convincing? Which is least convincing? Why? Compare the accounts.

Conclusion

In this chapter, we have briefly explored the history of marriage, especially within the Catholic tradition, and the two purposes of the practice of marriage. The descriptions of married love and of childrearing in this chapter are necessarily brief, incomplete, and unsatisfying. Nevertheless, they may begin to help us see why marriage is such an important and central practice in life and in society. Just as with dating, the identification of purposes also raises the question of whether there are some acts that can never aim at these purposes and ought therefore to be prohibited. Are there acts that married people should never do? To this question we turn in the next chapter.

8
Rules of the Practice
Sexual Activity in Marriage

So far we have not specifically discussed sex in marriage. By "sex" we mean more than just intercourse; the place of "sex" in marriage goes far beyond genital sex and is better understood as the gift of our bodies to one another. This physical mutual self-giving is not disconnected from the love that characterizes the whole of life, nor is it limited to intercourse. Our discussion will eventually lead us to more moral absolutes to consider: adultery and contraception. But first, we should talk about the rapidly increasing phenomenon of cohabitation. Is it dating? Is it marriage? What exactly is it? And why does the Catholic tradition have an absolute norm against it?

Marriage, Quasi-Marriage, and Cohabitation

If social trends are any indication, you can't talk about marriage these days without also discussing cohabitation. Cohabitation is notoriously difficult to define, beyond the simple fact that it involves sharing a living space with someone. Studies have shown that cohabiting couples differ in terms of the sharing of their lives and goods, their attitude toward marriage, and the possibility of children.

Roughly speaking, we can divide cohabitants into three groups on the basis of differences in their understanding of how cohabitation relates to marriage. First, there are serial cohabiters, who view cohabitation arrangements as temporary and not directed toward marriage. In these situations cohabitation has less to do with commitment and more to do with convenience. Second, there are premarital cohabitants, who choose cohabitation as a sort of prelude to marriage. Some have definite plans for marriage, others are simply considering marriage, but all view cohabitation as a stage on the path toward marriage. Third, there are permanent cohabitants who, for whatever reason, have made a choice not to marry, but nevertheless view the cohabitation as a quasi-permanent situation. Few cohabitants in our society fall into the third group; the vast majority are split pretty evenly between the first two groups.

Statistics on cohabitation show a dramatic and rapid rise in the practice. From a marginal practice just a few decades ago, a period of cohabitation has become the norm for couples. In 1965–1974, only 11% of couples cohabited, while by 1998–1999, over half of marriages were preceded by cohabitation. Other statistics show the number is growing even more rapidly. Such large-scale social change over a relatively short period of time is unusual. Moreover, it is known that survey rates for actual cohabitation underestimate the couples who are essentially practicing it; one survey indicates a significant number of couples who continue to maintain two "official" residences, usually because of family pressure, but who essentially live together.

There are many reasons for this rapid change. First, the rising marriage age combines with the earlier initiation of sex and long-term, marriage-like relationships to create a period of time where people are in long-term, quasi-marital sexual relationships and do not live at home. It is not surprising that couples in this situation are likely to cohabit, whether pursuing marriage or not. A second common reason is economics. Just as many young adults do not live alone for economic reasons, so too many couples who are already sharing the common household geography of "bed and board" find it absurd to bypass the economic benefits of sharing a house or apartment. The third reason, especially prominent in premarital cohabitants, is the fear of divorce and the desire to find out more about the other person and test the relationship before committing to marriage. As a thirty-year-old Boston law student puts it, "I don't know how people got married before living together first. This is crucial to see how you get along" ("Not Married Yet? You're Not Alone," 3A).

Is cohabitation an ethical issue, or merely a practical one? Some Catholic theologians have recently suggested that premarital cohabitation need not be seen as a problem. They cite the fact that, at various times in the history of Christian cultures, periods of betrothal were accepted. A couple announced to the community that they intended to wed at a future date and were then regarded by the community as married and committed to one another. They shared a life together, including sex, and eventually had a wedding and made the formal marriage vows. These theologians argue that rather than resist the contemporary trend toward premarital cohabitation, the church ought to acknowledge it and use the time as an opportunity to involve the couple in premarital catechesis and formation for their future vowed life together. This suggestion resembles the novitiate, or temporary vows, made by people exploring religious life—on the one hand, they are ordered toward final, permanent commitment to the religious community; on the other hand, such a commitment is a process, and stages facilitate the exploration and education in such a commitment of life.

Other theologians, however, contest these comparisons. The purpose of betrothal was often to test whether a woman was fertile or not, since children were so important, and the decision to marry was linked directly to that question. By contrast, modern advocates of betrothal have difficulty articulating when and why a couple would decide to go forward and marry. Moreover, since betrothal involved familial commitments, there were strong social forces discouraging careless or casual use of the practice. That is to say, betrothals were designed to convert to marriages. They constituted a trial period, to be sure, but not a trial of personal affection, but of fertility.

So opponents of cohabitation tend to point out two things. First, modern cohabitation often does not lead to marriage. Less than half of cohabiting couples ever marry, despite the fact that 76% of people cohabiting report "plans to marry." So even premarital cohabiters are not necessarily premarital. Admittedly, analyzing these numbers is difficult. Some might say they reflect a successful weeding-out process. Others point out that it is common for one partner in a relationship to hope for marriage, while the other does not share that aim. Such situations ordinarily involve a great deal of pain and conflict. The parallel with entering religious life is further eroded by the fact that no children need to be dealt with when novitiates take temporary vows.

However, the second reason is more important: cohabitation does not appear to work as a trial period or educational period for couples contemplating marriage. In other words, the common belief that cohabitation allows for a better, less-divorce-prone choice of marriage partner has been shown to be a myth. In fact, many studies show that cohabitants have a 50% higher divorce rate than couples who do not cohabit before marrying. These statistics must be read with care. Obviously many cohabiting couples do not divorce—in fact, their rate of divorce declines to match that of noncohabitants if they manage to stay married for seven years—and many noncohabiting couples do divorce. Further, some dispute the correlation of the two choices, divorce and cohabitation. There is some indication that, if the category is limited strictly to couples with firm plans to marry, and if we take into account more recent statistics where cohabitation is spread over a wider swath of the overall population, minimizing other contributing variables to divorce, the effect on divorce rates is small or nonexistent. Unfortunately, we don't have enough data to say conclusively.

To many it seems counterintuitive that premarital cohabitation would not lead to a more stable marriage. But let's recall how we defined married love. If married love carries the vow of permanency, and if it requires mutual commitment and work to build it, including "conversion" periods of dying to self, then we can see logically that there is no way to try out such a commitment. You are either committed or not. The sort of commitment present in a premarital relationship, particularly if partners view the cohabitation explicitly as a test, is simply not the commitment present in marriage. Thus, the notion of trying out married love is illogical.

When people say they want to test their relationship, they may mean they want to see if the feeling of love stays or not. They want to figure out if it is "for real." But two years of living together isn't going to test that; in fact, it might give you the illusion that the feeling does stay, only to discover that it fades several years later. Then what? Was the trial period not long enough? The point is that marital love is more than a feeling; it is a choice. Whether or not it's "for real" hinges not on the magic in the relationship but on the couple's commitment to make it real.

Furthermore, the economic logic that sometimes encourages cohabitation makes for a tricky setting in which to "test things out." Non-cohabiting couples who decide that they should not get married simply break up. If one party decides they are not committed, they can simply say so. Cohabiters are faced with a much more complicated situation. Perhaps they want to express doubts about the relationship, but then, knowing they have no place to go to while the other partner cools off, they avoid saying anything. But they quietly build some distance into the relationship. Or perhaps they are clear that the relationship should end, but they do not want to lose their part of the lease should they move out. Cohabitation introduces factors that inhibit free discernment about the choice to marry.

Surely prospective marriage partners should find out something about the living habits of the other person—cook some meals together, look at each other's bathroom to check on the toilet paper, and so on. It's good to have plenty of opportunities to observe one another, but the notion of a trial is mistaken. Worse, because of the cautious, trial nature of much cohabitation, couples develop patterns of living together-but-separately, which cannot be magically changed after the wedding. Perhaps they develop overly cautious communication styles or active social calendars or independent spending habits, things that will have to change after marriage, but which are not easy to change.

Traditionally the church's view on cohabitation has been dictated by its view on premarital sex. But the above discussion suggests that the issue involved in cohabitation is not simply sex. From what was said above about the patterns and attitudes towards commitment involved in premarital cohabiting, even those who disagree with the tradition's stance against premarital sex should still resist cohabiting before marriage in order to ensure complete freedom in making the final decision to marry and to avoid the setting up of poor relational dynamics that will haunt the couple later.

The Purposes of Marriage and Moral Norms

Remember absolute norms? We discussed them in an earlier chapter; they are the rules that direct us toward goods that fulfill us by ruling out actions that would contradict or undermine those goods. They are few but strategic, and none is more strategic than the norms that govern marriage relationships: the prohibition against adultery and the prohibition against contraception. Let's take the easier one first.

Adultery

Is the action we call adultery compatible with pursuing the goods involved in marriage? Particularly in the late 1960s and early 1970s, many saw a potential trend in this direction. Many married couples were "swingers" who had sex with others' spouses. They had "open marriages." Supposedly there was much more trust involved. And spouse-swapping is still around, although it no longer makes the news. A 1970s example is found in the film *The Ice Storm*, where a married couple on the rocks arrives at a social gathering and find out it is a "key party." That is, the men place their car keys in a bowl; at the end of the evening, women randomly draw a set of keys and go home with whatever man belongs to the keys.

Most people will not find these practices particularly compelling—but why not? Why is there still general agreement that adultery is wrong, even if consensual? When we investigate this question, we are forced to justify our stance, and that, in turn, may help us understand the reasoning behind other rules that are not as clear to us.

So why is adultery wrong? First, we should note historically that the prohibition against adultery is primarily concerned with assuring the paternity of children. Thus, many cultures have practiced a double standard: no adultery meant no adultery by women, or at least married women. However, it is clear that the prohibition has been largely maintained.

The "swingers" should indicate to us that the problem with adultery is not simply deception. Adultery usually does involve deception, but not always. Rather, adultery attacks a basic good of sex and marriage: the unitive good, or what we have been discussing in the last chapter as permanent and exclusive married love. We are skeptical of the swingers described above because we are skeptical that they really love each other in this sense. Adultery appears to be simply incompatible with being married, with the basic good of marital faithfulness. How can someone say he or she loves you and then cheat on you? He or she simply cannot coherently pursue both purposes.

What counts as adultery? This is the description question. Jesus famously expanded the adultery commandment by saying, "You have heard that it was said, 'You shall not commit adultery.' But I say to you that everyone who looks at a woman with lust has already committed adultery with her in his heart" (Matt. 5:27–28). Since Jesus goes on to say that if your eye is a problem, you should tear it out, we might question exactly what he means here. Nevertheless, Jesus is saying that adultery is really about your heart, about whether you are faithfully loving your spouse. Certainly to look "with lust" is more than just a passing admiring glance. Rather, it means seriously viewing someone as a sexual alternative to your spouse.

Imagine a possible scenario. You are an executive at a company, and you hire a new, young secretary. He is smart and handsome, and you begin chatting with him about your life and his, maybe even about your marriage and your kids. You both enjoy it, and since you work together, you start going out to lunch together. Some of those lunch conversations get pretty intense; maybe, you start talking to him about things that frustrate you about your husband, or you show him your writing and he shows you his. Suddenly, he asks whether you'd like to register for an evening writing class with him. You have wanted to do a writing class for a long time, but never took the initiative, so you sign up. The two of you drive there together, and regularly go out for a drink afterward.

For Discussion

1. Does the writing class scenario constitute emotional adultery? Why or why not?

2. Can there be emotional adultery? Why or why not?

3. Should adultery be a crime? Why or why not?

Contraception

Adultery consists of acts that undercut and attack the purpose or "good" of marriage: the love of the spouse. Contraception consists of acts that intentionally undercut and attack the procreative good, either permanently or temporarily. Most readers are likely to question this rule, and so more time will have to be spent discussing it.

Historical Background

Western culture used to think that procreation occurred when a man "deposited seed" in a woman. The man's seed contained the whole of the future human being; the woman's body provided a place for the seed to grow, nothing more. Hence Israel's scriptures are filled with agricultural metaphors for having children, and Jesus' parables often use the image of sowing seed to allude to the way in which the gospel works to produce new life.

In the nineteenth century modern science began to discover the process of conception as we know it today. In the older theories there was no conception: the seed itself was the human being. Therefore, practices that "spilled seed" unnecessarily were seen as, at best, a sort of waste of potential lives. Now we know that both woman and man contribute material to the new life. The union of the sperm and egg, like the union of man and woman itself, is the place where a new life is conceived.

In the early twentieth century the discovery of women's cycles of fertility and infertility shed even more light on the process of bringing new life into being. Under the earlier model, there was no place for "women's fertility" in this sense, since the woman did not materially contribute to the process. The observable fact that not all sex acts resulted in pregnancy did not preclude an explanation of conception that relied wholly on male semen deposited in the female. Perhaps this is one reason pregnancy was regarded as a gift and a blessing; people simply had no idea when it would occur and when it would not!

This background will help us understand why contraception has become such a controversial topic within the Catholic tradition. Until the early twentieth century, nearly all Christian churches maintained strict rules against the use of contraception—which, at that time, consisted of barrier methods or withdrawal. This opposition stemmed from the fact that contraception undermined and attacked the primary purpose of marriage (procreation), but also from a sense that contraception made the sexual act unnatural by spilling the man's seed unnecessarily.

By the 1920s, changes in biology, the movement of families to crowded cities because of industrialization, a gradual acceptance of the equality of women, and the rise of eugenics (scientific attempts to improve the human race through proper "breeding") all contributed to a strong pro-contraception movement. While Protestant traditions, starting with the Anglicans in 1930, increasingly accepted contraception, the Catholic tradition continued to reject it absolutely—though it did allow recourse to women's cyclical infertile periods.

In the 1960s, in the wake of the sense of change awakened by Vatican II and the development of oral contraceptives ("the Pill") by a Catholic physician, John Rock, it seemed quite likely that the Catholic teaching against contraception would also change. Vatican II documents no longer identified procreation as the primary end of marriage, and the Pill seemed to avoid the traditional argument that contraception blocked the natural finality of sex, since the Pill was not a barrier. There was a feeling of excitement in the air, particularly in the American and European churches. Pope Paul VI appointed an international commission, consisting of priests and bishops, medical experts, and even Catholic married couples, to study the question. A majority of the commission seemed to support a change in the teaching.

In August 1968, Pope Paul issued by far the most famous and influential papal encyclical of the twentieth century, *Humanae Vitae*. In it the pope sided with the minority report of the commission, and firmly reasserted the traditional teaching against all use of contraceptives. He cited "the inseparable connection, established by God, which man on his own initiative may not break, between the unitive significance and the procreative significance which are both inherent to the marriage act" (no. 12). *Humanae Vitae* set off a storm of controversy for many reasons. To some this seemed a sudden reversal of course from Vatican II just a few years earlier. Some had already anticipated a change in the teaching. For the first time in recent Catholic history, a group of American Catholic theologians (nearly all priests and religious) took to the media and told American Catholics they had a right in conscience to dissent from the teaching. It quickly became clear that the teaching was not going to be practiced by the vast majority of American Catholics: even in the 1970s, polls showed overwhelming dissent from the teaching. Many claimed that this issue essentially killed the credibility of the Church's teaching across the board. Once people got used to the idea that official Catholic teaching could be wrong on one thing, they ceased to listen to other things.

This is only one side of the story. For a dedicated minority, one's stance on contraception became a mark of genuine Catholic faithfulness. Some quietly taught methods of natural family planning to small groups of interested Catholics and others. In the appointment of Karol Wojtyla as Pope John Paul II, these Catholics found an ardent defender of the teaching, even as this same pope developed the most positive pro-marriage and pro-sex theology in the history of the tradition. These groups watched as Pope Paul VI's predictions of the concrete social effects of the "contraceptive mentality" spreading throughout society began to come true. They started saying that Paul VI was not conservative and backward-looking in this teaching, but prophetic and forward-looking.

Debating the Teaching

Let's look at the arguments. First, it is important to recognize that the tradition is not saying that you need to have a baby every time you have sex. On the contrary, the tradition clearly recognizes that couples can and should take responsibility for planning their families, so long as such planning is not an unjust or selfish restriction of love for possible children. Not every sexual act produces a child, and some couples are infertile. None of this is a problem.

Rather, the tradition teaches that you should not do anything to attack the procreative good or end of sex. "Attack" here means make a choice and do an action that intentionally separates the unitive and procreative ends of sex, in order to exclude the procreative end. To make a choice against a good is to attack it. Notice that the whole discussion about the purposes of sex and marriage is a necessary assumption here in order to debate specific acts. Once we've named the purposes of the game, the rules come into play to protect the goods involved in the game. We argued against adultery for similar reasons: it involves a positive choice against the unitive end, the two-in-one-flesh love that sex aims at.

Now just because something is a human good does not mean you need to make a positive choice for it every time. Nevertheless, you must avoid making choices that contradict it. So do you have to be overflowing with self-giving love every time you have sex with your spouse? That would be nice, but unrealistic. The point is not to do anything that involves a choice explicitly against that union. Adultery is clearly such a choice. Spousal abuse similarly involves bodily actions that are simply contradictory to the unitive meaning of sex. It is irrational to hit and make love to the same person.

In the same way, you don't have to choose to have a baby every time you have sex, but you ought not to choose something explicitly against that purpose. Declining to realize a good is not the same as attacking it. Contraception, the tradition argues, always, in every case, involves a choice to view the procreative good as bad, and to separate it from the unitive good. Hence, the failure rate of contraception is not really the issue here. The issue is the choice against the good, an action with a purpose that contradicts procreation.

So, for example, some women develop dire medical problems requiring an operation that will result in sterility. Ordinarily, the tradition views sterilization as a particularly bad form of choosing contraception—particularly bad because of its irreversibility. But in this case the woman and the doctors are not choosing sterility, but choosing the woman's health. If they could find a way to do that without sterilization, they would. The sterilization is regretfully accepted as a side effect, not directly chosen.

Some women take the Pill for medical reasons other than contraception. "For medical reasons" is a stipulation that has to be taken seriously. If there are other, comparable treatments for the same problem, even if they are somewhat more expensive or inconvenient, the other treatments without the contraceptive side effect should be chosen. However, in cases where the treatment is necessary and no other treatment is available, a woman may choose the Pill for the medical reasons without intending contraception. Similarly, in a case now hotly debated in the tradition, some argue that if a spouse has AIDs a married couple could use condoms, because the intention would be disease prevention, not the contraceptive side effect.

These cases are important because they are not "exceptions." That is, they are not actually cases of choosing contraception, not attacks on the procreative good. We discussed in the previous chapter how killing someone while defending yourself is not an exception to the rule against murder; it simply isn't murder, because you are not intending the death of another.

Under ordinary conditions, birth control methods are chosen with the express purpose of—obviously—controlling birth, and therefore do constitute an attack on an essential good of marriage. But what if there are extenuating circumstances? You have a good reason. You say, for example, "We have to get through grad school. We can't afford to have a baby—we're just barely making ends meet." Yes, good reasons. But when you choose to use contraception, you are still making the intentional choice to attack the procreative end of sex and separate it from the unitive end. The Catholic tradition firmly maintains that it is wrong to choose against a good in order to realize some other good. This is a crucial principle, as noted earlier when first introducing the idea of moral rules. If this principle is given up, then killing would be acceptable if it meant you could realize some sort of greater good. For example, if you were to drop a nuclear bomb on a Japanese city, you'd kill hundreds of thousands of people but you might avoid having to invade Japan and losing potentially many more lives. The tradition rejects this argument. Attacking basic goods in the name of other goods is wrong and dangerous.

We said at the start of this discussion that the tradition affirms that planning your family is a good thing—but how do you do that without contraception? There are a number of means that don't involve attacking the procreative good. These methods are known as forms of natural family planning (NFP). NFP makes use of knowledge of women's bodies and various signs that indicate ovulation. By a combination of daily temperature-taking and observation of cervical mucus, women can ascertain when they are fertile. The method works even for women with irregular cycles, for it is not based on a set calendar (as was the "rhythm" method). Rather, it is based on bodily awareness. Ordinarily, there is a five- to seven-day period during every cycle when women are fertile. If a couple has sex only on the woman's infertile days, NFP has a "perfect-use" effectiveness rate over 98%, as good as the best forms of contraception.

Doesn't NFP involve a choice to separate the ends of sex, just like contraception? The tradition says it is precisely the opposite. By respecting (rather than attacking) the natural connection of those ends—the fact that naturally they are not always connected—NFP shows exactly the opposite attitude toward the intrinsic connection between the goods. NFP is accepted by the tradition not simply because there is no physical barrier, or because it allows for God to intervene, but because it does not involve a necessary choice against the procreative good.

This point is often a sticky one for many people. The NFP couple and the contracepting couple may seem to be doing the same thing, intending the same thing, just by different paths. In some sense, this is true. Both are choosing to avoid pregnancy when it would not be responsible to have a child—a good thing. But one is using a means that respects the goods of sex, while the other is using a means that attacks and separates them. Theologians have used the example of two men seeking to provide food for their family: one gets a job, the other steals.

More importantly, NFP simply never involves the contraceptive choice against procreation. The choice to decline to have sex at certain times, the choice to decline to pursue the procreative good, is not a choice *attacking* the good. We might fruitfully compare this to standard Catholic teaching on persons who are dying. It is not always necessary to do everything you can to save someone who is dying. One may decline extraordinary means of treatment and allow the disease to take its course. But the official teaching strongly opposes euthanasia, which involves the active choice to do something that will kill the patient. In either case the result is the same: the patient dies. In the first case, however, death is allowed, not chosen, while in eutha-nasia death is directly chosen. Similarly, in NFP, the natural separation of the unitive and procreative ends is allowed, not chosen, whereas in contracep-tion, the separation is actively chosen. In NFP, there is no action taken where the goods are separated, and the procreative good discarded.

This may seem to be making a mountain out of a molehill, but a crucial ethical principle is involved: not to choose against certain goods as a way of pursuing other goods. That principle has wide application in Catholic moral theology, and to discard it allows one to attempt any sort of commensu-ration between incommensurable goods. Most importantly it justifies bad acts for the sake of greater goods, an idea the tradition has always rejected. Ultimately it is rejected on the grounds of the noncompetitive harmonious conception of God and God's creation that we outlined in chapter 4—doing evil to gain a good is the same as saying some people have to lose in order that others can win.

There is more at stake, as well. While the formal argument in favor of the prohibition is set out above, other theologians have pointed out that contraception is in fact an important social issue. Pope Paul VI, when writing *Humanae Vitae*, did not simply make the argument, but also added a sec-tion where he described the possibility of a "contraceptive mentality" that would creep into society (and sexual relations) if contraception was widely accepted.

> Responsible men can become more deeply convinced of the truth of the doctrine laid down by the Church on this issue if they reflect on the consequences of methods and plans for artificial birth control. Let them first consider how easily this course of action could open wide the way for marital infidelity and a general lowering of moral standards. Not much experience is needed to be fully aware of human weakness and to understand that human beings—and especially the young, who are so exposed to temptation—need incentives to keep the moral law, and it is an evil thing to make it easy for them to break that law. Another effect that gives cause for alarm is that a man who grows accustomed to the use of contraceptive methods may forget the reverence due to a wom-an, and, disregarding her physical and emotional equilibrium, reduce her to being a mere instrument for the satisfaction of his own desires,

no longer considering her as his partner whom he should surround with care and affection. (*Humanae Vitae*, no. 17)

Historians do not dispute the connection between the sexual revolution of the sixties and the development of easy, non-invasive birth control methods used by women. After all, how many of you would look at premarital sex the same way if no contraception were available? Ultimately, the view that procreation is an optional part of sex, over which we have control, is a dangerous one, since it will radically revise our view of sexual relationships.

Moreover, such a view is simply false. Sex is procreative. When we start thinking it isn't, we labor under an illusion. For one upper-middle-class college couple to use contraceptives, failure is unlikely, and there is a safety net if there is failure. But when the vast majority of society accepts contraceptive use, failure rates matter. Even a 5% failure rate matters when millions of unmarried people having sex results in tens of thousands of pregnancies. Some people remind you that birth control can fail in hopes of scaring you away from sex. But what should scare you is that your endorsement of contraception means that it will fail other people, and ultimately lead to abortions. Studies indicate that half of all women seeking abortion are there because of contraceptive failure. Indeed, the Supreme Court's own decision protecting abortion rights, *Planned Parenthood vs. Casey*, 1992, acknowledges the necessary connection between contraception and abortion both being readily available: "For two decades of economic and social development, people have organized intimate relationships and made choices that define their views of themselves and their places in society, in reliance on the availability of abortion in the event that contraception should fail."

Other theologians have pointed out that *Humanae Vitae* makes an underlying point about how we put naïve faith in technology and control, even in the most intimate areas of our lives. At the liberal, nonreligious college I attended I found some women without any Catholic leanings whatsoever who were interested in NFP precisely because it was natural. It was not going to mess up their hormones, it involved a process that was "organic," and cost only the price of a thermometer. The issue here wasn't the meanings of sex, but the way technology involves us in destructive illusions of control. Richard Gaillardetz asks, "Is there not a danger that our preoccupation with efficiency and convenience has led us to cheapen and even ignore altogether the distinctive blessings that come as we embrace the necessity of certain constraints?" (*A Daring Promise*, 106).

Most couples who practice NFP have testified to its benefits. While the presentation of NFP in the abstract inevitably leads to a focus on the infertile periods, couples who practice NFP point out that the whole process of cooperation, observation, and communication involved in using it has a unitive effect. By embracing the woman's body, instead of treating it as if it were diseased and defective, many couples report that they have a much deeper appreciation for their bodies. This is particularly true of men, who are often extraordinarily ignorant of the woman's cycle. Moreover, couples report that NFP spurs creativity in multiplying different ways of showing physical and emotional intimacy, rather than defaulting to sex. In all these ways, the constraints of NFP may indeed offer distinctive blessings.

Objections

The Catholic moral absolute against contraception has probably been the single most debated topic in moral theology over the last forty years. Obviously numerous objections have been raised to the teaching, and the major ones are outlined here. One possible objection not discussed here is overpopulation. Strictly speaking, since the official teaching accepts birth regulation (in the form of NFP), the overpopulation objection does not apply. In addition, the notion of overpopulation is highly contested. It is not at all clear that the earth is overpopulated; what is clear is that the earth's resources are not distributed evenly, and so some have far more resources than necessary while others lack basic resources. That is a problem of social justice, not birth control. So then, what are the other objections?

Not every act. The first objection to the teaching is that while the marriage as a whole may need to aim at and be open to having children, not every act needs to be open to procreation without exception. Prior to Vatican II, traditional Catholic moral theology tended to concentrate on the rightness and wrongness of individual acts ("Is it a sin or not?"), while tending to ignore the overall context or narrative within which acts took place. As the Catholic theology of marriage has become less juridical and more focused on the ongoing, relational character of marriage, it ought to become less centered on analyzing individual sex acts and instead concentrate on how those acts contribute to the overall purposes of marriage. Such acts should be considered within the totality of the marriage. Some married couples might use contraception wrongly, selfishly, in an attempt to avoid the generosity and self-giving involved in having children. But for many couples, especially those who have already had a number of children, it seems wrong to characterize the choice to use contraception as somehow selfish or an attack on the procreative character of marriage. Notice how our discussion has now shifted from the purposes of marriage to the purposes of sexual acts.

Physicalism. The second objection contends that the teaching of *Humanae Vitae* is based on a physicalist concept of morality. *Physicalism* refers to the attempt to read moral right and wrong directly from biological functions; it is sometimes called *biologism*. So for example, since I clearly use my teeth to eat, it would be wrong of me to use my teeth to tear open a stubborn package. Such a position is ultimately absurd, and it runs contrary to the clear acceptance by the tradition of intervention in biological processes (say, degenerative diseases) for the overall good of the person. At a basic level, it denies the freedom of the person and our ability to use our bodies rationally and creatively for many purposes.

This argument is really about whether or not it is moral to intervene in the biological processes surrounding sex. Part of the impetus for *Humanae Vitae* was a belief that the Pill would be an acceptable form of birth control because it is not a barrier. The notion of "barrier" is clearly physicalist. However, the physicalist objection is still raised, despite *Humanae Vitae*'s avoidance of any distinction between barrier methods and chemical methods of birth control.

No real difference between NFP and contraception. Some object that the physicalism of the tradition is evident in its acceptance of natural family planning, for the intent of couples who use contraception and the intent of couples who use NFP are the same. Both couples explicitly intend to avoid pregnancy. The tradition must be either physicalist or inconsistent in its defense of NFP. In either case, the tradition is consequently wrong about prohibiting contraception.

You will recall the analogous distinction between stealing and getting a job—both can provide food for one's family, but one is wrong and the other is not. My students often respond to this example by saying that the comparison does not hold, because stealing is obviously wrong, whereas the whole question at issue is whether contraception is wrong or not. The argument assumes what it is trying to prove.

Harmful to the good of marriage by preventing sex and spontaneity. The final objection to the teaching, and particularly to its advocacy of NFP, is that periodic abstinence can harm the unitive good by forcing couples' sex lives into an artificial and arbitrary schedule. Sex within marriage is meant to be a spontaneous expression of mutual affection and love, and such love cannot be scheduled like meals. Besides, women's cycles differ. Although progress in the study of the fertility cycle means that current methods of NFP, if followed correctly, predict infertile and fertile days with great accuracy, the number of certainly infertile days can be quite small for some women. Particularly if the couple avoids sex during menstruation, they are faced with the choice of enduring long periods of abstinence or taking a chance on ambiguous days. In either case, unnecessary tension is introduced into the relationship.

It is worth taking a moment to explore this objection a little further. Sometimes NFP is presented as if it were a mini-ascetical regime, a taste of celibacy for married people. As Rosemary Radford Ruether pointed out decades ago, this seems like a mistaken move by clerics who assume that sex within marriage is simply a matter of satisfying or suppressing selfish urges for intercourse. Her description is worth hearing at length.

> [NFP] treats marital love as an appetite which can be scheduled, like eating and sleeping. But marital love, if it is really developed, has been sublimated from the appetite level. It has been raised into the expression of a relationship, and therefore needs to follow the laws of that relationship, and to flow with the dynamics of that relationship. . . . Now it is obvious that if a couple were to really practice continence as a spiritual discipline, the last way they would do it would be according to the woman's monthly cycles of fertility. They would perhaps abstain for the forty days of Lent, or something of this kind, and meanwhile devote themselves to some special regime of prayer and contemplation. (*Contraception and Holiness*, p. 68)

"Spontaneity" may conjure up reckless, unrestrained sex on the living room couch on a Saturday afternoon when the urge hits, but in fact, it also means that at significant moments in the relationship, sex may seem entirely natural—upon the return of a spouse from a long business trip, on an anniversary, in celebrating the move into a new home, in consolation after returning from visiting a sick parent or relative, even after a hard fight between the spouses. In these cases and others, Ruether's point is that the choice to have sex is not a matter of simply following urges for pleasures, but of expressing love, intimacy, and union. The "spontaneity" is not a matter of following whatever biological urges hit, but a matter of allowing sexual acts to follow the uncertain, unpredictable contours of the marital relationship itself. Since the tradition grants that sexual intercourse is the most sacred and important expression of marital union and love, why deprive a couple of its use at times when that love and union will be embodied most appropriately?

For Discussion

1. What responses can you imagine to the four arguments above? Which seem most compelling to you? Why?

2. Many of those who agree with the Church suggest that the real force of the teaching against contraception can be seen in the fact that a society that adopts a "contraceptive mentality" eventually becomes promiscuous. They point out, reasonably enough, that American society changed radically since birth control became widely available, especially the Pill. How might one respond to this assertion?

A Brief Reflection on Temperance

Reflecting on Ruether's observations, we must again consider the virtue of chastity. Getting married doesn't suddenly mean you can give up chastity and have sex whenever you feel like it—as you will learn! Chastity is sometimes confused with celibacy, which is a vow to abstain completely from sexual acts. Chastity refers to our capacity to exercise appropriate control over our sexual desires and direct them to our final end. It is just as necessary for married couples as it is for people who are dating, for spouses must continue to show reverence for each other, rather than treating the other as an object for personal sexual gratification.

Now we have an odd relationship to chastity in our culture. On the one hand, conjure up a picture of ideal sex and it is likely to look something like this: two partners have been apart for a long period of time, they finally are able to reunite, and they are so overwhelmed that they cannot even make it to the bedroom before they are embracing, kissing, and tearing off each other's clothes. We find spontaneous sex or delayed sex attractive because it seems to arise from such strong, basic desires—as in Eric Carmen's song: "Take me over the edge, make me lose control." Some opponents of premarital sex actually encourage this attitude by depicting the wedding night in exactly this uncontrolled fashion: suddenly the external restraint is gone, and you are free to follow your urges.

But losing control isn't always a good thing. In a recent interview a serial rapist offered a seemingly sincere apology, then added that people needed to understand how strong his desires were. Without some sense of control over our sexual desires—that is, without chastity—the world would be an ugly place.

This sort of schizophrenia is better illustrated if we turn to food. Think about that triple chocolate cheesecake you've been craving. You are sitting at a restaurant, having eaten a decent meal. You really want the cheesecake, but you know you shouldn't. Then picture that glorious moment when you break down and triumphantly say, "OK, I'll get it!" That is the message much advertising sends us: go ahead and indulge your craving for the food, the car, whatever. Indulge. You know you shouldn't, but do it anyway—it will feel so good! If you're like most people, you don't usually give in. Most of the time you (grimly) do the rational thing. But those moments when you can indulge, when you can let go, are pure bliss.

This is what the virtue of temperance is supposed to fix. A temperate person is never grim about eating, but is quite pleased to eat in moderation—not too little, not too much. She may have the triple chocolate cheesecake, but not because she's succumbed to a craving. She eats it simply because she knows it's reasonable to eat cheesecake once in a while and enjoy it. And she doesn't feel grim when she's not eating cheesecake. She is the master of her appetite, and so when she eats, she can truly enjoy the food rather than just satisfy the craving. This is the free person: the one who eats what she wants when she wants it. She has the control to desire what is actually good to desire. The person who, for example, cultivates a taste for healthy foods doesn't have to struggle with a craving for a triple cheeseburger, because the triple cheeseburger doesn't even seem desirable. The same may apply to drink. The person who can stop at "buzzed" because she actually enjoys being buzzed is temperate with regard to alcohol; the person who has to force herself to stop at buzzed but would really rather get totally wasted and throw up lacks the virtue.

However, one of my students had this objection to the comparison with food and drink:

> I am a firm believer that in conjunction with an open, honest, communication-driven relationship, sex can be a great stress reliever/tension easer. . . . Without the use of contraceptives, there are times when this stress reliever can't do its job. If a couple is in the moment, but knows that they cannot have children because of financial distress or maybe they're just not ready for parenthood (which is okay for people to admit), they aren't able to express this deep love for each other when they need it most. One might argue that eating food is a good or drinking beer is a good, but can we categorize an expression of love in the same way? I understand that we can't realize the goods of eating, drinking, and being merry all the time, but can we ever express our love to one another too much? (Casey Campbell)

This student has raised the bar. The tradition is forced to reply that it is possible to express marital love too much *if* that expression of love always means sex. That may seem odd, but consider this: If we do not have some measure of control over our sexual desires, how can they possibly be a freely given gift? If we are "forced" by our urges to want to make out or have sex with someone, how is that more romantic than desiring to do it because we want to give the gift of ourselves to the other person? The nature of a gift is that it is free. And sex can only be a free gift if we possess it.

This is just as true after marriage as before. Some Christian marriage books make it sound like marriage is a license to have as much sex as you want. Restrain your urge until then, but afterwards open the floodgates. Given that we are aware of rampant spousal abuse and rape within marriage, you'd think people would stop saying such stupid things. If anything, the virtue of chastity is more necessary within marriage: it's not a matter of withholding the gift, but giving the gift only when it "fits." Advocates rightly point to testimony from couples who indicate that practicing NFP develops exactly this sort of mature chastity. That is to say, in response to sophisticated versions of the spontaneity argument, couples who use NFP have testified that the "rhythm" of the method has actually brought them closer together, perhaps because it has led the couples to more holistic forms of making love.

Wait, you say. You can see the need to cultivate chastity in a marriage in order for sex to be a free gift of self, but isn't Ruether saying exactly that? Don't we cultivate chastity by accepting periods of separation or late work nights or late childcare nights? Why follow the schedule too?

The only response I can think of to this point is that sex is not supposed to be any different from eating and drinking. What sets the "point of moderation" for how much to eat and drink? It is nothing more and nothing less than our bodies. And though we may complain to God about it, those bodies do not all have the same limits. Some people simply have a much higher tolerance for alcohol than others. Some people simply have a much faster metabolism than others. But our bodies are the limit, in all their peculiarity. So maybe we could say that NFP teaches us, in the end, to be the embodied finite creatures we are, to be ourselves (for our bodies are not separate from who we are), and to love as ourselves—not as someone else, and not pretending to be some godlike self-creator. Accepting ourselves bodily for who we are, and loving the way we are, are very good things for Christians to do. And it bears an uncanny resemblance to married love, that gift of self (body and person) described earlier. Maybe contraception isn't just about procreation, after all. Maybe it is about accepting ourselves (our whole selves, bodies included) as a gift from God, so that we can cherish our spouse in the same way.

Conclusion

Marriage as a human practice must have purposes. In these chapters, we have explored something of the common history of these purposes in Western culture and how they might be understood in marriages today. All of what we have said about marriage should make it clear that it is seen as an integral part of pursuing our overall ultimate end of love. Within other theories of our ultimate end, marriage might look different or it might cease to exist at all. But even the most skeptical critics of marriage in Western history have usually recognized the social issues involved in the procreation and raising of children, and so have recognized that even in a society devoted to pleasure, some form of marriage will still be maintained.

It might have seemed strange to discuss things like self-giving love and contraception in a chapter that specifically puts off discussing the Christian, sacramental aspects of marriage. Such teachings are part of what Catholics call the natural law, and they are meant to be applicable to all. While Christians may have stronger reasons for believing in self-giving love or avoiding contraception, they are not special beliefs or practices of Christians alone. That is to say, the tradition maintains that the arguments here, assuming the premises are granted, will apply to all, whether they follow Jesus or not.

That still leaves a lot to say, so we now turn to the Christian vocation to sacramental marriage, hopefully like a grand climax for our movement through our desires, to a place where our unique personal call from God and our unique personal love for another person come together in service to the world.

9

Practices of Sexuality

The Purposes of Sacramental or Vocational Marriage

What is God's will for your life? What does God want for you? For Christians, the question of what is our ultimate end, what is a truly happy life, is tied up with these questions about God's will. As historian Wayne Meeks writes, "'To do the will of God' is a phrase found often in the Bible, and the early Christians often use it to summarize the goal of life" (*The Origins of Christian Morality*, 84). Doing God's will is not like obeying some external authority, for God is the source of your life and knows you better than you know yourself. To do God's will is to find your place in God's creation, to be in harmony with all things. It is to discover your deepest longings, your deepest desires, desires so deep that it often takes work (which Christians call prayer and discernment) to discover them.

Another way of talking about finding God's will for your life is to speak of finding your vocation, your call from God. A vocation is the specific and unique way a person embodies the general, ultimate purpose of the Christian story: loving God and others. But when discussing marriage and vocation we may feel a disconnect. That's because vocation in Catholic circles has long been associated with priests and sisters, those called to the religious life and not to marriage. However, Catholic theology is developing ways of thinking about marriage as a vocation to the church and to the world, a vocation rooted in serving the kingdom of God, to which Jesus calls all—married and celibate—as one body. Each Christian has a unique call from God to be someone in particular. This call is received first and originally in baptism, where you are called by name into God's new family. All baptized Christians have a particular vocation to live out. To be baptized is to be set on a journey of discovery, to begin to unearth the call God has for you in the context of the fourth plotline of God's story. You don't do this alone; that's why you are baptized into the community we call the church. The community is the place where we celebrate and struggle with our calls together, where we encourage one another and challenge one another, where we fall and forgive together, where all of our different calls come together in a symphony to God. God's will for you is like playing a part in an orchestra: it is your part alone, played on your own instrument, but its beauty only shines through when it is played with all the other parts. Jesus called this great symphony the kingdom of God. It is ultimately why God created the world.

In this chapter we will develop the idea of marriage as a vocation, as a calling in service to the kingdom of God. First, we will explore the notion of the kingdom of God and consider why celibacy became historically a central Christian witness to the kingdom. Then we will explain how the tradition slowly but surely developed a sense that married people might have a similar call, through the development of the idea of marriage as sacramental. Finally, in the next chapter, we will explore the practical implications of the vocational purpose of Catholic marriage in today's society, how marriage might be oriented toward the work of building the kingdom.

Marriage and Family in the City: The Problem of Locating Love

Before talking directly about these ideas, we have to begin by looking at a key feature of our cultural context: marriage as a private relationship, separated from the public component of our lives. This strong separation of public and private is a unique feature of our culture, and unless we understand it, we will have difficulty seeing how sacramental or vocational marriage is a Christian way of locating marriage within a given cultural order.

Sociologists have long pointed out that one of the most profound social changes associated with modernization of cultures is the gradual detachment of various social or public practices from kinship or family ties. The examples of this are almost too numerous to mention. In most modern societies, family name and rank no longer determine class status, as they did, for example, in nobility structures in Europe. Instead, social class is now determined largely by education and by wealth. Education is no longer received primarily in the family but in large, state-run settings. Formative stories are passed along through mass media—books, radio, TV, or the internet—rather than through family channels. Careers are acquired by choice through the public channels of education and private business, rather than passed down from parents to children. Consumer goods are no longer produced within the family, but acquired by money in the public marketplace from anonymous institutions. Medical care, particularly long-term care for older persons, is also purchased in the marketplace rather than borne by younger generations of family members. Even religious beliefs, though still strongly associated with families, are increasingly perceived to be a matter of voluntary choice, rather than ancestral inheritance.

Such a dissociation of important practices from the family has surely influenced the waning importance of what we call the extended family. Previously the cultivation of more distant familial ties was a necessity for many areas of life, but now distant family ties can largely be seen as a matter of preference. Of course such dissociation also affects the nuclear family. Children are a great deal less reliant on parents, especially as they become older, or on each other. Parents too, particularly in the wake of the equality of women in the workplace, are less dependent on the family for their survival and flourishing.

This dissociation of the family sphere from the social sphere is most often characterized as the rise of the public/private distinction. We have already discussed the compartmentalization of modern life; this compartmentalization includes the separation of home from workplace, government from family ties, and sexual questions from political questions. All of these divisions rest on our common understanding of certain things as public and other things as private. Marriage and family, it is thought, clearly fall into the private compartment.

Why all this has happened is a matter of controversy. In fact the changes have been so large and so gradual that there is unlikely to be one neat, simple explanation. Clearly one cannot blame something as simple as selfish individualism for the weakening of family ties. While certainly the ideal of individual freedom and choice has been a major factor, it is possible that individualism is an effect, not a cause, of the changes. As noted above, many of these social changes arise from aspects of modern society that we take for granted: large private businesses, universal public education, a sharp separation between work and home, even universal equality before the law.

The evaluation of these changes remains a challenge. In the 1950s and 1960s, many sociologists regarded Western countries as a sort of vanguard for the whole world on these matters. Western patterns of freedom from family opened up possibilities for life that more traditional societies clearly lacked. In more recent years, as Western societies have experienced the further breakdown of the family unit, a drop in fertility rates, a massive upsurge in divorce, a large increase in children being raised in non-nuclear units, and the feminization of poverty, observers have become significantly more divided about what is happening and what can be done about it.

How do we place marriage within the larger social context? Theologian David McCarthy, who has done groundbreaking work in this area, suggests that our society thinks of love, romance, and marriage as if they were a plant with no need of a supporting ecosystem. It grows almost magically, by its own strength. Psychologists, pastors, and books are brought in to help if it is stumbling, but all tend to pay attention only to what is happening in the plant, not in the plant's environment. They focus on issues like the attitudes of the spouses, their communication skills, their sex life, and their interactions with the children.

McCarthy suggests, "The modern problem of love is a question of its location. Where is the dwelling place of love?" (*Sex and Love in the Home*, 25). In the name of freedom we have cut off married love and family life from genuine community. By doing so we have not made marriage happier, as we might have hoped. We have made it like a stunted plant, deprived of the nourishment it needs to grow and bear fruit. As McCarthy puts it, "Interpersonal love does not create a loving environment as much as it requires existing practices of love as a place to grow" (p. 22). Love is like the seeds scattered by the sower in Jesus' parable: there are many, many seeds, and there is no plant without the seed, but the growth of the seed depends on whether it falls on good ground or rocky ground or among thorns.

The modern desire to remove marriage from its dependence on other social obligations and links certainly grew out of a sense that there were a lot of thorns involved! However, not everything was thorny, and modern society didn't pick and choose but razed the whole thing in order to allow us to build a structure from scratch, all shiny and new, exactly to our desired specifications.

Rather like Wal-Mart, the independence and newness are illusions. Wal-Mart exists within an ecosystem of sorts, too, and depends on that ecosystem just as much as older ways of doing business might have depended on family connections. Thus modern marriage appears to have no location, but in fact it does exist within thorns and rocks of a different sort than in the past.

In recent times considerations of sexual ethics and social ethics have been split apart from one another, as if sex were merely a question of "personal morality," but this is quite contrary to the tradition. As Herbert McCabe explains in regard to sexuality in the Genesis creation narrative, the serpent "in Middle Eastern mythology is the symbol of autonomous sexuality, sexuality operating in isolation from a total human context, sexuality going quietly mad by itself" (*The People of God*, 110). McCabe notes, "The isolation of sex from its total human context, which is a result of the Fall, is linked closely with the isolation of the individual from his total communal context" (p. 111). This is the limitation of comparing eating and sex: eating is merely a matter of biological need for individuals, but sex is a necessity for the entire human community, not for each individual. This is exactly why the theologians of the early church and the Middle Ages put so much emphasis on procreation: they saw our sexuality as profoundly communal, oriented not so much toward our own personal good as to the good of the whole human community. The community was the ancient "location" of sex. While we cannot simply echo their way of naming the context for sexuality, we nevertheless need to appreciate the underlying point that sex is a communal reality. So the question is, where do we locate sexuality and marriage?

Marriage and Family within the Horizontal God Story

As we have seen, Christianity places marriage and sexuality within God's story, a narrative of God's character and work that revolves around the twin commandments of loving God and neighbor, orienting all our relationships around the story of God's love. We have seen that the plotlines draw us away from idols and from the self in order to be able to love truly, not competitively or possessively. But for Christians, this is not simply an end in itself. In the previous two chapters, we recognized that marriage, as an action, has two purposes: love and procreation. This is true for any marriage. However, marriage also points beyond itself for Christians. It is a sacrament, a way of playing out the plotline of God's call to his "chosen people" to live out an alternative way of life as an attractive witness for the world, so that they can see God's love. This happens not individually, but in a community where such a sacrament is located. That community we call the church. Early Christians sought God's will by following Jesus' proclamation of the kingdom of God. Their vocation, God's call to them, was seen as a social movement, a movement from one king to another, in the playing out of the horizontal dimension of God's story, God's desire to reconcile the world. To locate marriage within the Christian story, therefore, we need to look closely at this proclamation of the kingdom of God.

Jesus, Israel, and the Kingdom of God

Jesus' first words in the Gospels are, "The time is fulfilled, and the kingdom of God has come near; repent, and believe in the good news" (Mark 1:15).

Most scholars agree that Jesus' entire message is about the kingdom of God, especially about how he and his work are inaugurating it here and now. His preaching of the kingdom of God is what identified Jesus as the Messiah (anointed one, Christ). Many of the Jews expected that God would send a messiah to usher in Israel's ultimate destiny, which they called the kingdom of God. The Gospels tell how Jesus is that figure. Look at Simeon, a "righteous and devout" man, "looking forward to the consolation of Israel" (Luke 2:25). Upon encountering Jesus he says, "Master, now you are dismissing your servant in peace, . . . for my eyes have seen your salvation, which you prepared in the presence of all the peoples, a light for revelation to the Gentiles and for glory to your people Israel" (Luke 2:29–32). Jesus is the fulfillment of God's messianic promises to Israel to restore God's kingdom.

Jesus' message is that the kingdom of God has begun, has "come near" (Raymond E. Brown, *Introduction to the New Testament*, 128). What does this mean? This is a crucial and complicated question. Let's begin by pointing out a few things it can't mean. It can't mean that Jesus was simply preaching about an afterlife. The *inbreaking* of the kingdom is present all over the Gospels, and there is no extant Jewish notion that would support a message simply about some other "heavenly" place. First-century Jews were concerned with Israel. This misunderstanding of the kingdom is encouraged by the use of the phrase "kingdom of heaven" in Matthew, but Matthew simply used a conventional Jewish substitution so as to avoid speaking the divine name.

Another thing it can't mean is a kingdom in the usual, earthly sense—if that were the case Jesus utterly failed. Far from being installed as the new and glorious King of Israel, he was humiliated and crucified by the people he was supposed to defeat, the Roman occupiers of Israel. So Jesus is neither a purely otherworldly king nor an earthly king.

How shall we understand this kingdom? We should think in terms of political slogans. The coming of the kingdom of God is a sort of handle that encapsulates Jesus' mission, which is the culmination of the larger mission of Israel, first seen in Abraham's call. Biblical scholar W. D. Davies describes it as "the beginning of a new order and the culmination of an old order" (*Introduction to the New Testament*, 147). Davies and other scholars also say we could translate the Greek to mean "rule of God" or "reign of God." It is as if Jesus is saying, God's authentic rule is making itself felt, but has not fully arrived yet.

In a nutshell, the kingdom of God is a proclamation of a new and radical change in the relationship between God and humans, and of humans with each other. Before, humans and God were not at peace, for humans sought power and control and saw God as a rival or created other gods they liked better; before, humans were not at peace with each other, but were competitors for power. *Now* is the time when all that can change—indeed, is changing. This is not a timeless message, but a timely one; "the time is fulfilled" here and now, and the real question of the whole New Testament is how people will respond to what God is doing. Will they turn and accept the kingdom? Specifically, will Israel turn and receive its greatest gift? Of course, the answer to that turns out to be more complicated than a simple yes or no.

The Kingdom and Marriage in Scripture

So what does the kingdom have to do with marriage? Or to put it another way, how do marriage and family get transformed by the inbreaking of the kingdom? One historian summarizes by saying that the kingdom "placed marriage in a larger framework" in which the "messianic family is more basic to human identity than marriage and family" (Glenn W. Olsen, "Progeny, Faithfulness, Sacred Bond," 102). One's identity becomes centered on relationships in and around Jesus rather than biological families.

We need to look at the specific ways this is manifest in the New Testament and the early church. Near the beginning of Mark's Gospel, Jesus does some dramatic things: he calls disciples, drives out demons, and eats on the Sabbath. Word is getting out about him, and it is not good. We are told, "When his family heard it, they went out to restrain him, for people were saying, 'He has gone out of his mind'" (Mark 3:21). So they go to find him. Jesus is in a crowd when he is told, "'Your mother and your brothers and sisters are outside, asking for you.' And he replied, 'Who are my mother and my brothers?' And looking at those who sat around him, he said, 'Here are my mother and my brothers! Whoever does the will of God is my brother and sister and mother'" (Mark 3:32–35).

This is not the only recorded incident of Jesus in some sense rejecting his biological family. In Luke's Gospel we are told that Jesus at twelve years old stayed behind in Jerusalem after his parents left "but his parents did not know it" (Luke 2:43). They were frantic and spent three days searching for him, finally finding him in the temple among the teachers. They were upset, but he asked, "Why were you searching for me? Did you not know that I must be in my Father's house?" (Luke 2:49).

Not the Jesus you met in Sunday school, is it? What is going on here? The first story most vividly illustrates one of the main themes of Jesus' ministry: the constitution of a new family, based not on blood, but on allegiance to God and to Jesus' own ministry. As you may remember from the previous chapter, the ancient family was the crucial institution for identity. Family and marriage defined who you were, often in a closed way that excluded or looked down on others. In short, family relationships are distorted, particularly if you are poor or weak or female. That Jesus calls God "father"—and that he commands his disciples specifically not to call anyone on earth "father" (Matt. 23:9)—should be taken seriously here. Jesus wants to found a new family.

Because of this, Jesus often presents ordinary, untransformed family responsibilities and obligations as a hindrance to the kingdom. When one "of his disciples said to him, 'Lord, first let me go bury my father,'" Jesus replies bluntly, "Follow me, and let the dead bury their own dead" (Matt. 8:21–22). When someone comes to him and asks, "Teacher, tell my brother to divide the family inheritance with me," Jesus refuses and takes the opportunity to warn people of the dangers of desiring wealth and possessions, which are related to the family (Luke 12:13–21). In another place, Jesus tells a parable of many guests invited to a feast, who make excuses for not attending: they have bought land, or oxen, or just gotten married. Enraged, the host instead invites "the poor, the crippled, the blind, and the lame" to the feast (Luke 14:15–24). Those who are excluded or marginalized from ordinary family life are not tied up in its obligations, and so can wholeheartedly respond to the kingdom.

Jesus goes on to summarize this line of teaching: "Now large crowds were traveling with him; and he turned and said to them, 'Whoever comes to me and does not hate father and mother, wife and children, brothers and sisters, yes, and even life itself, cannot be my disciple'" (Luke 14:25–26). And he offers an odd parable about the cost of discipleship, which concludes, "So therefore, none of you can become my disciple if you do not give up all your possessions" (Luke 14:33).

Jesus is calling us away from idolatry, from the ways in which possessions and family obligations lead away from God and into idolatry. That the criticism is quite harsh is seen above all in Jesus' own choices. Not only was Jesus homeless and without possessions, but he apparently did not marry and have children. It was extremely uncommon to refuse to do this task, perhaps the most important in the life of a Jewish male at the time. Only small, extremist groups we would today call "sects" or "cults" did as Jesus did.

Lisa Sowle Cahill nicely sums up the idolatry of the ancient family and Jesus' critique of it: "Today's phrase 'family values' connotes a solidarity in family identity that the first Christians found highly suspect, if not condemnable. Families in the ancient world commanded intense loyalty and in return secured one's status and advantages in society. Christians, on the other hand, commit themselves to a new community of believers in Christ, one in which loyalty to the family hierarchy is superseded by solidarity with other believers in a mix of family and class standings. The new family of Christ subverts customary ways of allocating power and resources within the larger society" (*Family*, 18). Jesus is out to disrupt the family, because its relations, both internal and external, are distorted by power and control that creates oppression. Instead, he is founding a new family in which relationships are more open, equal, and sharing.

Early Christianity quite clearly took this line of reasoning to mean that celibacy, the intentional opting-out of the marriage and family status game, was the ideal path for the Christian who wished to follow Jesus and work for the kingdom. Some have argued that early Christian praise of celibacy stemmed primarily from some perceived "anti-body" or "anti-sex" sentiment. But Peter Brown, perhaps the leading scholar of early Christianity, states that "this is a secondary cause and may well be quite a superficial one" ("The Notion of Virginity in the Early Church," 433). Instead, "the virgin body was abnormal largely because it was, by normal categories profoundly asocial—it did not belong to society as naturally defined" (p. 435). Early Christian celibacy asserted "the right of the individual to seek for himself or herself different forms of solidarity, more consonant with the high destiny of free persons" (p. 436).

These Christians sought a different sort of society, a new family that was not based on ascribed social status or blood ties. The indications of this in the early tradition are too numerous to cite more than a few examples. Paul urges his followers to remain unmarried, if they can, so that they are not divided and distracted by family responsibilities. Early Christians are depicted in Roman writings as "home-wreckers," because they bring new converts into their community regardless of their family obligations. The fact that early Christians also urge celibacy on women is particularly disruptive—in the patriarchal family systems of the time, women had to be attached to a man in order to receive recognition. Early Christians reject this, and allow women to live free of these patriarchal bonds.

Celibacy

As we see above, Christians conceived of celibacy as a countercultural action, a "declaration of independence" for one's body, particularly from the cultural imperatives contained in marriage. We often fail to realize that today. For many, the whole notion of celibacy seems bizarre at best and sick at worst, so accustomed are we to modern psychological theories that equate our sexuality with our other natural appetites for food. It's like starving your sexuality to death, you might think. What could possibly be the purpose of that?

We cannot possibly offer a full spirituality of celibacy here, but we can suggest certain themes that are important in coming to understand the value of celibacy. First and foremost, celibacy is meant to serve and form community, not cut a person off from community. Early on, Christian monasticism developed a strong preference for the communal, rather than the hermitic, lifestyle. Obviously living in a large community is facilitated by celibacy and hindered by marriages. Marriage introduces a necessary inequality, competition, and exclusion into the community's relationships, making it much harder to embody the "brothers and sisters" ideal of monastic community life. The Vatican II document on priestly formation suggests that, through celibacy, priests "gain extremely appropriate help for exercising that perfect and unremitting love by which they can become all things to all men through their priestly ministration" (*Decree on Priestly Formation* [*Optatum*

Totius], no. 10). A freedom for greater and wider community is why celibacy has always been seen as a "gift," and not simply a matter of strenuous personal discipline.

Such should be the case for all Christians who are not married. But some single Christians today, who are not necessarily vowed to celibacy, have been vocal about how unwelcoming and isolating it is to be a single in Christian communities. Laura Smit, in a wonderful book about Christian singleness, notes that, according to scripture, "Christians should assume that they will be single unless and until they have a godly reason to marry" (*Loves Me, Loves Me Not*, 77). Instead Christian communities often push marriage on everyone as the norm and leave no place for singles. Christians are pushed into marriage by social imperatives, particularly fear of loneliness and exclusion, instead of seeking marriage only if and when it will be vocational, in service to the kingdom of God. Smit concludes, "People need help leading godly single lives, and instead the church for the most part continues to act as though everyone is married or soon will be" (p. 253). Were we to recover the ideals of the early church, the situation would more likely be reversed, or at the least, single Christians would be welcomed into family households. The fact that celibate Christians often feel cut off and isolated is not a problem with celibacy, but a problem with the way many Christians are living out marriage, in closed, inhospitable, private households.

Second, celibacy has to be understood as an eschatological sign, a sign of the kingdom to come. Jesus explicitly asserts that in that kingdom there are no marriages (Mark 12:25 and parallels). This is disturbing news to some, but there really is no other way to read this passage. Vatican II states that celibates "bear witness to the state which the resurrection will bring about in the world to come" (*Priestly Formation*, no. 10). Marriage, though a great human reality and even a sacrament, ultimately will pass away; the celibate lives out a witness to the ultimate marriage of Christ and Christ's church. As one text puts it, "celibates experience . . . a persistent desire to commit themselves single-heartedly to the person of Jesus" (Marie Theresa Coombs and Francis Kelly Nemeck, *Discerning Vocations to Marriage, Celibacy, and Singlehood*, 120). The unity we experience in marriage is only a pale foreshadowing of the promised union between all of us and God. In our society we are quick to scoff at such notions, but it is only against such a background that the practice of celibacy can be understood.

Finally, celibacy must be seen as a form of freedom if it is to be appreciated. It is true that, like voluntary poverty, it is a paradoxical sort of freedom. But those who have shed possessions in their lives recognize how freeing it can be not to have so much stuff. So too celibacy, while perhaps initially challenging, ultimately supports a freedom of movement, vision, and ministry that can be truly liberating. Writers in the early church were not ashamed to remind their hearers that marriage and childbearing, while good, are also tremendously sacrificial and taxing work. Particularly in light of the prohibition against divorce that Jesus issues, celibacy can look positive. I once had dinner with a Benedictine monk in his fifties, who described all the places he had lived and all the different kinds of work he had done. He did not sound pained about his life; on the contrary, it sounded amazing. And it would have been impossible in the context of marriage and childrearing.

Catholics are responsible for considering the overwhelming New Testament witness in favor of celibacy when discerning their own vocation. It simply cannot be avoided or dismissed. If we are unwilling even to consider it, perhaps we have not yet understood Jesus' preaching of the kingdom and the real significance of our own faith. Having said that, it is a longstanding tradition that celibacy is a charism, or gift, given by God to some Christians but not to all. We face all sorts of social pressures to ignore or dismiss the possibility that we have received this gift, and these must be recognized. On the other hand, we cannot manufacture the gift.

For Discussion

1. What would you see as the advantages of celibacy? What are its disadvantages? What language of ultimate purpose and strong evaluation underlies your judgments?

2. Does college life on your campus put pressure on students to be involved as couples? If so, how is this pressure exerted?

Recovering Marriage as a Vocation for the Kingdom

Even in the early church's celebration of the value of the celibate life, Christians were quick to affirm the goodness of marriage, although not always in the most glowing of terms. Sections of Christianity where sex and marriage were perceived as bad were rejected by the orthodox tradition, even as the tradition maintained and reinforced a preference for celibacy. Eventually, this led to a two-level ethic, a sense that the Christian community has two tiers of members in it: the elite and the ordinary. When the emperor converted and Christianity went from a small community to the religion of the empire, such a two-level view became reinforced, since winning a large number of the general population to celibacy seemed impossible.

Little is done to mine the New Testament witness that might suggest that marriage and the family, properly transformed, might also serve the kingdom. That witness is most visible in two places. The first is Jesus' most obvious and prominent sexual teaching, his rejection of the option of divorce. Divorce was common and accepted in both Jewish and Greco-Roman circles, and yet Jesus' well-attested teaching rejected divorce, without exception, according to Mark and Luke. Matthew records a controversial exception for cases of *porneia*.

We will discuss divorce in the next chapter; here we need only note the extreme position Jesus takes on this question by rejecting all divorce and even equating it with adultery. Biblical scholars observe that Jewish experts in the law were debating the grounds for divorce in Jesus' day. One school of thought allowed for divorce in cases of sexual infidelity, another for any matter that displeased the husband (the example used is that his wife spoils his dinner), while a third suggested that divorce could even be valid in cases where the man simply found a different woman he liked better. In this context, Jesus' stance is radical indeed. Some research suggests that a few Jewish sects (such as the Essenes) may also have rejected divorce absolutely, but that only makes it clearer that Jesus was outside the Jewish mainstream on this question.

What does this teaching mean? The disciples reply in shock, "If such is the case of a man with his wife, it is better not to marry" (Matt. 19:10). Similarly, when I surveyed two of my classes on the question of whether they would ever consider divorce as an option in their own marriages, the vast majority indicated that they did not want to rule out divorce. Few people aim at divorce, but most want to keep the option open.

Why does Jesus take such a hard line? Jesus is upholding marriage as the model for the complete faithfulness between God and God's people that God intended it to be in the first place. The purpose of marriage is faithfulness itself, two people making a promise to one another that is unbreakable, despite all their failures. Such a marriage witnesses to God's kingdom, for it testifies to the steadfast love of God. God does not keep his options open. God commits forever.

The second point is found in the so-called household codes, present in several Pauline letters. An example of the household codes is found in the letter to the Ephesians.

> Be subject to one another out of reverence for Christ. Wives, be subject to your husbands as you are to the Lord. For the husband is the head of the wife just as Christ is the head of the church, the body of which he is the Savior. Just as the church is subject to Christ, so also wives ought to be, in everything, to their husbands. Husbands, love your wives, just as Christ loved the church and gave himself up for her to sanctify her, in order to make her holy by cleansing her by the washing of water by the word, so as to present the church to himself in splendor, without a spot or wrinkle or anything of the kind—yes, so that she may be holy and without blemish. In the same way, husbands should love their wives as they do their own bodies. He who loves his wife loves himself. For no one ever hates his own body, but he nourishes and tenderly cares for it, just as Christ does for the church, because we are members of his body. "For this reason a man will leave his father and mother and be joined to his wife, and the two will become one flesh." This is a great mystery, and I am applying it to Christ and the church. Each of you, however, should love his wife as himself, and a wife should respect her husband. (Eph. 5:21–33)

The code continues to provide similar orders to masters and slaves, and parents and children, the other components of an ancient household. Instructions of a similar sort appear in a number of other New Testament letters, underscoring the importance of this sort of instruction in the earliest Christian communities. As in the divorce passage, the one-flesh union described in Genesis 2 is cited directly, indicating its importance to the early gospel.

These codes are often a source of heated controversy among modern Christians. For some, the codes contain a sacred endorsement of a certain form of the family, in which the male is the head and the female follows. For others, the codes offer blatant proof that biblical authors were not exempt from the social biases of their time. Many scholars distinguish between the codes and Jesus' original message of equality, which apparently proved "too hot to handle."

However, a more compelling reading transcends this debate. The form of the household code is indeed borrowed from standard Roman advice literature, as if Paul were borrowing something from Dear Abby or an etiquette book. What is striking about this standard advice is how mutual it is. The passage begins by telling both parties to be subordinate to one another in Christ (Eph. 5:21). The passage addresses the "lesser" party first—and the fact that such a party is addressed at all is noteworthy. Further, the actual duties turn out to be mutual, rather than one-sided. Headship itself is transformed by the model of Christ, who suffered as the servant of all. All in all, a case can be made that while these passages do not necessarily present us with a once-and-for-all picture of exactly how marriage is supposed to work, they do show us how the earliest Christian communities were interested in taking up the family structures around them and transforming them through Jesus' gospel.

We can tie together the anti-divorce teaching and the household codes by recognizing that, in both, married love is supposed to take on the character of God's love, so that Christian marriages can show the world something about who God is. Marriage is a mission, a vocation given by God. In order to carry out the mission we have to practice marriage in a counter-cultural way.

For Discussion

1. Is divorce compatible with the vow of permanency in marriage? Why or why not?

2. In what other ways might married love look like God's love for us? How have you seen it (or not seen it) in your own family?

The Kingdom and the Sacraments

In the household codes Paul indicates that marriage is a sign of the union between Christ and the church. Though the texts are slim, the tradition has found them sufficient to designate this relationship as a sacrament. But what exactly does that mean? Here we need to draw a connection between the biblical witness and the sacramental theology worked out over the centuries by the Catholic tradition.

Sacraments, as every Catholic is taught, are visible signs of God's grace. But in the context of God's story it may be more helpful to say that sacraments are the "place" where Christians most intensely display the kingdom, the transformed realities of the world when there is love of God and neighbor, when the world is reconciled. When we speak about God's will or God's plan, we are talking about bringing the kingdom of God into reality "on earth as it is in heaven." The kingdom of God, as Jesus announces it, is both a present and a future reality, both "already" and "not yet." It is both true and not yet true. The future world coming into being in the sacraments is the world of love, peace, joy, reconciliation, and wholeness, as opposed to the world as we now experience it, a world of conflict, war, anxiety, hatred, and dividedness. Sacraments are a witness to the world of this transformation of reality.

We would do better here to see the seven sacraments as ecclesial realities tied to the kingdom of God, rather than appeal to abstract notions of

God's grace. In exploring marriage as a sacramental reality for Christians, we will consistently highlight the ways in which Christian marriage is tied to the mission or vocation of the kingdom of God proclaimed by Jesus, and the ways the practice of marriage is fundamentally a communal, and specifically ecclesial, project for Christians, thus countering the particular bias of our present culture, which regards marriage as a private contract between two individuals entirely dependent on their two wills.

So what does it mean that marriage is a sacrament? Michael Lawler takes the traditional definition ("an outward sign of an inward grace instituted by Christ") and explains, "A sacrament is a prophetic symbol in and through which the Church, the Body of Christ, proclaims, reveals, and celebrates in representation that presence and action of God which is called grace" (*Marriage and Sacrament*, 14). He agrees that a "prophetic symbol" must be a "two-tiered reality." In this case, the communion of love between spouses is the foundational reality, while the "more profound" level it symbolizes is "the intimate communion of life and love and grace between God and God's people and between Christ and Christ's people, the Church" (p. 14). Lawler's description maintains the importance of the divine and human levels of a sacrament, and also ties the notion of sacrament firmly to the overall life of the ecclesial community.

Yet his definition lacks adequate reference to the vocation of that community, and thus to the notion of the coming of the kingdom of God, which has a mission to reveal God's love to the wider world. By calling the symbol prophetic, Lawler indicates the key feature of any sacrament, its direction toward the future reality. But a full appropriation of the present–future dynamic allows us to avoid the problems associated with "two-level" imagery. "The presence and action of God" remains a static, rather than dynamic, reality associated with specifiable appearances and events.

More specifically, the action of God is not clearly specified as saving—and hence, a matter of pure gift, as indicated by the term *grace*. By connecting marriage more fully to the notion of vocation, to our call to discipleship, we can get a much better sense of the saving character of grace and of the sacrament. Often enough, the idea that sacramental marriage confers grace conjures up images of supercharged commitments or a special, secret force that somehow strengthens the couple to live out their marriage vows better than non-graced marriages. As we shall note later, strengthening is certainly one way—but only one—that marriage as sacramental functions as an effective sign of the kingdom of God. Strengthening, however, should be seen as one of a whole range of ways that Christian marriage is saved and graced by God—all of which serve not so much the marriage itself, but as support for the vocational call of the marriage.

We might fruitfully compare this orientation of saving grace to Karl Barth's comments on the "personal liberation of the Christian." Barth notes that many Christian preachers and thinkers have offered the "saving grace" of Christianity as a message that makes us feel better, particularly in times of trial. That is to say, grace really benefits us by making us feel less afraid, more confident, or more free. All this is true enough, Barth says, but the danger is to believe that this personal comfort and liberation is somehow the point of being a Christian. Rather, Barth argues strongly that the point of being a Christian is to witness to Christ in the world—that is, to fulfill a particular vocation. Any personal comfort we receive is given by God in order to support the primary task of the vocation. Put simply, the gifts are given for the sake of the task, and not for our personal happiness. A proper reading of the Old Testament story of Israel supports this view. People are often troubled by God's "favoritism" of Israel over other nations in the Old Testament. But, properly understood, this favoritism is not an end in itself. The point of favoring Israel is not so Israel can be happy, but so that Israel can fulfill its mission. So too a proper understanding of the saving grace of marriage places any personal strengthening of the spouses in the context of the vocation sending the spouses into the world. The fact that the spouses take joy in each other's love is a consequence of their shared mission. The saving is for the mission, because the sending exceeds anything we could accomplish by our own strength.

For Discussion

1. How does this discussion affect your view of what goes on in a "church wedding"? How is this view of the sacrament of marriage different from your preconceptions?

2. The sacrament of marriage is said to be a "participation in the life of God by the community." What does this mean in practical terms?

Sacramental Marriage in the Kingdom-Household: New Families in the New Family

Sacramental marriage is not giving you special treatment, but giving you a special task, a vocation. Sacramental marriage, beyond love and procreation, is a vehicle by which we see God's kingdom come. It is a vocation to a new, different, and sometimes countercultural family life lived out in the midst of God's new family, the Christian community.

Thus it is the answer to the previously identified problem of the location, the ecosystem, in which love grows and flourishes. By placing marriage within the sacramental system, tying it especially to baptism and Eucharist, marriage and family are given a new home and the possibility of transformation.

To understand what this might entail, let us turn to St. John Chrysostom, one of the greatest authors of the early church, whose work on marriage and family is extensive. Chrysostom lived in the fourth and fifth centuries, and began his Christian journey seeking the peace and detachment of the ascetic life, living in caves and nearly starving himself with extreme fasting. However, he eventually returned to the city and became a bishop. He was given the nickname Chrysostom ("golden mouth") for his preaching; his sermons were legendary in their time and remain a profound legacy.

His treatment of marriage and family is remarkably focused on the practical matters of the Christian household—possibly because it was given in the form of sermons. His work affirms the traditional two ends of marriage: chastity and procreation. But he also shows profound interest in the pernicious influence of money. By all accounts, Chrysostom's city was wealthy, and he takes no prisoners in his all-out assault on the influence of wealth and greed in family life. In this way Chrysostom attends to the location of love in ways that many other writers of the tradition do not.

He argues that many problems in the family, especially between husband and wife, arise from concerns about money. By contrast, he insists that the Christian household should do things differently, beginning specifically with the marriage celebration itself. Strikingly, he condemns the feasting and merriment of pagan marriage celebrations, insisting instead that a Christian's wedding should symbolize the couples' vocation to the Christian life together. One way they can do this is by inviting the poor to the wedding celebration (Homily 1 in Rogers, *Theology and Sexuality*, 87-92). This suggestion was not received any better by his audience than it would be today if someone suggested we go down to the homeless shelter and bring in a dozen people to our wedding banquet. But Chrysostom presses the point: "Are you ashamed of this idea? Do you blush? What could be more unreasonable than this? When you drag the devil into your house, you do not think you are doing anything shameful, but when you plan to bring Christ in, you blush?" (Rogers, 88–89). In fact, hospitality toward the poor should not just happen at the wedding. It ought to become a regular characteristic of the household. The couple should invite the poor person in, for he or she "is able to bestow all God's blessings simply by setting foot inside" (Homily 20 in Hunter, 94).

Why would we not want to do this, despite Jesus' repeated insistence that when we care for the poor, we care for him? Surely part of the reason is our concern to protect our property. We worry what a stranger might steal from us. Chrysostom, in his own way, indicates that real hospitality involves a cost, and yet the alternative is to live in fear, to close off our riches from others by enclosing ourselves in our family life.

We might also say that we would feel uncomfortable inviting poor strangers into our home. Is our discomfort related to class, to a feeling that they are worse than we are, that it would soil the dignity of our home to invite someone dirty and different?

Chrysostom's specific and provocative examples point toward a general theme best summarized in the recent work of Lisa Sowle Cahill. She writes that New Testament and early Christian writers were concerned about sexual issues because they sought to "use sex and gender conduct to enhance solidarity, not as mere conformity, but as inclusion of the excluded and as unified resistance to oppressive social structures" (*Sex, Gender, and Christian Ethics*, 137). Chief among these oppressive structures was the family, which institutionalized and reinforced social hierarchies and patriarchy. We have seen that the early Christians, following the example of Jesus and Paul, saw that the most effective way to oppose these structures was to free oneself from them entirely by choosing the life of communal celibacy.

However, Cahill argues, the instruction about sexual practice and marriage was also subversive. It "often functioned in the early Christian communities to challenge social hierarchy, especially as embodied in the Greco-

Roman family" (p. 141). Of course this involved sexual restraint, but the reason for the restraint was not a matter of individual heroism. Rather, sexual restraint was needed so as to manifest "the unity of the community" of Christians (p. 151). The even more prominent restraint with regard to possessions had the same aim. The teachings about giving up greed and giving up lust were unified in their purpose of manifesting a community that was neither divided nor competitive. The family unit, the fundamental unit of society, was faced with a stark choice: either serve the oppressive structures of the society, or become transformed in service of the kingdom of God.

For Discussion

1. In today's culture, how might Christian marriages work against oppressive social structures? What oppressive structures might be supported by marriage in our society?

2. John Chrysostom was particularly concerned about the role of money in marriage. How does love of money affect Christian marriage today?

Conclusion

This chapter introduced a number of possibly unfamiliar ideas. Most importantly, we have come to see that the Christian God story has a horizontal component, which is the promised and partially begun social transformation Jesus called the kingdom of God. To be a Christian is to have a specific and unique role to play in this historic drama, a countercultural role as part of the ensemble of the Christian community in the world. That is to say, God calls Christians by name to a unique vocation, and while sometimes that means a call to a life of celibate service, it also can mean a call to a particular way of married life, a sacramental way that emphasizes the transformation of married life and love in service to God's kingdom.

The unfamiliarity of some of these ideas is partially a result of the relatively late recognition of the sacramental and vocational character of married life. It is also partially because Christians unknowingly accept the public/private compartmentalization of life, therefore avoiding the question of locating love within a social structure, an ecosystem that fosters the marriage and is in turn fostered and transformed by it. Hopefully, these difficulties have been somewhat overcome by the historical and theological analysis of the vocational purpose of Christian marriage. But what does it mean concretely? How can a couple live out a vocational marriage in practical terms? To that we now turn.

10

Rules of the Practice
Society and Sacramental Marriage

What can a marriage do for the world and for God? In this chapter we develop a number of issues, which we can roughly divide into exterior and interior transformations needed for marriage and family to serve the purpose of a vocation to show God's kingdom. In treating the internal transformations of marriage, we will look at how the focus on the kingdom affects "natural marriage," love, and procreation. But first we need to look closely at the external issues of how marriage and family fit into the Christian vocation of witness to the world, by representing the future kingdom.

The External Transformations of Vocational Marriage

Our first approach to external issues comes in the form of a challenge to some particular arguments. Early Christian marriage sought to overcome oppressive features of the ancient family such as forced marriage for money and family status, the absolute hierarchy of the husband over the wife, and the role of the family in perpetuating social hierarchy and privilege. Early Christians thought it important to make a break from their families in order to display an alternate form of living, consistent with love of God and neighbor.

Is this view out of date? No longer do we live in a society where wealthy clans and nobles marry in order to hold on to their power and possessions, nor are marriages the means of maintaining social oppression and exclusion. No longer is marriage necessarily patriarchal, nor is the household the basic unit of society. It is no longer a place of production and economics. It is private, sequestered away from questions of riches and economic justice, which are the affairs of government and business. Haven't we achieved some of the ideals of the early Christians? Their countercultural view, important for its time, seems no longer applicable. According to Bruce Malina, Jesus' criticisms of family forms belong with his overall teaching on self-denial—meaning not the modern individualist self, but the "collectivist" self identified by adherence to social hierarchies and the families that sustain them ("Let Him Deny Himself," 118).

However, a crucial challenge can be made to this positive view of the modern family. David McCarthy insists that the modern construction of marriage and family may be just as tied to structures and systems of oppression as ancient ones, but in different ways. He begins by noting that our "unconditioned conception of marriage and family" does in fact serve certain political and economic ends (*Sex and Love in the Home*, 66). What McCarthy means by an "unconditioned conception" is a view that familial relationships are established solely on foundations of affection, rather than out of any practical aim. As he puts it, "The politically vested household of the ancient world has been replaced in modern times by a home founded on love between husband and wife rather than social alliances and financial exchanges between families" (pp. 67–68).

That description says nothing about what replaced the family's role in politics and economics. The socioeconomic order of noble families and clans has been replaced by the modern nation-state and the market economy. Both the modern nation-state and the market economy are competitive in nature. Both are impersonal systems of social exchange that rely on self-interest to drive and maintain a certain social order. Cooperation happens only when interested parties perceive possible gain for themselves; they are managed by contract, limiting and controlling the scope of cooperation. Success in either the economy or the government relies more on competition than on cooperation. The Philospher Alasdair MacIntyre quipped that one could call capitalism "constant civil war carried on by other means" (*After Virtue*, 273). Personal affection, love, has no place in this.

This sounds harsh, but there is also truth in it. We could not live in a world where life was competitive all the time. This is where the family comes in. McCarthy says, "Family has the function of performing what our economic and social organization cannot—a natural and necessary . . . set of affective bonds" (p. 71). Families are based on unconditional love; but schools, workplaces, and governments are based on ruthless application of merit (see also Christopher Lasch, *Haven in a Heartless World*).

This organization of our culture creates peculiar tensions. For example, the family is constantly threatened by competitive "market values"—the sexual and even parental roles become competitive and self-interested. It is hard be self-interested all day long at work and then come home and morph into a giving, generous person. The state and the market rely on families, yet do not allow their values to creep in.

But doesn't this impersonal public sphere at least give everyone a fair shot? Here lies the second problem McCarthy uncovers: the illusory idea that we've gone from a pre-modern family system where family ties inhibited freedom to a modern system that, while competitive, at least leaves us without ties. The illusion here is that the modern family lacks ties when actually it is tied directly to the market and the nation-state. McCarthy argues that you are basically enslaved to the government and the market for all your needs.

This radical dependence is a reliance on impersonal forces. The bonds of market and nation-state are necessarily impersonal, contractual, and competitive. They are not susceptible to transformation by love. A CEO in a large organization may be persuaded that treating employees well is ultimately good for business, but this is still self-interest, not a relationship of love.

Definition and Description of Closed Household

The deeper problem, McCarthy argues, is that such a system creates a household ideal—the "closed household" or the suburban household. It is reliant on personal income, such that two wage-earners are ordinarily required. This household is empty in the sense that its time must go to earning more so that it can buy more contracted services so that it can continue to be a "happy home." The home itself has no productive purpose; it is a unit of consumption. McCarthy summarizes, "The suburban home represents the separation of the family from wider social life." The household itself is not enmeshed in transformed relationships of love; it is a fortress of affection dependent on external, competitive, contractual relationships to sustain its happiness.

Such an ideal is detrimental to those who are exploited by the closed household's consumption, and also to the household itself. First, for those who can afford it, the closed household empties meaning from the common life of the family. The "wider social life" that it abandons has traditionally formed a support network for the household itself, allowing internal tensions to be dissipated and overcome. Second, for those who cannot afford it, the closed household functions as a goal, driving the lower class to work enormously. And as richer households isolate themselves and rely on contractual relationships, poorer ones no longer have more fortunate neighbors with which to share. Poorer households are deprived of the informal commerce with richer ones that formerly allowed for bonds of charity to develop.

The geography of contemporary homebuilding reflects this. Today, houses are usually built in large, isolated subdivisions that are largely segregated by income and class. Such neighborhoods are designed to cater to a certain elite. They are isolated from any community business, and are completely reliant on the automobile. Few things are as isolating as the car; you encase yourself to travel, avoiding any contact that might come from walking, biking, or using public transit. Combined with attached garages, there is not even an opportunity to chat with a neighbor.

The houses in subdivisions provide further opportunities for isolation as they are built on larger lots than are city homes, and the front porch has been replaced by the back deck. Inside the household, space has expanded so that individual family members can achieve maximum isolation. Consider the following statistics: despite the fact that the average World War II era household had 3.67 people in it (compared to 2.6 in 2002), the average new home size has increased by almost 250% from 1950 to 2003 (983 sq ft to 2330 sq ft). A tiny 1% of homes built in 1950 had four or more bedrooms, while 37% of 2003 new homes had that many.

Is There an Alternative?

The point is that the modern family is dependent on a system that creates competition and even eats away at the love inside. McCarthy suggests that Christian marriages have a vocation to model an alternative way of living as family that is connected by love with neighbors, relatives, church, and the local economy. McCarthy's ideal is the "open household." The open household is enmeshed in a web of relationships in which it both gives and receives. These relationships are sometimes messy, but they are genuinely personal and susceptible to transformation by love.

Let's look at the way "intermediate associations" play a central role in Catholic social teaching. Intermediate associations are networks where resources are shared instead of bought. These associations stand between the immediate bonds of family and the impersonal bonds of market and state. They connect the household to a complex social life, rather than just to the economy and the government.

The importance of intermediate associations in Catholic social teaching is driven by what McCarthy calls an "organic" vision of how society is supposed to look. Catholic social teaching rests on its resistance to the modern visions of both capitalism and communism. Both systems, in different ways, seek to eradicate intermediate associations in favor of the abstract whole. Both are inherently totalitarian, in that they oppose a view of the world in which each person has a unique and inherent dignity.

Pope John Paul II writes, advocating the social vocation of the family, "Far from being closed in on itself, the family is by nature and vocation open to other families and to society, and undertakes its social role" (*Familiaris*

Consortio, no. 42). McCarthy suggests that by failing to see the importance of intermediate associations for household life, we are constantly either retreating inward or becoming overwhelmed at the magnitude of social problems. Intermediate associations give us a place to "act locally," while also providing support and bonding within the family itself. They offer a place where productive human relationships can be sacramental, signs and manifestations of God's love.

Yet intermediate associations have been disappearing in American society for decades. This retreat from our neighbors leaves the family adrift. A key vocation of the Christian family in today's world, McCarthy argues, is to exist and become rooted in a place where our lives have the opportunity to become intertwined with others.

For most families today, the actions involved with this must be intentional. McCarthy offers a key example from his own life: when moving to a new job, his family decided to buy an old row house on the main street of the town. Many of the stories that illustrate McCarthy's book arise from that choice, which forced his family into closer relationship with neighbors. The home ought to facilitate associating with others in and around the household. In choosing where to live, we cannot forget that the gospel reminds us that Jesus comes in the form of the stranger, and not the warm and close personal friend. An open household is a place of hospitality where we welcome the stranger and are open to the possibility of his or her gifts.

As with all vocations, the church community has a responsibility to couples to teach and nurture their call to be an effective sign of God's love. These calls to live as a sign and realization of the kingdom are ecclesial in the sense that every Christian marriage will be filled with a vision and with practices that embody and reflect the core mission of the church. They will be parts of the one Body of Christ, acting in love, mercy, peace, and community with God's world.

The Interior Transformation of Vocational Marriage: Natural Marriage Transfigured

Such a specifically Christian vocation in the larger society is an essential characteristic of Christian marriage. Such a family has a task beyond itself;

it becomes something other than a place of consumption. A mission-less marriage will lack this vocational bond in Christ. Marriage with a mission allows us to see marriage on par with religious and sacramental life, oriented to the larger mission of the Christian community, the mission of the larger "new family" within which our own families find their place.

Following the classic theological axiom that grace builds on nature—that God's work elevates the natural goods of creation—we should expect that the traditional purposes of natural marriage will also receive new meaning and definition in Christ when pursued in the context of the kingdom. How might we consider love and procreation as transformed by the kingdom?

Love Transformed: Indestructible and Sanctifying

Let us begin by considering the common aspiration to marry one's "best friend." It is a hallmark of what Judith Wallerstein calls "companionate marriage," a type of marriage that is relatively new and non-traditional compared with other forms. Other marriage models include the "romantic marriage" (where the marital bond is based on a vivid sexual attraction and passionate intimacy) and the "traditional marriage" (where the bond is based on the stability and security of two partners working hard, one at work and one at home). Companionate marriage is much more like an equal partnership, where work, home, love, and everything else are subject to ongoing negotiation. Wallerstein depicts this type of marriage as potentially rewarding since "every aspect of a companionate marriage, including serious issues such as the child's religion, are traded back and forth and settled by negotiation and compromise" (*The Good Marriage*, 167). The partners successfully maintain this type of marriage by being involved in every aspect of the other's life. They tend to be interested in each other's work, they share childrearing and other household responsibilities equally, and they articulate their bond in terms of shared interests and worldviews. One of Wallerstein's interviewees said that when she dated she kept having "relationships that were too passionate and destructive. . . . I was always looking for the messed-up guys who were exciting, guys who came in and out of my life" (pp. 170–71). Eventually, she realized she was addicted to the "melodrama." Then she found Kit, with whom she was already friends. Instead of relying on "the initial attraction," she chose Kit for their "similar ways of being," and the "attraction and sexual passion" followed (p. 172).

This presents an interesting example of marriage because a bond is based on a shared outward orientation to the world, rather than an inward attraction. The shared outward orientation is not simply a matter of sharing leisure interests; genuine companionate marriage shares more substantive ground. The cores of worldviews overlap.

This model certainly challenges some of our assumptions about the sort of love shared between partners. But we should not imagine such a relationship to be asexual, simply because it is not based on sexual attraction; similarly, romantic marriages are not based on the sharing of substantive worldviews but do include discussion and action. The question is, what forms the center of the relationship?

Many recent Catholic theologians have begun to mine the notion of friendship as a model for Christian marriage. Even in the second century Tertullian offered one of the strongest endorsements of such marriage: "What a bond is this: two believers who share one hope, one desire, one discipline, the same service. The two are brother and sister, fellow servants. There is no distinction of spirit or flesh, but truly they are two in one flesh. Where there is one flesh, there is also one spirit. Together they pray, together they prostrate themselves, together they fast, teaching each other, exhorting each other, supporting each other" (quoted in Hunter, 38).

We are reminded, both by Tertullian and by our earlier discussion of friendship, that friendship is not merely a matter of closeness or support, but a sharing of vision, goods, and being moved toward the same ultimate end. It needs to be based on the shared vision of the parties. The love involved in such a Christian friendship, such that the marriage reflects God's love to the world, is sanctifying and indestructible.

Sanctification

To sanctify something is to make it holy. To make something holy is to dedicate and make something pleasing to God. When God expresses a desire for Israel and the church to become "a holy people," God means that the people's life together is dedicated to God. Everything that is done is dedicated to the glorification of God. For a person to grow in holiness, or to become sanctified, is to have more of his or her life glorify God.

Vatican II repeatedly emphasized that all Christians are called to holiness and have a vocation to develop their lives in the service of God. Most commonly, religious men and women grow in holiness through shared prayer and through community life. Their vows—poverty, chastity, and obedience—are meant to dedicate them totally to their community. The dedication to a life of shared prayer and shared community aims at the glorification of God, at making members of the community into "living sacrifices" to the praise of God.

It is essential to recognize here that sanctification as a process is a matter of living into holiness through life and prayer with others. According to Christian teaching, we do not grow in holiness through our exertions, but through our weakness and through grace, most often receiving holiness from another, who draws us along the path of sanctification.

The chief "other" here is God, but in religious life it is also the brothers and sisters of the community. Marriage also becomes the life of shared prayer and shared community by which growth in holiness can and does happen. We should be careful here; this is not merely a matter of becoming better morally. A marriage where each partner makes the *other* a better person is a better exemplar of God's love. Such support involves a life in prayer and mission centered in and on God. It is noncompetitive love. Spouses find their relationship to God deepening as their own relationship deepens.

Christians most often describe sanctification using language about the Holy Spirit. If we follow biblical usage, the Holy Spirit designates a reality both inside and outside the person. The Spirit both dwells within the person and works to form bonds between persons. A sanctifying marriage is one where the Holy Spirit is seen both within and between spouses. Richard Gaillardetz reminds us that God is not a "third party" in a Christian marriage (*A Daring Promise*, 41–43). Rather, God makes his home precisely within the communion of the couple. God is not an external responsibility, adding to the pressures of the marriage, but is the substance of the couple's shared life, and is often met in the other person, as someone filled with the Spirit. Little theological work has been done to develop the insight of Tertullian nineteen centuries ago that the marriage of two Christians results in one flesh *and* one Spirit. Such reflection shows great promise.

Indestructibility

It is natural, then, to consider a marriage bound by the Holy Spirit in this way as indestructible. The Holy Spirit is the bond that unites the Father and the Son, the greatest relationship of love we know. That bond is not even shattered by death, but overcomes death. It is by the Holy Spirit that the Father raises Jesus from the dead. Because the Spirit dwells in Jesus, death cannot contain him. In killing the Son of God, we humans try to break the bond of Jesus and the Father, but even death—sin's greatest weapon—cannot break that bond. When Christians share in Jesus' body, they also come to find the Holy Spirit dwelling within them and so share the same bond with the Father, and the same promise of eternal life.

If we take all of this language seriously, a marriage bound by the Holy Spirit has the same sort of strength. Wallerstein notes that one of the dangers of companionate marriage is its constant negotiation, which extends to the bond itself. Beth and Kit quite casually indicated that divorce would be an option. This is natural; their marriage is a partnership, and were one of their worldviews to change or were their work to take them in some other direction, the substance of their shared bond would be lost. The reliance upon a sense of equality and shared substance in such a marriage also makes it fragile.

Because of this danger, it is not surprising that the most vivid New Testament teaching about marriage between Christians is that there is no divorce. A Christian marriage of friendship shares a love that it not merely an interest, but is God's own love. The bond is dependent not so much on how they feel about one another, but on their faith itself. If their commitment to their faith is unshakable, their commitment to their marriage will be too.

Perhaps no other action is lifted up as clearly in the New Testament as a contradiction of God's story as is divorce. As we noted previously, the debate in Jesus' time centered on reasons for divorce, but Jesus asserted that the whole point of marriage is to put an end to such competitive love, such trading up to a "better" marriage. We need to be careful here: Jesus aimed his criticism of divorce squarely at the spouse who divorces "and marries another." The problem here is with those who regard their marriage not as an effective sign of God's self-giving love but as a self-interested proposition, which they may leave when they no longer feel fulfilled.

Both St. Paul and St. Augustine address divorce, and their comments point to the importance of this sacramental character of the marriage bond between Christians. Paul is the first to make the distinction between the marriage of two Christians and the marriage of a Christian and a non-Christian (1 Cor. 7:10–16). Marriages between two Christians cannot be undone; even if they separate, their options are to remain single or to be reconciled. He offers this as a direct interpretation of Jesus' own teaching. However, he indicates that marriages between Christians and non-Christians play by somewhat different rules. He indicates that if such marriages are happy and are not resisted by the non-Christian spouse, the Christian spouse should stay married. If the non-Christian will not live in peace with the Christian, then Paul suggests they should divorce, "for Christ has called us to peace." Even today, this teaching is enshrined in Catholicism in what is called the "Pauline privilege," where the church is able to dissolve a marriage such as Paul indicates "in favor of the faith."

Similarly, Augustine, in the first extended treatment of marriage as a sacrament, connects the teaching against divorce to the "sacramental bond" between the couple (see Hunter, 108). As we have seen, Augustine argues that procreation is the primary purpose of marriage. However, he asserts that the sacramental bond is even more important. Marriage "in the City of our God" has a "sacramental quality," such that "the marriage cannot be dissolved in any way, except by the death of one of the spouses. The bond of marriage remains, even when children, for the sake of which the marriage was entered into, do not result from that bond due to sterility. Therefore, it is not permissible for married persons who know that they will not have children to separate from each other and have intercourse with others, even for the sake of having children" (Hunter, 115). He is well aware that this practice is countercultural: "But who does not know that the laws of the non-Christian are different?" (Hunter, *Marriage in the Early Church*, 109). However, the "sacramental significance" of the bond makes the difference.

Today, childbearing is less important in marriage. More emphasis is put on the mutual love and communion of the spouses. So if you were to think of the most likely reason you would want to divorce a spouse, what would it be? For many, that reason would be cheating. Beth and Kit, our companionate marriage couple, certainly follow this line. Beth speaks strongly about the solidity of the bond between her and Kit, but when asked what might break the marriage, she responds, "Infidelity would. . . . For us, [faithfulness is] essential, because it's a basic trust issue that lets each of us be ourselves" (Wallerstein, 181). Beth goes on to say that they are not afraid this would happen, but she rightly points out that a marriage based on respect and trust cannot abide a choice that undermines that basic mutuality in favor of someone else.

Would this also be true of a Christian marriage? The logic of the argument suggests that it would not. Even adultery, *if there is repentance*, would not be sufficient to destroy a bond cemented in the Holy Spirit. While such a situation would be extremely hard for both parties, here friendship would have to give way to the love of God, love that pursues us relentlessly even when we sin.

But doesn't Matthew's Gospel explicitly state that adultery would be an exception to the divorce prohibition (Matt. 19:3–9)? Indeed, some Bibles translate *porneia* as "adultery," and there is a long tradition of understanding adultery as an exception to the teaching. However, there are important reasons to contest this reading, for the usual Greek word for adultery is *moicheia*, not *porneia*. In another passage Matthew speaks of both *porneia* and *moicheia*, suggesting that he sees these two terms as describing two different things (Matt. 15:19). Later in the divorce passage, Matthew speaks of adultery using a form of the word *moicheia* (Matt. 15:9). It would seem extremely odd for Matthew to use a different word in the same passage if *porneia* already meant adultery. Even more importantly, the Mosaic law to which Jesus and the scribes refer in the passage virtually mandates a husband to divorce an adulterous wife. Jesus is explicitly contesting this passage; why would he make an exception in favor of the law that he is overruling? Many contemporary scholars agree that *porneia* is more correctly translated to refer to an incestuous marriage between two persons who are too closely related, or to a marriage between a believer and a non-believer (or between a Christian and a pagan as discussed in 1 Cor. 7). Finally, the notion that the sacramental bond between husband and wife mirrors the marriage of Christ and the church supports a call to faithfulness even in the face of infidelity. Surely it is a great thing that Christ loves his church even when that church is unfaithful to him.

Great, perhaps, but the reality that elicits such faithfulness is ugly. This emphasis on indestructibility even in the face of adultery should not overshadow the more positive implications of indestructibility. The indestructible sacramental bond in the Spirit between Christians is obviously a source of new life, strength, and reliability. And it is increasingly a countercultural witness to the world, a living out of plotline 4. To recognize the other person's commitment to me, even when I struggle with my own commitment, even when I fail to love, is a witness to me and to the world. It is a witness of a love that is stronger than death, stronger than anything the world can throw at it.

Debating Divorce

Indestructibility in a Divorce Culture

The prohibition against divorce as a form of adultery brings strong objections in today's culture. This biblical teaching cuts against a commonplace of our society that divorce is a necessary way out of a potential lifelong prison sentence in an unhappy marriage. To work through this complex clash of morality and culture we need first to look at contemporary culture's claims about our present situation. Then we will take a look at the practical issues surrounding divorce in today's Catholic Church.

We often hear that half of all marriages end in divorce, but behind this common aphorism lies a tangle of statistical data (see Popenoe, "The State of Our Unions"). In the United States the divorce rate has increased steadily since the nineteenth century. Starting in the mid-1960s, the rate of divorce began a rapid increase, peaking around 1980 at levels more than twice as high as the 1960 rate and more than four times higher than the 1900 rate (see omsoul.com). Since then, the divorce rate has slowly but steadily dropped about 25% below its peak.

What caused this massive and rapid shift in a social practice surrounding such a central institution? The issue is much debated. Often the debate centers on a shift in the meaning of marriage, particularly among women, who have come to see marriage less as obligatory self-sacrifice and more as a source of personal fulfillment. People now demand happiness in marriage and are far more likely to end unsatisfactory marriages. But is this pursuit of marital happiness liberation or the triumph of selfishness over commitment?

Barbara Dafoe Whitehead argues that over the course of the twentieth century divorce gradually moved from a tolerated but exceptional case for dealing with marital problems to a positive lifestyle choice. She calls this the shift to "expressive divorce," in which the choice to divorce is seen "as a form of psychological entrepreneurialism" (*The Divorce Culture*, 56). She cites a 1970s divorce narrative in which the author states, "The decision to separate is like Martin Luther nailing his theses to the door. . . . You start on your emotional reformation" (quoted in Whitehead, 59). The shift in attitudes toward divorce indicated an underlying shift in attitudes toward marriage and family: "People began to judge the strength and health of family bonds according to their capacity to promote individual fulfillment and personal growth" (p. 5). Whitehead makes a clear connection to market capitalism, in which freedom of choice for personal gratification trumps any and all concerns about larger community goods, such as the environment.

Whitehead is critical of this shift, which she attributes to emotional immaturity and a blatant disregard for "other stakeholders," particularly children. However, other commentators suggest such concerns are overblown. Pamela Paul details the rise of the "starter marriage," the phenomenon of a brief, childless marriage during one's twenties. The phrase "starter marriage" indicates an acceptance of the market logic; Paul even describes some as suggesting that in the future we will develop the idea that there is a marriage for every season and stage of life (*The Starter Marriage and the Future of Matrimony*, 251). Such a change in marital practice results from an underlying view that marriages should indeed contribute to and maintain individual happiness. The only alternative would seem to be reverting to a day when people stayed in unhappy marriages out of obligation or economic necessity.

The issue of children and divorce is critical in this social debate. Extensive studies have called into question two myths about children and divorce, both of which undermine the ideology of expressive divorce. The first myth is that if the parents are happier, the children will be happier too (Judith Wallerstein, Julia Lewis, and Sandra Blakeslee, *The Unexpected Legacy of Divorce: A 25-Year Landmark Study*, xxiii). In a 1994 national survey, only 15% of people agreed with the statement, "When there are children in the family, parents should stay together even if they don't get along" (Popenoe, "State of Our Unions"). In fact, children of divorce are often plagued by personal, academic, and psychological struggles connected to the divorce. While in certain extreme instances (i.e., abuse), divorce may produce benefits, these are exceptions rather than the rule. This myth, which the authors of the study call the "trickle down effect," indicates adults' inability to understand how children view and make sense of their world.

The second myth is that the divorce itself is the most traumatic time for children. The study indicates that divorce leaves developmental scars that surface throughout the lifetime of children of divorce. Moreover, the experience of living in a post-divorce family often takes a much deeper toll than the actual separation (Wallerstein, *Unexpected Legacy*, xxv). As the authors argue, the real struggle for children of divorce is likely to come when they enter into serious adult relationships (p. xxix).

The above argument traces the rise of divorce to a shift in the purpose of marriage, from self-sacrifice to self-fulfillment. There are also "harder" social indicators. The shift coincides with a tremendous increase in women's education and the ability of women to support themselves through satisfying work, removing the economic necessity that kept marriages together. The advent of no-fault divorce laws, which make the process of civil divorce far easier, also plays a role. Finally, a massive shift in the overall social acceptability of divorce makes a difference. The social stigma associated with divorce has largely disappeared.

More complications surface as we break down the data. For example, as of the mid-1990s, divorce rates in some states (mostly in the South) are two to three times higher than those in the lowest-divorcing states (mostly in the North). Do cold winters keep couples together? Couples with higher incomes and more education also have significantly lower divorce rates, as do couples who are childless at the time of marriage. Finally, marriage postponed at least until age twenty-five is much less likely to result in divorce than marriage at twenty years of age or younger. The overall divorce rate masks significant variation among different cultural subgroups.

What can be done about this shift? There is great concern to "find the right person," but this over-romanticized view creates as many problems as it solves. Instead, we might consider the divorces that do not need to happen. Divorces fall easily into two groups: those that result from serious conflicts in the relationship, and (the majority) those that arise out of boredom, immaturity, communication problems, and a sense that the "grass is greener on the other side." One study puts 70 to 75% of all divorce in this low-conflict category (Paul R. Amato and Alan Booth, *A Generation at Risk*, 220). Strikingly, since the early seventies, 95 to 98% of married couples describe their relationship as "very happy" or "pretty happy"—only 2 to 4% are described as "not too happy." According to one recent survey, only 2% of couples rate their chances of breaking up as "high" or "very high" (*Statistical Handbook on the American Family*, pp. 25, 57). The statistics imply that many divorces happen in marriages that were once genuinely happy. Often couples hit a rocky period in the relationship and are unable to ride it out. Numerous studies confirm that a strong majority of couples who describe their marriage as troubled and who stay together report they are happy five years down the road.

Catholic tradition has long held that separation is appropriate and even necessary in cases of abuse and negligence (though it also maintains that remarriage is impossible, given the permanence of the marriage vow). Are these low-tension cases simply a matter of one or both partners wanting a "better" spouse, exactly the attitude Jesus condemned? Most divorces are initiated unilaterally and are resisted by the other spouse, who wants to save the marriage. The numbers are striking: nearly half of divorces are not desired at all by one partner, and only 23% indicate that the divorce was desired equally by both parties (*Statistical Handbook*, 58). Is the abandoned spouse, who did not choose divorce in the sense of a moral choice outlined in this text, simply stuck with the action of the other? And what of those who later regret their decision to initiate divorce? Can their sin be forgiven?

Indestructibility and Catholic Teaching on the Bond of Marriage

The Catholic tradition has enshrined the ontological character of the marriage bond—and that constitutes a chief difficulty in the discussion of these matters. To say something is ontological means that it simply *is*. The Catholic tradition holds not that the bond *shouldn't* be broken, but that it *can't* be broken. Consequently, divorce shifts from being a problematic moral choice to an absolute impossibility. So a spouse who chooses civil divorce is, in a sense, pretending to break a bond that continues to exist in the eyes of God and the Church.

Recently, two theological arguments have been advanced against this claim that divorce is impossible. The first points out that, even in canon law and magisterial documents, the theology of marriage has shifted from a legalistic or juridical conception to a personalist or relational conception. Some theologians have spoken of a shift from a contractual view of marriage to a covenantal view, while others have pointed out that the 1983 revision of the Code of Canon Law clearly defines marriage as primarily a "communion of the whole of life," rather than vows or bonds. Whatever language is used, the result ought to be a change in thinking on the impossibility of divorce. It made sense, under the old juridical view, to posit the existence of a bond that persists even when the entire marriage has broken up. But if we define marriage in terms of the communion of life of the spouses, how can one say that the marriage "continues to exist" when there is no communion of life?

The second argument against the impossibility of divorce comes from within the tradition. Even the New Testament seems to allow divorce in exceptional cases. St. Paul argues that a newly initiated Christian may divorce his or her non-Christian spouse *if* the non-Christian wants to leave, for "it is to peace that God has called you" (1 Cor. 7:15). Paul articulates Jesus' prohibition against divorce for Christian spouses, and he likely shocks the Corinthians by insisting new Christians should stay with their pagan spouses—unless the non-Christian insists on leaving. The entire discourse is delivered in the language of "should" and "should not"—in moral, not ontological, terms. Biblical scholar Richard Hays observes that this and other New Testament passages show that the early Christians took the teaching against divorce seriously, but they also felt free to amend it to deal with particular situations (*The Moral Vision of the New Testament*, 372–73).

Luther, expounding on 1 Corinthians 7, criticizes "the senseless laws of the pope, which, in direct contradiction to this text of St. Paul, compel and force the one mate not to change his status on pain of losing his soul's salvation, but to wait for the runaway spouse or the death of the same" (*Luther's Works*, 28:37). He insists that a spouse who abandons a marriage is a "false Christian," and so can be regarded as the non-Christian described by St. Paul. Otherwise, Luther says, the spouse who was abandoned would have to "follow after the non-Christian mate or live a life of chastity without the will and capability to do so, and he would be the prisoner of another's caprice and live in danger of his soul" (p. 36). Luther denies this liberty to the spouse who runs away, however. Luther's underlying point is that a person's life and salvation are endangered if one is still tied to a spouse who runs away; Paul's teaching indicates that the Christian life itself is more important than saving a particular marriage.

Interestingly, Paul's exception has become enshrined in canon law as the "Pauline privilege," whereby the bishop of Rome can dissolve marriages "in the favor of the faith." Against the claim that marriages cannot be dissolved, this Pauline privilege seems to say that they can—and are. Defenders of the traditional teaching hold that such privileges are "divine," maintaining Jesus' absolute prohibition on any *human* breaking of the bond.

However, critics of ontological indissolubility also point out that the Eastern Christian tradition allows for divorce in exceptional cases. In the practice of *epikeia*, or judgment, divorces do occur. The church allows the parties involved to go through a period of penance, after which they may remarry (John Meyendorff, *Marriage*, 60–65). Again, critics point out that if *any* dissolution of marriages occurs in the tradition, the claim of ontological indissolubility falls.

Indestructibility and Annulment

Parallel to the claim about ontological indissolubility is the claim that, for such a bond to come into existence, certain specified conditions must be met. In some cases these are not met, resulting in an "apparent marriage"—not a marriage at all, or more precisely, not a valid marriage. So, for example, a marriage must be entered into freely by both partners. Consent makes the marriage and coercion invalidates it. If one member of the marriage is forced into marrying, such consent is not present and there is no bond. Consider another example: marriage involves openness to children, but one spouse secretly conceals the desire to avoid having children. They do not truly promise in marriage what the tradition says marriage is, and so they do not in fact marry.

Until the 1960s annulments—cases where an apparent marriage is declared invalid—were uncommon. However, since then the number of annulments has skyrocketed, especially in the United States. As with most issues, there are two perspectives on this rapid rise in annulments. Advocates of the annulment process point to changes in the canon law and the theology of marriage since Vatican II as reasons for the rise. They claim that Vatican II offered a much higher standard for marriage than in the past, and the new Code of Canon Law allows for much broader application of psychological criteria, such as immaturity or emotional dysfunction, as grounds for finding a marriage invalid. In addition, the tribunals have simply become much more efficient, particularly in America.

David McCarthy defends the process of annulment precisely on the grounds that it illuminates "the communal nature of Christian marriage" by providing "a set of procedures in the Church where former husbands and wives, along with family members and friends, are able to give an account of marriages gone wrong." He carefully notes that annulled marriages are "not erased," but "retrospectively understood to be faulty or invalid as permanent covenant, precisely at the point where a couple formed the union" ("Marriage, Remarriage, and Sex," 285). As Pope Benedict puts it in his address to the Roman court charged with reviewing annulment cases, the procedures are not simply juridical nor simply pastoral, but involve "a love for the truth" ("Speech to the Roman Rota," 600). Ideally such a process helps both parties understand what went wrong and enables the Church to give further account of the nature of the marital commitment, by offering descriptions where it is misunderstood.

On the other side are two groups—strange bedfellows—who are highly suspicious of this rise in the number of annulments. They largely agree that the present system is a widespread exercise in pastoral deception, with couples and tribunals essentially collaborating to manage the fallout of the rapid rise of divorces in the culture. Since most Catholics do not grasp the subtle distinction between divorce (dissolving an existing marriage) and annulment (declaring that an apparent marriage never really existed), the number of annulments creates a scandalous situation in which the Church essentially supports divorce. Some also point out that the whole system is painful and disingenuous, since it continues to allow Church officials to pretend that there is no such thing as divorce even as they render verdicts that are divorces in everything but name. In contrast with the Eastern churches, which have a discipline for dealing with divorce, the Catholic Church simply denies the real story of marital failure. This is not only deceptive but also

potentially destructive for spouses trying to understand what went wrong in their marriages. Beyond this, the two groups split, one group concluding that the Church should call a spade a spade and acknowledge the reality of divorce, the other asserting that the annulment process should be made much tougher in order to discourage divorce.

What is at issue here? The annulment problem is really not a matter of the annulment system itself, but of the context in which Catholic marriage and Catholic civil divorce go on today. Advocates of the present system of annulments argue that many who get married today have neither the intellectual grasp of what marriage is supposed to mean nor the emotional maturity to practice the relationship. This raises two questions. First, what exactly is the necessary level of knowledge and maturity? And, if it is achievable by only a small group, then can such an idea be reconciled with centuries of permanent marriage? Annulment critics point out that the knowledge needed is relatively basic: knowledge that the commitment is permanent and lifelong, involves a sharing of life, and leads to children. They also point out that marriage, as permanent, is precisely the place where we learn maturity.

The more serious question is why so many people are being allowed to marry in the first place if the Church believes they lack the necessary knowledge and emotional maturity. Why allow Catholics whose marriages were annulled to try marriage again without extensive therapy? Whatever one's take on the annulment situation at present, the problem has to go back to formation and marriage preparation. Catholics enjoy a right to a sacramental marriage, and therefore priests and others who prepare married couples are only allowed to deny the sacrament in extreme cases (John Paul II, *The Role of the Christian Family in the Modern World [Familiaris Consortio]*, no. 68). This is a "leftover" from older canon law and a more juridical view of the sacraments. If a more sophisticated view of the marital vocation has been developed and affirmed by the tradition, then a more substantial and selective process of formation and discernment would seem logical.

For Discussion

1. How does this section compare with the views about divorce with which you began? What are the similarities and differences?

2. Does divorce fit into the Christian God-story or not? How would you justify your answer?

3. Can you think of examples where marriage vows would be invalid, and therefore null?

Parenting Transformed: Children as Sacrifice

Many of my students plan on delaying marriage until their late twenties and delaying parenting a few more years after that. They feel the need to establish themselves, to be settled into their career and a house before they can begin to have children. These students do not view this as selfish; on the contrary, they want to be well prepared so their kids will have "the best."

True, having and raising a child are not easy propositions. Fundamental matters such as health care and parental leave are hard to come by. Yet one might question the notion of "being ready" for children. Is anyone ever ready for children? Rodney Clapp notes that having children for Christians is a matter of welcoming the stranger, for your child will always surprise and challenge you with his or her difference.

The phenomenon of delayed parenthood is a helpful place to start examining our notions about what sort of a vocation parenting is for Christians, and how the theological and vocational context of Christian marriage will transform the purpose of having and raising children. Culturally, the rise of delayed parenthood elicits two immediate explanations. The first has to do with the changing nature of work in our society. Instead of inheriting a job or working straight out of high school, many people in our society go on to numerous years of additional schooling as professional preparation.

Such schooling is often expensive and time-intensive. Often both partners are juggling the relationship and the foundation of a career. Adding kids to this picture seems to be prohibitive. The first years of a job, in many careers, are particularly grueling.

The second explanation is different. For many couples, a prime reason has to do with a desire to enjoy the marital relationship itself prior to the "intrusion" of children. It is a time for the young couple to establish their personal relationship on a firm footing. In this view, the arrival of children places a strain on the relationship, just like the demands of establishing a career. Most see postponing children as ultimately beneficial for everyone, since security gets established prior to having children.

Theologically, the primary challenge to the above picture has to be the question of sacrifice. On the one hand, no one argues against the idea that having children means sacrifice. Indeed, *both* arguments are based on the premise that everything changes when children come along. But the decision to postpone stems from a desire to avoid sacrifice. The couple hopes to "have it all." The sense of sacrifice is not present.

Unfortunately, sometimes this spirit of sacrifice cannot magically be conjured up when children arrive. The spouses are established in hard-working careers and routines of personal enjoyment—then all of a sudden these require drastic reconstruction. "Family" cannot instantly become the first priority, or the quality of the relationship or one's work will suffer.

The Catholic Family: Questions of Structure, Questions of Purpose

What are the purposes of specifically Catholic families in regard to raising children? We saw how the sacramental reflection and realization of God's faithful love and commitment amplifies the unitive purpose of natural marriage—staying together is not simply a matter of sticking by one's word or putting children first. It aims at reflecting a Christian vocation to follow Christ, who is God. What about parenting purposes? How is raising children sacramentalized by Christian vocation?

Questions of purpose are often obscured in this debate by questions about family structure. Some claim that raising children well involves a certain structure: the two-parent family with one wage-earner. The loss of that structure is why we're in such a mess. Women, they say, must sacrifice career ambitions in order to be mothers. It's that simple; take the variable out of the equation, and suddenly it becomes a lot less complicated. For women, there is a certain order that must follow, according to Pope John Paul II: "There is no doubt that the equal dignity and responsibility of men and women fully justifies women's access to public functions. On the other hand, the true advancement of women requires that clear recognition be given to the value of their maternal and family role, by comparison with all other public roles and all other professions" (*Role of the Christian Family*, no. 23). While the language is slightly awkward, the message is straightforward. Women can have public roles, so long as those roles are considered less important than the role of motherhood.

Theologian Julie Hanlon Rubio criticizes this position, but not on the usual grounds that it rejects the full equality of women. Rubio instead looks to the Gospels, and specifically to the idea of every Christian's vocation to discipleship, as the ground to affirm the dual vocation of both parents to nurture the family and to serve Christ in the world. Rubio particularly hones in on the "anti-family" passages of the Gospel: "Jesus' followers are called first and foremost to discipleship in community. He tells them that discipleship with him means *not* putting their families first" (*A Christian Theology of Marriage and Family*, 98). Discipleship in scripture "presumes a public vocation," (p. 99) and cannot be limited to living a virtuous and good family life. "Public vocation" need not mean career or job in a narrow sense, but it does mean engaging in work outside the home in witness to the gospel. Rubio is quick to note that such a dual vocation should be held "with caution," since "the idea of public vocation is not meant to justify high-paying or high-power jobs that do not allow for adequate time with children" (pp. 108–9). The point here is not careerism versus self-sacrifice, but a real tension within the Christian life itself, in which vocation challenges certain traditional arrangements of home life.

Work, Home, and Sacrifice as a Parent

Sometimes in the "balancing work and home" debate we fail to notice the dominant social structures, which need not be accepted without question.

For example, prior to industrialization women and men both worked at home and spent significant time with children, co-parenting them and educating them, even in the absence of universal public schooling. What is at issue in the present society is the demands of the workplace. Rubio points out that while nearly everyone subscribes to the "family first" ideal, in reality parents devote substantially more resources to the workplace than to children. Often enough, a workplace demand is seen as nonnegotiable, and family life must adjust accordingly. One may want to put family first, but it simply cannot be done. Since children react and feel much more in response to our actions than to what we say, many children conclude that the job is more important than they are.

If we begin to see how this works, we can recognize that the sacrifice of parenting may involve adjusting work ambitions rather than abandoning them. For example, one faculty couple I know has constantly juggled teaching schedules and leaves of absence in order to avoid day care for their three children. Doing so has meant that neither spouse has been able to do everything that he or she might want to do as an academic. Another mother chose to work in a freelance independent housecleaning service and the local city council because she can do these jobs with her children—indeed, the children help with the work. In these cases, the issue is not "work or family," but the ability to adjust expectations so that work and family are less likely to come into competition.

Some would say the sacrifice here is income, pure and simple. This is true in both cases cited above: the academics make less than if both worked constantly, full-time, and the industrious mother foregoes the larger salary and security possible from a different work situation. How does this sacrifice help the children? In poor and working-class families, work is so essential and tyrannical that parents are often enough virtually enslaved to it. Unfortunately, not everyone can follow the examples cited above. The lack of a just wage and the erosion of reasonable hours and benefits, as authorized for nearly a century in Catholic social teaching, are major social justice issues. It is insufficient to point to hard-working immigrants of our grandparents' or great-grandparents' generations. Large families and close-knit ethnic neighborhoods formed a support network, children were more independent, and most importantly the work and income needed to support a family was often less and sometimes available on a much less formal basis. The income problem is not a matter of extravagance; costs for housing, transportation, and medical care are all a great deal higher today than they were in previous generations. So for many in our society today, the tyranny of high expenses, low wages, and poor job security deals a terrible blow to the best parenting intentions.

But the problem of work can and does affect those who are not struggling to make basic expenses. David McCarthy points out that income can begin to justify increases in family consumption, sometimes in the name of providing "the best" for a family. The families I mentioned above are economically stable, but they could be better off. The latter family, for example, loves the outdoors, but cannot afford a boat or a snowmobile or fancy camping equipment. They often remark that many people could make similar choices if they were willing to sacrifice these "toys," which are supposed to buy "time together" for the family.

Sacrifice here is not simply parental. It means that, in the name of greater goods, children sacrifice too. We need to drop our competitive social aspirations that our children deserve "the best" of everything. In our society, "the best" often translates into "the best money can buy," which then translates into more and more parental work. If we recall what was earlier said about the need to shift our conception of the household from closed to open, these financial sacrifices are exactly the place where such shifts take place. It may mean living in less-expensive housing and different neighborhoods, using more public facilities, and sharing more with neighbors. The mother I spoke of above never rents videos or buys books, but makes extensive use of the local library. The faculty couple lives in a neighborhood that is less posh, has fewer amenities, and poses more parenting challenges. In each case, there are real sacrifices. The sacrifices ultimately free them from the tyranny that governs parenting in the closed household.

The Purposes of Catholic Parenting

Debates over better and worse family structures, then, are not misplaced. But we will do a better job of identifying better and worse if we attend to the sorts of structural features discussed above. This draws us back to the question of purpose. While structural considerations are important, they do not determine good and bad parenting. We need to look instead at the purposes or aims of parenting.

The general purpose of countercultural witness and service to the world, explained above by McCarthy, is specified for parenting in a number of ways. First, parents assume responsibility for forming and shaping their children as disciples of Christ. Recent Church documents speak of the family as a "domestic church." This is not meant in a strict sense, but in the sense that the family is the first and perhaps most important force of formation in children's lives. Put more bluntly, parents have a responsibility to introduce and build their child's relationship with God.

This responsibility is exemplified by the practice of infant baptism. Why do we baptize babies? Do we really believe that they will go to hell if they are not baptized? Some now see it as merely a welcoming ceremony, but actually it is a commissioning. The promises are made to follow Christ, and the sacrament is received, moving a person from darkness to light, from sin to forgiveness, from solitude to the Church community. However, isn't this problematic? I mean, do you want your parents making promises and doing things for you on your behalf? In doing so, the parents are committing themselves to being church for the helpless baby, introducing the child, step by step, to what it means to be a Catholic and live in a church community. They impose a responsibility on their children, one that is permanent, and counter to the social slogan that everyone is free to develop his or her own way.

A second responsibility has to do with educating children. Perhaps the most distinctive feature of the human animal is language, by which we communicate with one another, form relationships, and create culture. Since our ultimate purpose is love, we need to be taught what love means.

One of the most decisive moves in American Catholic history happened at the Third Plenary Council of American bishops in Baltimore in 1884. There the American bishops decreed "the establishment of parochial schools, the pastor's obligation in this matter, the people's obligation to support such schools, and finally the obligation of parents to send their children to Catholic schools" (Jay Dolan, *The American Catholic Experience*, 271–72). In practical terms, the bishops ordered that any church without a parish school was to build one within two years, cementing the need for a form of education different from the ideas and textbooks of nineteenth-century

American schools, which promoted a "generalized Protestant ethos" (Martin Marty, *A Short History of American Catholicism*, 134).

The parochial school, however, is no longer available to everyone as it once was. Is it, perhaps, no longer necessary? While a form of generic Protestantism is certainly no longer taught in most public schools, the idea of a value-neutral or value-free education is problematic. As many have argued, the vacuum of values in the schools simply allows certain values to slide in under the radar: blind faith in government, capitalism, consumerism, and a weak religious pluralism where all religions are essentially the same. In effect, children are educated as if there were no "master narrative," which in practical terms means they learn the dominant master narratives of an individualist, consumer society.

Parents must make choices in overseeing their children's education. It is no coincidence that the rapid rise of home-schooling over the past few decades has drawn strongly from the ranks of Christians and highly educated secular liberals. These groups may look different politically and may teach their children differently but they share a deep suspicion of supposedly value-free education and fear its destructive effects on their children. By noting this example I am not suggesting that home-schooling is the best way. I merely want to point out that the sacramental, Catholic responsibility of parents in educating children is not simply to learn the alphabet, math, and enough other stuff to get a job. It requires an effort to form children who are able to be creative, especially in building loving relationships in the world.

The third responsibility of Catholic parents is to raise their children with a sense of service toward the world, and specifically toward their neighbors in city, state, and country. That is to say, Catholics need to raise good citizens, even if these citizens live in ways that challenge aspects of the dominant culture. The danger in focusing simply on religious and parochial education is becoming a closed, fearful community in the midst of a hostile world—something that many say was true of the Church prior to Vatican II. Catholics, no matter how critical of the culture, still have a responsibility to serve their communities. As John Paul II wrote, families "can and should devote themselves to manifold social service activities, especially in favor of the poor" (*Role of the Christian Family*, no. 44). John Paul II here confirms the theme of this chapter: the Christian family has a particular vocation to the transformation of society.

For Discussion

1. What sacrifices are you willing to make for your children? How do you see the work–home tension?

2. How does a Christian vision call children to sacrifice in terms of "fitting into" the larger society? Is this good or bad?

Special Issues: Vocation and Mixed Marriages

I recently attended a large Sunday evening mega-church service in the sub-urbs, filled to the brim with people under age thirty-five. The main attraction was a talk on "marrying well." The speaker identified three mistakes people make: rushing, not seeking the counsel of others, and "ignoring spiritual compatibility." He offered a combination of research, humorous anecdotes, and basic advice on the first two, but the third point was the overall aim of the sermon. And he knew it would not be an easy point. He admitted that his message could be hard to accept, because it might mean that some people would have to break up with their significant others. An expectant silence filled the room. Earlier he had made them laugh; now he made them think.

For a long time, especially in the Catholic tradition, marrying someone of another religion was virtually unthinkable. One's religion, one's under-standing of God and the world, is the center of one's identity, right? How could one overlook that in such an important relationship? Of course, for many centuries it was a matter of family custom and of raising children in the faith, but today, with ever greater emphasis on personal compatibility, you would expect this to be a major issue for couples. You'd expect, "Oh, we totally don't like the same movies, but we have the same faith." Instead you're likely to get, "We just click so well on so many different things that the religious difference is no big deal."

For some, this entire chapter will have been problematic because it's based on the premise that two Christians are marrying one another, and understand that marriage as a step in their common response to God's call for their lives. What about "mixed" marriages? Some may even be offended by this discussion. It may feel like we're discriminating on the basis of religion. Doesn't love matter most? But how can we fulfill these goals, all the things we've talked about here, especially with raising children, if both spouses are not of the same faith?

Today mixed marriages are common. The Church still imposes obligations on the Catholic spouse in such a marriage: the marriage must not hinder their practice of the Catholic faith, and the children "as far as is possible" are to be brought up in the Catholic faith (John Paul II, *Role of the Christian Family*, no. 78). However, such marriages are not officially discouraged, as they formerly were. Especially in light of the development of a much richer and more thoroughly sacramental view of marriage, the situation seems incongruous.

The general question of mixed marriage is a practical one, however. Properly, Catholics need to consider different sorts of marriage. The first is a marriage between a Catholic and a non-Catholic Christian. Here, while there are real differences in some of the issues discussed in this chapter, there is also the possibility for a great deal of common ground. Such couples will have to deal with the sad and painful division of Christianity in their own household, negotiating between ecclesial communities, technical belief systems, and rituals. However, such negotiation can also be done in a spirit of ecumenism, a spirit that recognizes but seeks to overcome the sad divisions among Christians.

Another sort of marriage involves a "disparity of cult" (as Canon Law calls it). These marriages are between a Catholic and a practicing member of another, non-Christian religion. John Paul II himself insists that in such cases, the non-Christian's beliefs "are to be treated with respect," in accordance with the Vatican II understanding of the value of non-Christian religion. In such couples, sharing a vocation is considerably more challenging, though certainly not impossible, given the genuine overlap between Christianity and other religions. Nevertheless, truly committed members of a particular religion should be none too eager to sacrifice their devotion for a marriage or, worse, for "falling in love." It becomes difficult for the religion to remain a full expression of one's life; instead, it becomes more like a private hobby, pursued on the side.

The question of the religious practice of the children will be difficult. Many people today say, "We'll do both, and the children can pick one when they're older." But this view fails to understand the nature of child development. With such an upbringing children are more likely to view religion as a whole as arbitrary and self-made. Genuine religious difference is complicated enough for adults to understand. It may be better to bring the children up in one tradition, recognizing that they may inquire into the other when they are older.

Finally, there are mixed marriages between a Catholic and a secular person with no religious commitment at all. The pope seems far more concerned about these marriages than about mixed religious marriages. Again religious commitment is likely to turn into a private hobby. More seriously, the children will not understand the partner who does not practice a religion. The tradition warns against any involvement with a person who is hostile to God or to Christianity or to Catholicism. Even a person who is indifferent will pose a challenge to everyone in the family. Of course, each case is different, and the specific roots of lack of interest in religion must be considered.

Doubtless, readers will offer examples of great mixed marriages, but we must consider what is meant by "great." Do we mean what this chapter has discussed about the sacramental character and work of Catholic marriage? It is undeniable that there are exceptions. But what constitutes a *reasonable* exception? And has the exception become the rule? The point here is not to issue a simplistic, blanket condemnation of mixed marriages. But one must ask whether a mixed marriage can take on the purposes described, particularly in this chapter. Many people in our society fail to understand these purposes, and hence they think that the religious affiliation of the partners is no big deal. If the sacramental character of marriage is understood, it is a big deal.

Conclusion

One of John Paul II's writings may serve as a sort of summary of the varied themes of this chapter.

> In particular, note must be taken of the ever greater importance in our society of hospitality in all its forms, from opening the door of one's home and still more of one's heart to the pleas of one's brothers and sisters, to concrete efforts to ensure that every family has its own home, as the natural environment that preserves it and makes it grow. In a special way, the Christian family is called upon to listen to the Apostle's recommendation, 'Practice hospitality,' and therefore, imitating Christ's example and sharing in his love, to welcome the brother or sister in need. (*Role of the Christian Family*, no. 44)

Here the importance of the household, and the household of a particular sort, shines through. Hospitality is the mark of the vocational marriage, opening its doors to the world rather than closing them. Each family may find its own response to this call, but in our American context the counter-cultural witness of the early Christian family has renewed relevance, particularly in combating individualism and consumerism. This call is not primarily political in the sense of specifically political activity, but it is a call to society with others and building a household that is open to society, rather than caved in on itself.

Beyond this vocation the natural aims of marriage are also transformed by the sacrament. Love becomes a means of sanctification and produces a bond so filled with grace that, when validly contracted, it can never be broken. The indestructibility of the bond undergirds Catholic teaching and debate on divorce and annulment. Sometimes receiving less attention are the specific responsibilities of Catholic parenting, particularly in terms of ecclesial membership, education, and public service.

In all these ways, then, Christians are called to marriages that are truly vocational, that truly live out plotline 4 of God's story. And that means Christians can't marry just anyone, or for any reason. As Laura Smit summarizes,

> Christians should never marry out of insecurity, fear, a desire to escape the parental home, a need for affirmation, or a search for financial stability. Christians should marry only those who enhance their ability to

live Christlike lives, those able to be true partners in Christian service, those who give them a vision of the image of God and the glory of Christ. (*Loves Me, Loves Me Not*, 77)

Put simply, recalling the language of Lewis in our first chapter, Christians are called to marry their "best friend," the friend who actually shares the vision of the kingdom. If that seems overwhelming, then you have properly understood Jesus' New Testament proclamation of the kingdom. For us it is impossible, but not for God. That is why celibacy is so important to the tradition. However, with the help of grace, Catholic marriages can also become means and instruments to a more boundless love, rather than a restriction of love. The pathways to be trod in this area over the coming centuries are exciting because it is such new territory.

11 *Epilogue*

Forgiveness and Reconciliation
The Final Word of Ethics

Moral theology can seem dismal. A lot of it consists of talking about all the things we do wrong, the ways we screw up and fail to pursue the good. A hopeful vision is constantly put forward, of course, but even reading about that vision can remind us of how far we are from it. This is especially the case in regard to Catholic sexual teachings, at least in today's world. We might feel a little better about debating killing or abortion or stealing, comforting ourselves with the thought that we do not do such things, we are better than that. But the illusion of our goodness is much harder to maintain when surveying our sexual lives. Whether or not you accept the particulars of the Catholic tradition, we can agree that we all muddle through human relationships making mistakes, hurting ourselves and others, regularly falling short of our vision of love.

Our illusion about our goodness is the greatest stumbling block to Christian faith. Jesus comes to defeat the power of sin, and sin is never more powerful than when it is hidden. Dietrich Bonhoeffer, discussing the need for confession, says, "The expressed, acknowledged sin has lost all its power. It has been revealed and judged as sin" (*Life Together*, 113). Only when we see our sin can we come to know the heart of the good news, which is the possibility—indeed, the certainty—of forgiveness and reconciliation.

So maybe this section on forgiveness and reconciliation should have been the first chapter of the book instead of the last. Rightly understood, moral *theology* begins with a recognition of forgiveness and reconciliation, not with an accounting of all of our right and wrong actions. The Christian life begins, for all of us, at baptism, a sacrament of pure and complete forgiveness of sins, symbolized by our washing in the waters and our being clothed in a white garment. By beginning with God's love, we were really beginning with forgiveness. After all, God's love is not something we deserve, it's not a right that we have. God does not love us because of some independent worth on our part; all of our worth, our existence, comes from God in the first place. God's love then magnificently continues to aim at our lives, even when we aim at something completely different. God's love in this world, as John Paul II has eloquently said, always looks like mercy. It is always a love that we do not deserve and cannot earn, for which we can only be grateful.

But if forgiveness is the first word in Christianity, it is also the last word, and so it is fitting to end with it. God's love for us, for all, and for the world is never to be confused with a patronizing, "Well, everything's OK." Everything is not OK in this world or in ourselves, not by a long shot. Such a false gospel is part of the reason people then get mad at God when things don't go well, or stop believing in God when they see the enormity of evil in the world. God is not OK with evil. The real question that is raised by the fallenness of the world is, how will we deal with it? How will God deal with it? God's answer is Jesus, and Jesus does not fight evil with evil's tools of violence and hatred. Rather, God's answer to hate and sin is love. Consequently, Jesus is not God's magic trick for doing away with evil. Love is long hard work, and its greatness is always seen in perseverance, in its triumph over time, not in an instant. Jesus, in gathering Israel and forming the church, is part of something larger, of God's strategy for defeating evil and reconciling the world through forming a people who love and who return love when faced with hate. That will not work quickly. But with Jesus' resurrection and the sending of the Holy Spirit into the world, we Christians believe that it cannot ultimately fail. That means the end of the story is the final and ultimate reconciliation of everything, of all people, in Christ. That's your story, my story, and the story of the whole world. It is the final word.

As Christians we live in the process of love triumphing over sin, and so we are faced with the task of forgiveness and reconciliation. What disappears, when there is forgiveness and reconciliation, is sin. Sin gets erased. That doesn't mean it never happened, but it means that we, the living, deny sin all of its power and relegate it to the past. It means that the past need not determine the present and the future. If we think of a time in our lives when sin has broken a relationship, we can see how the continued existence of the sin in our mind and in the mind of the other party is precisely what continues to keep us apart.

To cite a key example, would you forgive your spouse who has committed adultery? Or would the marriage, its present and its future, be destroyed by that past sin? If it is destroyed, the final word is sin, the final word is the past. But if it is not destroyed, love wins. That is not to trivialize the issue; it is not a case of you and your spouse saying, "Oh, well, what's a little adultery now and then?" Adultery has in fact harmed, or perhaps even destroyed, the relationship. That is the reality. The question is, can there be redemption, resurrection, hope? The Christian answer, to this or any problem, is always yes, yes, yes.

Forgiveness, Guilt, and Righteousness

There are some roadblocks to understanding this correctly. For one thing, we should make clear that the point of recognizing sin and the need for forgiveness is not to make us feel guilty—or righteous. Both reactions are wrong, although the Christian community is full of people who are either stuck in guilt or self-righteousness.

This book may have critiqued all sorts of actions you have done or are doing. You may come away, in classic Catholic fashion, feeling like God is angry with you—or the Church is, or I am. You may try all sorts of strategies to get yourself off the hook, to dodge the potential accusations. You may reject the whole idea of moral theology and tell the Church to mind its own business. Or you may feel so guilty that you despair.

Despair is the opposite of hope. Despair is what comes when you feel like you've failed and there is no possibility of going on or reconciling. Your future is imprisoned by your past actions. But the tradition says that's totally false. The path to hope and freedom is recognizing one's sins and repenting of them. Repenting means you really acknowledge the sin and hurt and injury involved in your past actions, and you sincerely do not want to repeat them. The good news is God forgives them. God has already forgiven them. That doesn't mean you get a free pass to the afterlife; it means that your future need not be burdened by your past, in God's eyes. You have sinned, but God's forgiveness has made you whole. Just think about how powerful it is when this happens in your own life (Herbert McCabe, "The Forgiveness of God," 119–23). Think about a time when you have really hurt someone, really insulted her or him or attacked that person intentionally. Maybe you knew by the next day that you had indeed hurt him or her. Maybe it triggered a long breakdown in your relationship. Within the Christian narrative, that relationship can be repaired when you apologize, truly apologize, and the other person accepts your apology sincerely. That person has given you a gift, given you grace, in the complete sense of the word—you deserved condemnation, and he or she gave you love. That story is the story Jesus tells again and again in relation to God, and he insists that the Christian community play out that story in their lives together. We must forgive each other our trespasses as God forgives ours.

The danger in the Christian tradition is not in recognizing our sins, but in *not* recognizing them—or holding others hostage to their sins. This is self-righteousness. In its darker forms, it is the desire for vengeance. Maybe you read through this book, and you've always been a faithful Catholic, and you've actually followed all these paths carefully. Well, that's good! So, what are you thinking about your classmates who have not lived this way? What are you thinking about the prostitutes, or the adulterers? What are you thinking about the ex-boyfriend or ex-girlfriend who did you wrong? Christians are not called to righteousness. They are called to witness to the truth, which includes living good lives; but part of that truth is the invitation to forgiveness and reconciliation, even for the worst sins.

In this way, I think it's safe to say that righteousness is a far worse condition for the Christian than is guilt. The one who says, "I've done wrong," is far better off than the one who says, "I never do anything wrong." Christians struggling with guilt have not yet seen or heard or appreciated the genuine grace of God offered in Jesus, the full forgiveness of God. But Christians struggling with righteousness or with vengeance are in much more dangerous territory. They have not even acknowledged their need for forgiveness. They have not followed the only command for Christians in the Our Father. And the New Testament writings say, over and over again, that these people will not receive forgiveness. They will receive the same judgment they inflict on others.

Jesus illustrates this with a parable (Matt. 18:21–35). He depicts a king calling in a debtor to collect what he is owed. The man owes more money than he has, so the king orders the man, his wife, and his children to be sold to pay the debt. When the debtor begs for more time, the king is "moved with compassion" and forgives the debt entirely. Essentially, the debtor owes the king his life for the debt, and the king gives it back to him.

But then the debtor, happy and free, encounters a co-worker on the street who owes him a much smaller amount and demands his money back. The co-worker begs for patience, but instead of forgiving the debt or staying it, the man sends his co-worker to prison to work off the debt. Others see this and report it to the king, who angrily chastises the man and commands him to be "handed over to the torturers." The parable is clear: you can be forgiven only if you forgive others; if you are unforgiving, the forgiveness you have received is taken away.

This is not about God magically erasing black marks in a little book. It really means that relationships are repaired and recreated. And so we must recognize that forgiveness and reconciliation are a process, the single greatest, most important process we can practice. It is totally insufficient to picture sin and forgiveness as "no big deal," with love easily vanquishing our little mistakes. Forgiveness is hard. Being forgiven by someone else may even be harder, but it is the most radiant human reality we can find. It is the path of humanity being transformed to share in God's own life.

The Process of Reconciliation

How does this process work? Gerry O'Hanlon is an Irish Jesuit theologian who has been closely involved in the "troubles" of Northern Ireland, for centuries the scene of destructive conflict between factions loyal to England and others loyal to Ireland. Like certain areas in the Middle East, it is a land where rival claims have not been settled. In the course of this conflict much blood has been shed. We in the United States often fail to recognize that conflict becomes interminable when blood is shed, for bloodshed constitutes a serious grievance against the other side. They have killed one of ours. What shall we do? If we do not respond, have our sons and daughters died for nothing? It is like the problem the United States has had in places like Vietnam and Iraq. Once blood is shed, we must have victory. And of course, the same goes for the other side.

O'Hanlon writes on the necessity and process of reconciliation from this perspective. How, in the midst of a history of bloodshed, can both sides move past the past, beyond past actions, to achieve peace? In this process, we find that small-scale reconciliation between individuals is no different than political negotiations, or even the reconciliation that has to go on between God and God's own world. The process is the same. One option is being imprisoned by the past, forced interminably to take revenge in pursuit of total victory. Sin wins. The other option is the possibility that the past can be the past, can be "killed" by love in forgiveness.

O'Hanlon suggests that reconciliation always involves three steps. The first step is that the truth must be told, preferably by the one sinned against. Nothing mucks up forgiveness more than someone denying that he or she did anything wrong, or worse, insisting that he or she, and not the one injured, get to name what went wrong. Think about the adultery situation outlined above. To say, "It's no big deal," or, "It wasn't really adultery because we didn't have intercourse," or simply to refuse to talk about it cuts off the possibility of reconciliation before it can even begin. Denial of sin makes forgiveness impossible.

The only other option is facing our sin—as expressed to us by the one whom we've sinned against—and affirming it as the truth. How will that feel? For most of us, it may be the moment in our lives when we feel the most powerless. We say to a person with a real grievance, "Yes, I did that; yes, you are right about that; yes, I broke the relationship." It is, to put it bluntly, ego-destroying. It is also scary because we have placed ourselves in the hands of another—another whom we've wronged. We are "at the person's mercy."

Of course, sometimes it is not a clear situation of victim and accuser. But that does not mean we can respond, "Well, what about what *you* did?" We've all done it, but how does that help? That just becomes another way of avoiding the truth about ourselves, inevitably evolving into a competition of who has been injured more, and so who has to be in the powerless position. It's better for both parties to move themselves into the powerless position by acknowledging the whole truth and listening to the other, not by refuting the truth by calling the other person into question.

But there may be plenty of situations where there is a clear victim and a clear accuser. And the truth must be spoken by the accuser. It needs to be real truth, not a trumped-up, exaggerated story, but it nonetheless belongs to the accuser. This is of course what God does for us, throughout the Christian tradition, by sending laws and prophets to tell us the truth about how we've screwed up. Like so many of old, we are not really interested in hearing the truth about ourselves, particularly if we're rich and powerful (by the skewed standards of the world). But God is relentless. The truth must be acknowledged, and ultimately God speaks the truth.

This is only the first step. The process goes haywire if we stop here. Ironically, in our culture, where we often deny our sinfulness, we also take pride in being the pure victim. Pure victimhood in our society often seems to convey status and power, and in some sense it does. To be a victim is to have a social voice, to be able to say to your friends or your neighbors or Oprah, "Look how I got screwed." Victims can be just as vicious as sinners, precisely insofar as they hold onto their status as victims. That status is based on past actions, and so, once again, sin wins.

Thus the second step is to offer unconditional forgiveness. The accuser feels pained by the prospect of the first step, the victim feels the pain of the second step. In some sense, these two steps go together, like a dance, in that the accused will feel able to handle the truth insofar as he or she believes that the victim is not out to destroy him or her with it. The difference is, however, that the victim deserves the truth, whereas the accuser does not and cannot deserve forgiveness. Forgiveness has to be purely gratuitous.

Forgiveness may be scandalous to us—first and foremost because it seems to let the sinner off the hook. Think of the adulterer. Your spouse cheats on you, confesses, you tell him or her how this has hurt you and made you feel, and then you offer forgiveness. This is where the "unconditional" part becomes crucial. The victim can make forgiveness into a tricky power move by making it conditional ("Well, I'll forgive so long as you . . ."). The worse the offense, the more power can be packed into the withholding of forgiveness. When past sins are constantly whipped out in the heat of conflict, the effect on relationships is absolutely deadly. That is not forgiveness at all. Real forgiveness is not earned in any way; it is simply given or withheld.

Why in the world would anyone forgive like this? Although there is a lot of psychological truth in the value of "letting go of the past," ultimately this is not a matter of personal happiness but of genuine love of the other—the one who has screwed us. It is the greatest sort of love, because it is a giving of space, a giving of life, in which you say, "I do not have to do away with you in order to survive and prosper." In the adultery example, the victim says, "I do not have to hurt you in order to make up for the ways you've hurt me." This is love. Maybe it is also the great secret of "make-up sex," for that is sex in the light of this kind of love.

There are two things to note, however. First, we go wrong if the forgiveness comes without the first step. If the truth is not told and acknowledged, forgiveness may just be a matter of personal self-destructiveness or even stupidity. Forgiveness without truth is a sure sign that the love present is not mutual. Second, this forgiveness is not a denial of the present broken state. It's not a case of "let's pretend." Nor does it fix things, but things can't get fixed without it.

Fixing—genuine reconciliation—requires a third step involving both parties. Think of this third step in a spatial way. The sinner has done something bad and so has moved away from the victim, has put a separation between them. That separation is still there after the victim tells the truth and offers forgiveness. So the third step has to involve closing the space. The first two steps name the space and defuse its terror, but the space is still there. How is it to be closed?

Remember the point in the famous story of the Prodigal Son where the son is walking toward the father's house and then the father comes dashing out of the house to greet him. Both parties are moving. So, O'Hanlon writes, both parties must do things in the third step. Both of them must close the space.

The accused needs to acknowledge the space and begin to close it by taking steps toward the victim. These are not, we must stress, ways of "making up" for the sin. The adultery cannot be healed by flowers, but only by truth and forgiveness. However, the proper response from the accused, now forgiven, is gratitude. That new love needs to be shown in action, gratuitous action that tells the victim we love him or her, too. If there is no such movement, forgiveness may indeed defuse the conflict, but there will be no reconciliation.

The victim's task is actually living into the forgiveness that has been granted. O'Hanlon describes this as "absorbing the pain," almost like a sponge soaking up the distance between the parties. Even if forgiveness has really happened, it is doubtful that the pain of the separation has been forgotten. This could involve self-deception. The other temptation would be to take part of that pain you still feel and direct it toward the accused. You can say to yourself, "He hurt me so much, I have the right to hurt him a little, to put a little distance between us." No, this is not going to result in reconciliation. Your pain is real, and you can't place it where it belongs (on the one who has caused it), so what do you do? You absorb it.

This may be the most difficult part of the process of reconciliation. If you avoid it, you will bury and refuse to acknowledge pain that is really there. As Rowan Williams describes forgiveness, he rejects the idea of "forgive *and forget*": "We know this is not true: if we have been badly hurt by someone, then whatever happens the scars and memories will still be there, even if we 'forgive' them. And if we have hurt someone, the same is true: we may be 'forgiven,' but we can see the effects of what we have done, perhaps for years after" (*A Ray of Darkness*, 49–50). The hurt is real, so what to do with it? We can perpetuate the cycle of hurt and violence and sin by striking back, or we can absorb it.

Or, more precisely, we can share its absorption with the community and with Christ. Christ's suffering and death, contrary to some recent movies, is not a heroic endurance test that shows up the devil. It is, as theologian Robert Jenson puts it, God really absorbing the sin of world, through suffering it. It is "what it cost the Father to be in fact—and not just in somebody's projected theology or ideology—the loving and merciful Father of the human persons that in fact exist" (*Systematic Theology*, 1:191). This may not be much comfort, since our pain is not magically taken away. But it does mean that, in a certain sense, God shares our pain. And of course, God has given us the Christian community so that we need not bear hurt and pain and suffering alone, but may share its burden with others.

Sex, Confession, and Forgiveness

This discussion may not seem relevant to our sexual sins, whatever they may be. It may sound more pertinent to cases of betrayed friendships or violence or war crimes. In contrast, our sexual sins may seem somewhat comical. Sure, there are really serious sexual sins—rape and adultery spring to mind—but what about our more trivial sexual misdeeds?

Even our more tame sexual sins are still sins. They are still a matter of turning away from the good, from our true purpose. And undoubtedly they still involve pain. The consistent claim that "no one gets hurt" from consensual sexual relationships is simply false—and we all know that. Often enough, the hurts inflicted and suffered in relationships, the sex given or taken for false and destructive reasons, the lies and manipulations given or taken in order to feed our egos or cover over our loneliness, these may be among the deepest hurts we experience. Our unwillingness to acknowledge this publicly and forcefully is the surest sign that sin has won the battle. So many of us must pretend that love is not a battlefield, or that even if it is, we can take it.

What we fear, collectively and individually, is confession. Confession is the tradition's way of dealing with sin and forgiveness, not through fear, but in a context of forgiveness and reconciliation. As Bonhoeffer puts it, "In confession, the breakthrough to community takes place. Sin demands to have a man by himself. The more isolated a person is, the more destructive will be the power of sin over him, and the more deeply he becomes involved in it, the more disastrous is his isolation" (*Life Together*, 112). But the liberation offered by Christ comes precisely in being able to overcome that isolation. "Christ made the Church, and in it our brother, a blessing to us. Now our brother stands in Christ's stead. Before him I no longer need to dissemble.

Before him alone in the whole world I dare to be the sinner that I am; here the truth of Jesus Christ and his mercy rules" (p. 111). This blessing comes from losing the pride that keeps us hidden, that makes us put on righteous disguises before others, and which ultimately leads us to be in competition with one another.

But if you are anything like me, you hate the idea of confessing sin *to someone*. Why not just confess to God? Bonhoeffer notes that, unlike our brother, God is perfect, holy, sinless, whereas our brother "knows from his own experience the dark night of secret sin" (p. 115). If we prefer God, "we must ask ourselves whether we have not often been deceiving ourselves with our confession of sin to God, whether we have not rather been confessing our sins to ourselves and also granting ourselves absolution" (pp. 115–16). The sacrament of confession and reconciliation is not for God, but for us, so that we may actually receive the grace of forgiveness concretely and physically, just as we receive concretely and physically the body and blood in the Eucharist or our spouse's body in marriage.

That is not to say the sacrament always works well. But if we recognize what is going on—that we are receiving forgiveness without paying a cost or without needing to justify ourselves—we can see the amazing grace in it. Rowan Williams describes forgiveness by comparing it to someone saying, "Yes, you have hurt me, but that doesn't mean it's all over. I forgive you. I still love you" (*A Ray of Darkness*, 50). Those are rare words indeed, words of "enormous liberation."

Conclusion

Moral theologians are sinners, too. I have been in need of forgiveness from God and others just as much as anyone else. The accounting done throughout this book could not have been done without the experience of such forgiveness. It is imperfect, painful, and in process, but it is real. And it allows us to consider our actions truly in the light of the gospel, rather than bend the gospel in order to conform it to our actions. This is the ultimate task of Christian ethics, placing our actions within the God-story, the story of a God and a community of sinners where reconciliation can and does take place.

Endnotes Appendix

Chapter 1

The initial descriptions of love are drawn from Plato's *Symposium*, from *The Works of Plato*, ed. Irwin Edman (New York: Modern Library, 1928), pp. 353–358; and Helen A. Regis, "The Madness of Excess: Love Among the Fulbe of North Cameroun," in *Romantic Passion: A Universal Experience?*, ed. William Jankowiak (New York: Columbia University Press, 1995), pp. 141–151. One surefire way to get students thinking about these descriptions is by watching certain movies that offer pictures of romantic love in our culture. Possible recommendations: *Jerry Maguire, Say Anything, Fatal Attraction, American Beauty, Sweet November, Pretty Woman, Little Children*, and *The Bridges of Madison County*.

The various loves are described by C. S. Lewis, *The Four Loves* (New York: Harcourt Brace, 1960). I have repeatedly begun my class with this text, and it always seems to work, not least because it is so well written and students can argue with it. Also mentioned, by the same author, is *The Screwtape Letters* (New York: Macmillan, 1961), especially letter 18, which deals with the temptations of romantic love. Aristotle's descriptions of the types of friendship are found in Book VIII of the *Nicomachean Ethics*; it is another great discussion starter. The comparison of friendship and romantic relationship is a topic of much interest. Amy Laura Hall's *Kierkegaard and the Treachery of Love* (New York: Cambridge, 2002) adds a helpful voice in seeing agape not simply as completing human love, but also *challenging* it.

Most of the "Reason" discussion here is a basic Thomist/Aristotelian account of action, one which is consistent both with the Catholic tradition and with much contemporary moral philosophy. The distinction between purposes and "results" or consequences is particularly crucial from a pedagogical standpoint; Cathleen Kaveny suggests in an article that instrumentalization, not relativism, is the greatest challenge to teaching Catholic students today, and she is right. See "Young Catholics," in *Commonweal* 131, no. 20 (November 19, 2004), pp. 19–20. On human beings as human becomings, see Herbert McCabe, *God Still Matters* (New York: Continuum, 2001). Also see C. S. Lewis, *The Screwtape Letters* (New York: Macmillan, 1961). The very brief treatment of virtue takes some liberty with the term

akrasia by using it as a catchall for the state between virtue and vice, which in fact is quite complex in Aristotle. For a nice description, see Amelie O. Rorty, "Akrasia and Pleasure: Nichomachean Ethics Book 7," in *Essays and Aristotle's Ethics*, ed. Amelie O. Rorty (Berkeley: University of California Press, 1980), pp. 267–284.

Chapter 2

The importance of sexuality as a category can be found in Congregation for the Doctrine of the Faith, *Declaration on Certain Questions Concerning Sexual Ethics (Persona Humana)*, in *Vatican Council II: Volume 2: More Post Conciliar Documents*, new revised ed., ed. Austin Flannery, OP (Northport, NY: Costello Publishing, 1998), pp. 486–499. The chapter introduces a narrative treatment by means of the movie; other movies might also be used, most importantly to help students more concretely grasp the theories presented later. I find Joseph Bristow, *Sexuality* (New York: Routledge, 1997), a reliable and readable resource for contemporary secular constructions of sexuality. On the biological view, see Helen Fisher, *Why We Love: The Nature and Chemistry of Romantic Love* (New York: Henry Holt, 2004). For an overview of this entire discussion, under the heading of "mating intelligence," see Dan Jones, "The Love Delusion," *New Scientist* 193, no. 2597 (March 31, 2007), pp. 14ff, and Lori Gottlieb, "How Do I Love Thee?" *The Atlantic* 297, no. 2 (March 2006), pp. 58–70. Foucault's masterwork is *The History of Sexuality, Volume 1: An Introduction*, trans. Robert Hurley (New York: Random House, 1978). The reference to food in Judaism is from Arthur Hertzberg, *Judaism* (New York: Touchstone/Simon and Schuster, 1991). The closing comment is from Ronald Rolheiser, OMI, *The Holy Longing: The Search for a Christian Spirituality* (New York: Doubleday, 1999).

Chapter 3

This chapter is an attempt to condense an introduction to Christian theology into one chapter—a nearly impossible task that demands certain decisions. The approach to theology as God's story owes debts to the "school" of narrative theology and especially to Hans Urs von Balthasar's *Theo-Drama*, but more importantly it seems the best way for theology to be truly scriptural. Here I do not distill abstract "concepts" out of the biblical story, but instead present "plotlines" that help students understand "what God is doing." The idea that Scripture constitutes a coherent overall narrative is, of course, highly contested and is a theological claim, not a historical or literary one.

The first plotline on idolatry draws heavily on the work of Herbert McCabe (already cited) and on Robert Barron, *The Priority of Christ: Toward a Postliberal Catholicism* (Grand Rapids, MI: Brazos Press, 2007). All "god-talk" will tend toward the irrelevant unless the fundamental categories of "true" and "false" gods come out on the table. The second plotline is presented most briefly here, a recognition that ultimately Jesus' story is a story about the union of human and divine, but one not abstractable from the person of Jesus as presented in the Scriptures. The third plotline is certainly the most challenging, as it involves the scandal of the cross, and the material on the false self and fear is drawn from Henri Nouwen's *Lifesigns* (New York: Doubleday, 1986). The fourth plotline gives full integrity to the "horizontal story" of Scripture and is deeply indebted to many works by N. T. Wright, whose thoroughly Jewish Jesus appears to make the most theological sense of any of the available pictures of "the historical Jesus" today. In particular, this aspect of the story counters the "anti-purity-law" Jesus that influences much Protestant scholarship about sex in the Bible.

Benedict XVI's encyclical *Deus Caritas Est* is available online at http://www.vatican.va/holy_father/benedict_xvi/encyclicals/documents/hf_ben-xvi_enc_20051225_deus-caritas-est_en.html (accessed December 12, 2007). Particularly its first part is worthwhile student reading. Hans Urs von Balthasar's conception of love is detailed in one of his most accessible short works, *Love Alone Is Credible*, trans. Edward T. Oakes (San Francisco: Ignatius Press, 2004; orig. 1963). Balthasar's corpus also contains fine expositions of love in *The Christian State of Life* and the short section on the experience of mother-child love (also worthwhile for class discussion) in *The Glory of the Lord: A Theological Aesthetics, Volume V: The Realm of Metaphysics in the Modern Age*, trans. Oliver Davies, et al. (San Francisco: Ignatius Press, 1991), pp. 615–618.

Chapter 4

The gender stereotype lists are much more fun to generate from students themselves, but popular literature has no shortage of such generalizations, notably John Gray, *Mars and Venus on a Date* (New York: Harper Paperbacks, 1999). Augustine's reflections are from his *Literal Commentary on Genesis*, as quoted in *Women in the Early Church*, ed. Elizabeth A. Clark (Wilmington, DE: Michael Glazier, 1983), pp. 28–29. Plato's articulation of the potential equality of the sexes is in *The Republic*, Book V. Lisa Sowle Cahill's comment is from her *Sex and Gender and Christian Ethics* (Cambridge, MA: Cambridge University Press, 1996), pp. 1–2. This book is something of a minor classic in its comprehensive scope, and my debt to it should be obvious. The story about gender and dorm rooms is Terry Collins' "Macalester may let men, women share dorm rooms," *Minneapolis Star Tribune*, November 20, 2003, 1B. Gender complementarity is seen compactly in Pope John Paul II's *The Role of the Christian Family in the Modern World (Familiaris Consortio)* (Boston: Pauline Books and Media, 1981), nos. 22–25. I use this text as the most definitive statement of the pope's vision of marriage and family. Joseph Ratzinger's comment on nature and gender is made in *Salt of the Earth: The Church at the End of the Millennium* (San Francisco: Ignatius Press, 1997). Wendell Berry's classic essay is found in *Sex, Economy, Freedom, and Community* (New York: Pantheon, 1993), pp. 117–173. Berry's essay could be worth several days of study by itself. Its attention to social issues marks it off from Freud/Foucault AND the Catholic tradition. I have tried to capture some of its spirit in the later chapter on marriage as a vocation.

The treatment of homosexuality and homosexual acts here, rather than in later chapters, arises from a recognition that the question is much more closely tied to the question of gender than to questions about procreation or extra-marital sex. The analysis of homosexuality here draws primarily on two works, neither Christian and both pro-homosexual: David F. Greenberg, *The Construction of Homosexuality* (Chicago: University of Chicago Press, 1988), and Edward Stein, *The Mismeasure of Desire* (New York: Oxford University Press, 1999). The issue requires careful detail due to the many popular misconceptions now afoot, whether pro or anti. Examples of language-bending abound in *The Lesbian and Gay Studies Reader*, eds. Henry Abelove, Michele Aina Barale, and David M. Halperin (New York: Routledge, 1993). The citation on lesbian desire is from Elizabeth Grosz, "Refiguring Lesbian Desire," in *Race, Class, Gender, Sexuality: The Big Questions*, eds. Naomi Zack, Laurie Shrage, and Crispin Sartwell (Malden, MA: Blackwell, 1998), pp. 268–281, here 278.

The literature on Christians and homosexuality continues to proliferate, although the basic issues are relatively simple. John McNeill's *The Church and the Homosexual* (Boston: Beacon Press, 3rd ed., 1988) remains accessible and easy for students to understand. More complex works are represented here by Elizabeth Stuart, "Authority, Sexuality, and Friendship," in *Embracing Sexuality: Authority and Experience in the Catholic Church*, ed. Joseph A. Selling (Aldershot, UK: Ashgate, 2001), pp. 89–100, here 93–96. The standard work in this vein has become Eugene Rogers' *Sexuality and the Christian Body* (Malden, MA: Blackwell, 1999). Such work, while conceptually interesting, seems not to have had a great deal of pastoral impact (yet?), partly because of its reliance on sophisticated theological arguments that are not widely accessible. Nevertheless, it is far more careful than more popular defenses of homosexual relationships based on "freedom to love." The magisterial arguments are found in *Persona Humana* (1975) and Congregation for the Doctrine of the Faith, *Letter to the Bishops of the Catholic Church on the Pastoral Care of Homosexual Persons (Homosexualitatis problema)* in 1986. The more recent documents (2003 and 2005) are not treated here in detail, because none of the basic arguments from the earlier documents are changed; however, the increasingly strident resistance to the increasing social acceptance of homosexual relationships has undoubtedly raised some questions about the overall conceptual argument of the magisterium on orientation and acts. The earlier 1975 document has no difficulty calling homosexuality a "deformity"; this is probably an accurate indication of the magisterial position all along, although it is understandable why Catholics might want to soft-pedal it. The social trend toward understanding homosexual orientation as inborn is reported in George Gallup Jr., *The Gallup Poll 2003* (Lanham, MD: SR Books),

p. 161. The argument for considering committed homosexual couples as anomalies to be included in the understanding of marriage is from David McCarthy Matzko, "Homosexuality and the Practices of Marriage," *Modern Theology* 13 (1997), pp. 371–397. An illuminating piece on homosexual parenting is an interview with Gregory Maguire by Daria Donnelly, "A Gay Parent Looks at His Church," *Commonweal* 130, no. 18 (Oct 24, 2003), pp. 20–22, here 21.

The definition of a *practice* is drawn from Alasdair MacIntyre's *After Virtue*, 2nd ed. (Notre Dame: University of Notre Dame Press, 1984), p. 187. One potential orientation of this entire text was around this central notion of practices; instead, the final half of the book is essentially a consideration of practices. Analyzing sexual relationships in our society as "practices" is particularly tricky because, while evidently fitting the definition, they are also considered "private" in terms of the modern public/private distinction. Consequently, while we all recognize relationships as a central social preoccupation, we are increasingly unable to subject them to any forms of social regulation, whether legal or customary. This is a conceptual problem that runs deeply in students, and probably in all of us, and directly unearthing it (in my judgment) isn't terribly productive. However, attending to the confusions it creates and attempting to redirect questions and debates in more "social" directions is productive, and that is what I have done throughout the rest of the text.

Chapter 5

The historical portraits of the evolution of dating draw on the following sources: John D'Emilio and Estelle Freedman, *Intimate Matters* (New York: Harper and Row, 1988), and Beth Bailey, "From Front Porch to Back Seat," in *Wing to Wing, Oar to Oar*, eds. Amy and Leon Kass (Notre Dame: University of Notre Dame Press, 2000), pp. 27–37. I should note here that the *Wing to Wing* reader is one I have used in classes in the past and is probably the broadest anthology out there of source material. In telling a coherent story, the issue of class differences is elided, but it may be important to raise it with a more sophisticated class. The study of the 1950s town is from Robert J. Havignurst, et al., *Growing Up in River City* (New York: Wiley and Sons, 1962). The volume interestingly says almost nothing about dating, focusing instead on the rise in "delinquency," which is much lamented in the 1950s. Roughly 30% of both boys and girls from the River City cohort go on to college or some other post-secondary education.

The treatment of the contemporary scene summarizes data from the following sources: *The Blackwell Handbook of Adolescence*, eds. Gerald R. Adams and Michael D. Berzonsky (Malden, MA: Blackwell, 2003), especially articles by Heather A. Bouchey and Wyndol Furman, "Dating and Romantic Experiences in Adolescence," pp. 313–329, and Lisa J. Crockett, Marcela Raffaelli, and Kristin L. Moilanen, "Adolescent Sexuality: Behavior and Meaning," pp. 371–392. Also see National Survey of Family Growth (NSFG) 2002, conducted by the National Center for Health Statistics (NCHS), at http://www.cdc.gov/nchs/about/major/nsfg/nsfgback.htm (accessed December 19, 2006); Michael J. Hunt, *College Catholics* (Mahwah, NJ: Paulist Press, 1993), pp. 53–55; George Gallup Jr., *The Gallup Poll 2003*; "The New Virginity," *Newsweek*, December 9, 2002; Davis and Smith, 1994, cited in Linda Rouse, *Marital and Sexual Lifestyles in the United States* (New York: Haworth Press, 2002); Jeffrey J. Arnett, *Emerging Adulthood* (New York: Oxford, 2004); and Norval Glenn and Elizabeth Marquardt, *Hooking Up, Hanging Out, and Looking for Mr. Right: College Women on Dating and Mating Today* (New York: Institute for American Values, 2001). More anecdotal analysis is provided by Allan Bloom, *The Closing of the American Mind* (New York: Simon and Schuster, 1987); Ellen Fein and Sherrie Schneider, *The Rules: Time-Tested Secrets for Capturing the Heart of Mr. Right* (New York: Warner Books, 1995); and the incomparable Tony Clink, *The Layguide: How to Seduce Women More Beautiful Than You Ever Dreamed Possible No Matter What You Look Like or How Much You Make* (Camp Sherman, OR: Citadel Books, 2004). In addition, although not cited, the ambiguity of our culture is interestingly displayed in the book-length reflection/rant by Katie Roiphe, *Last Night in Paradise: Sex and Morals at Century's End* (Boston: Little, Brown, 1997). Particularly useful may be Roiphe's interview with a pro-virginity young adult (which Roiphe definitely is not).

Books on the Christian dating debate are Joshua Harris, *I Kissed Dating Goodbye* (Sisters, OR: Multnomah, 1997) and *Boy Meets Girl: Say Hello to Courtship* (Sisters, OR: Multnomah, 2000); Jeramy and Jerusha Clark, *Define the Relationship: A Candid Look at Breaking Up, Making Up, and Dating Well* (Colorado Springs: WaterBrook Press, 2004); Eric and Leslie Ludy, *When God Writes Your Love Story: The Ultimate Approach to Guy/Girl Relationships* (Sisters, OR: Multnomah, 2004). While less systematic, Jason Evert's *If You Really Loved Me: 100 Questions on Dating, Relationships, and Sexual Purity* (Cincinnati: Servant Books, 2003) reflects some of this influence coming into Catholic circles. A fine (though somewhat overedited) survey of different "positions" in this debate is found in *5 Ways to the Love of Your Life*, ed. Alex Chediak (Colorado Springs: THINK, 2005), where a number of authors here mentioned are represented, including Lauren Winner ("The Countercultural Path") and Jerusha and Jeramy Clark ("The Purposeful Path"). Hayley DiMarco's high-school version of Christian dating is found in *The Dirt on Dating* (Grand Rapids, MI: Hungry Mind/Revell, 2005). The above books, while surely making theological arguments, are definitely aimed at popular audiences. Two others—Donna Freitas and Jason King's *Save the Date: A Spirituality of Dating, Love, Dinner, and the Divine* (New York: Crossroad, 2003) and Lauren F. Winner's *Real Sex: The Naked Truth About Chastity* (Grand Rapids, MI: Brazos Press, 2005)—are also somewhat popular, but edge toward scholarly. Each book has much to recommend it; I find *Save the Date* a particularly useful class text because students are prone to disagree and argue with it, partly because it is so obvious that the two authors do not agree. For my money, Winner has mapped out the most fruitful territory for future theological reflection—this chapter itself is an attempt to manage this conceptual debate a bit more academically, but we all are waiting for a more robust theological treatment of "dating relationships." Or are we?

Karen Lebacqz's readable article is "Appropriate Vulnerability," in *Sexuality and the Sacred: Sources for Theological Reflection* (Louisville: Westminster/John Knox Press, 1994), pp. 256–261. Furlong's comment is from Monica Furlong, "Sex Before Marriage," in *Sexuality and the Sacred*, p. 262. Ronald Rolheiser treats sexuality in *The Holy Longing: The Search for a Christian Spirituality* (New York: Doubleday,

1999). Rolheiser's chapter is a wonderful piece, perhaps as a class-closing summary.

Chapter 6

The treatment of specific sexual acts is prefaced by a section on moral absolutes. My analysis is consistent with defenders of moral absolutes, while leaving open the question of whether this or that action falls under an absolute, because, as shown best by Charles Pinches, *Theology and Action: After Theory in Christian Ethics* (Grand Rapids, MI: Eerdmans, 2002), the whole question ultimately hangs on description. The best treatments of the need for moral absolutes are John Finnis' *Moral Absolutes: Tradition, Revision, and Truth* (Washington, DC: Catholic University of America Press, 1991) and Alasdair MacIntyre's extraordinary "How Can We Learn What *Veritatis Splendor* Has to Teach?" in *The Thomist* 58 (1994), pp. 171–195. The Vatican document quoted is *Persona Humana*, in Flannery, *op. cit.*, no. 3. I refrain from defending a specific theory here, though Grisez/Finnis is useful for sharpening the moral reasoning of students. The key learning goal here, though, is to get students to stop thinking in terms of rule-and-exception, and instead recognize that "exceptions" are really a matter of saying that the rule does not apply to a particular case. With more advanced classes, it is advisable to spend some time on (a) the importance of purpose or intention in evaluating actions and (b) the inadequacy of an approach that prioritizes consequences (the approach that comes most naturally to students).

Lurking in the background of the direct discussion of premarital sex is Herbert Chilstrom and Lowell Erdahl, *Sexual Fulfillment: For Single and Married, Gay and Straight, Young and Old* (Minneapolis: Augsburg Fortress, 2001), a humorous but frank text by two retired Lutheran bishops that, for all its argumentative flaws, articulates common attitudes that are at work in students' everyday conceptual reasoning about their sexual lives. As a teaching exercise, I have also found that dividing the class up into three "camps": consent-only, committed-relationship sex, and nothing-until-marriage, is extremely useful. If the teacher helps the (usually smaller number of) defenders of consent-only, you can easily provoke the "middle group" into defending relationship sex on the grounds of commitment and the possibility of pregnancy. Almost like magic, the classic goods of marital sex are introduced as the key consideration, often to the delight of the minority on the no-premarital-sex side. References for the scholarly debate are: from the pro-premarital sex side, Philip S. Keane, SS, *Sexual Morality: A Catholic Perspective* (New York: Paulist Press, 1977), Richard McCormick, SJ, *Notes on Moral Theology 1965–1980* (Lanham, MD: University Press of America, 1981), pp. 447–462, Anthony Kosnik et al., *Human Sexuality: New Directions in American Catholic Thought* (New York: Paulist Press, 1977), and Gareth Moore, OP, *The Body in Context: Sex and Catholicism* (New York: Continuum, 2001); from the anti-premarital sex side, see Ronald Lawler, Joseph Boyle, and William E. May, *Catholic Sexual Ethics: A Summary, Explanation, and Defense* (Huntington, IN: Our Sunday Visitor Books, 1998), Lauren F. Winner, *Real Sex: The Naked Truth About Chastity* (Grand Rapids, MI: Brazos Books, 2005), and David McCarthy, *Sex and Love in the Home: A Theology of the Household* (London: SCM Press, 2001). Lawler/Boyle/May offers a comprehensive treatment of the magisterial position, not only on this question, but on all the normative questions dealt with later in the text. It is recommended as an accessible substitute to magisterial documents, though its complete reliance on Grisez/Finnis begs a question some teachers may wish to leave open. The survey numbers are from the National Marriage Project 2001 report (full citation in next chapter). In one sense, placing this argument before the argument on contraception is awkward, especially when attending to the classic argument against premarital sex. Helping students recognize the connection among all these debated questions is important.

On other sexual actions, the literature is sadly scant. A wonderful paper was presented at the Saint Louis University undergraduate theology conference in October 2005 by Christina Gebel, a Saint Louis University undergraduate, entitled "Is Oral Moral?" Gebel's work, like Winner's, indicates an important direction for moral theologians to take. Also cited here is Jason Evert, *If You Really Loved Me: 100 Questions on Dating, Relationships, and Sexual Purity* (Cincinnati: Servant Books, 2003). On masturbation, see the articles collected in *Readings in Moral Theology, no. 8: Dialogue about Catholic Sexual Teaching*, eds. Charles Curran and Richard McCormick (New York: Paulist Press, 1993), as well as Kosnik et al. and Lawler/Boyle/May. The data is taken from the chapter on masturbation in Robert T. Michael et al., *Sex in America: A Definitive Survey* (Boston: Little, Brown, 1994).

Chapter 7

Some readers will find my organizational decision here to distinguish strongly between natural marriage and sacramental marriage the most controversial editorial decision of the entire textbook. A good part of the impetus for this division is pedagogical. The tradition is evidently messier than this, but the distinction is present throughout, and students are apt to become confused on many questions if this distinction is not kept in mind. For example, the whole social debate over gay marriage is often couched in whether "religion" should be written into law; the problem here obviously is an inability to recognize that much of what Catholicism claims about religion is claimed on natural law grounds and is susceptible to support from non-Christian sources. But the division is also designed to highlight the emerging conception of marriage as a full-blown Christian vocation, central to the concerns about holiness and discipleship in the New Testament. The two-level ethic, as both Vatican II and Pope John Paul II (in *Veritatis Splendor*) demonstrate, is over. Hence, the sacramental character of Catholic marriage must be given real and sustained attention.

Because this decision is organizationally highlighted, certain decisions about where to place topics will raise eyebrows. Specifically, the inclusion of the contraception debate in natural marriage, while technically correct, is likely to strike some as deeply implausible. On the other hand, the inclusion of divorce and indissolubility in the subsequent chapter on marriage as a sacrament is technically incorrect, because the tradition has asserted that natural marriages are also indissoluble. However, the importance of considering the New Testament witness on divorce, and especially how it is related to Old Testament law and practice, needs to override the technicalities of indissolubility that crept into the tradition when the Church assumed more responsibility for civil marriage in the Middle Ages. In point of fact, natural marriages are dissoluble under the practice of the Petrine Privilege, whose logic seems to fit

more naturally with the New Testament witness and the richness of the sacramental theology of marriage than does the more barren assertion that natural marriage is indissoluble.

The sacramental theology introduced and assumed here (though expanded at some length later) is rooted in *Lumen Gentium (Dogmatic Constitution on the Church)*. Expanded treatments of it are found in Herbert McCabe, OP, *The People of God: The Fullness of Life in the Church* (New York: Sheed and Ward, 1964) and Alexander Schmemann, *For the Life of the World: Sacraments and Orthodoxy* (Crestwood, NY: St. Vladimir's Seminary Press, 1973). This sort of "time-based," present/future sacramental theology seems to me to fit best with the New Testament eschatological conception of the Kingdom, certainly better than more "timeless" or vertical accounts of sacramental grace found in much sacramental theology.

Contemporary sources on marriage in our society are Jeffrey Arnett, *Emerging Adulthood* (New York: Oxford, 2004); Alan Wolfe, *Moral Freedom: The Impossible Idea that Defines the Way We Live Now* (New York: W. W. Norton, 2001); Census Bureau Current Population Survey 2003; "Not married yet? You're not alone," *St. Cloud Times*, December 2, 2004, 3A; and David Popenoe and Barbara Dafoe Whitehead, "The State of Our Unions: The Social Health of Marriage in America 2001: Who Wants to Marry a Soul Mate?" (Rutgers, NJ: National Marriage Project, 2001). The polarized state of the situation could probably be seen theologically by comparing the volume *Sexuality and the Sacred* (Louisville: Westminster/John Knox Press, 1994), and many of its essays, with David Gushee's recent book, *Getting Marriage Right: Realistic Counsel for Saving and Strengthening Relationships* (Grand Rapids, MI: Baker Books, 2004), which is in full-blown crisis mode. I was surprised initially to find Stephanie Coontz, *The Way We Never Were: American Families and the Nostalgia Trap* (New York: Basic Books, 2002), to be an intriguing and balanced commentary that particularly directs us to the socioeconomic conditions of forms of marriage and family. All her conclusions may not be what a Catholic would want, but she does alert us to the problem of trying to fit a square peg into a round hole—if we are unwilling to question certain social changes, it is just an exercise in frustration to wish for a particular family form to reappear by sheer willpower.

The extensive use of Old Testament Scripture here, in a chapter on natural marriage, proceeds from the assumption that both Greek and Jewish sources depict something about creation. Though the stories of Israel *also* point forward to sacramentality and vocation, they are used here as narrative examples of the standard two purposes of marriage. Historical sources, in addition to Scripture, are Augustine, *Of the Good of Marriage*; John Chrysostom, "Homily 20 on Ephesians"; Thomas Aquinas, *On Evil*, trans. Richard Regan (New York: Oxford, 2003); and the articles collected in *Marriage and Family in the Biblical World*, ed. Ken M. Campbell (Downers Grove, IL: InterVarsity Press, 2003). This last collection is a useful summary, except for its highly biased and ahistorical treatment of Scripture. John J. Collins comments on Tobit in his article "Marriage in the Old Testament," in *Marriage in the Catholic Tradition: Scripture, Tradition, and Experience*, eds. Todd A. Salzman, Thomas M. Kelly, and John J. O'Keefe (New York: Crossroad, 2004). The separation of sexual passion and marriage into different relationships in the Roman world is explored in Glenn W. Olsen, "Progeny, Faithfulness, Sacred Bond: Marriage in the Age of Augustine," in *Christian Marriage*, ed. Glenn W. Olsen (New York: Crossroad, 2001), p. 109. Tertullian and Chrysostom, as well as other ancient readings, are collected well by David Hunter, *Marriage in the Early Church* (Eugene, OR: Wipf and Stock, 2001). The twentieth-century Catholic developments draw on John Gallagher, "Magisterial Teaching from 1918 to the Present," in *Human Sexuality and Personhood* (St. Louis: Pope John Center, 1981), pp. 191–210, and the still-very-useful John C. Ford, SJ, and Gerald Kelly, SJ, *Contemporary Moral Theology, vol. 2: Marriage Questions* (Westminster, MD: Newman Press, 1964). Debates over "Schema XIII" at Vatican II are exhaustively surveyed in *History of Vatican II, vol. 4*, eds. Giuseppe Alberigio and Joseph Komonchak (Maryknoll, NY: Orbis/Peeters, 1995), pp. 269–331. Some Council Fathers objected to the absence of primary/secondary language, as well as the absence of praise for large families and the assignment of responsibility for deciding how many children to have to the couple themselves. Others suggested that the Council did not go far enough in integrating modern psychological perspectives on human sexuality and human love, and therefore remained too tied to the biological and to the past. For representative comments, see the speeches collected in *Third Session Council Speeches of Vatican II*, eds. William K. Leahy and Anthony T. Massimini (Glen Rock, NJ: Paulist Press, 1966), pp. 214–233. Studying a bit about this debate might help students understand not only something about Vatican II, but also something about how the Church works. The theology of the body is found in John Paul II, *The Theology of the Body: Human Love in the Divine Plan* (Boston: Pauline Books and Media, 1997). An accessible summary is given by Christopher West, *Theology of the Body for Beginners: A Basic Introduction to Pope John Paul II's Sexual Revolution* (West Chester, PA: Ascension Press, 2004). My comments here are based on an as-yet-unpublished article by myself and William Mattison III on the pope's theology. The absence of an extended treatment of TOB may concern some, but in this textbook I have refrained from taking any particular theological exposition of sexuality as THE dominant picture. This is not to be taken as a criticism of TOB.

Students ought to look at the wedding vows themselves when studying marriage. A wonderful commentary on the vows is Julie Hanlon Rubio's chapter on the wedding ceremony in her *A Christian Theology of Marriage and Family* (New York: Paulist Press, 2003). My debt to Rubio in the following chapters may only be exceeded by my debt to the works of David McCarthy. The quote from Jules Toner is found in *The Experience of Love* (Washington: Corpus Books, 1968). Judith S. Wallerstein and Sandra Blakeslee offer extended and helpful descriptions and categorizations of good marriages in *The Good Marriage: How and Why Love Lasts* (Boston: Houghton Mifflin, 1995). The central portion of the treatment of marital love is drawn from Richard Gaillardetz's excellent *A Daring Promise: A Spirituality of Christian Marriage* (New York: Crossroad, 2002). I have used this text in courses, with good effect. Its theological connections are excellent, and his treatment of the paschal character of marriage is crucial (and obviously connected to the discussion of the false self in the initial chapter on love). I doubt Gaillardetz would disagree with the fact that I have included his comments in the chapter on "natural marriage"; it seems that his treatment is meant to be universally applicable, regardless of the theological language. Supplementing Gaillardetz are Evelyn and James Whitehead, *Marrying Well: Possibilities in Christian Marriage Today* (Garden City, NY: Doubleday, 1981); Robert Farrar Capon, *Bed and Board: Plain Talk about Marriage* (New York: Simon and Schuster, 1965); Jean Vanier, *Community and Growth* (New York: Paulist Press, 1979); and Ronald Rolheiser, *The Holy Longing* (cited earlier).

On parenting, see Helen Stanton, "Obligation or Option? Marriage, Voluntary Childlessness, and the Church," in *Celebrating Christian Marriage*, ed. Adrian Thatcher (New York: T&T Clark, 2001), pp. 223–239, and Rubio. Christopher Ruddy's essay "The Sacred Heart of Jesus" is found in *Awake, My Soul: Contemporary Catholics on Traditional Devotions*, ed. James Martin, SJ (Chicago: Loyola Press, 2004), pp. 1–7. Statistics on out-of-wedlock births are from the National Marriage Project 2001. For comments on the socioeconomic sources of family instability in inner cities, see William Julius Wilson, *When Work Disappears: The World of the New Urban Poor* (New York: Vintage Books, 1997). The examples cited here are all too brief, and a further introduction to the sociological question of parenting and society is highly recommended.

Chapter 8

On cohabitation, statistics and stories are available at Sharon Jayson, "Cohabitation Is Replacing Dating," *USA Today*, July 18, 2005, 6D, and United States Conference of Catholic Bishops, *Marriage Preparation and Cohabiting Couples* (1999), found online at http://www.usccb.org/laity/marriage/cohabiting.shtml (accessed December 11, 2007). The arguments for reviving a form of betrothal are offered by Adrian Thatcher, *Living Together and Christian Ethics* (New York: Cambridge University Press, 2002), and (in compact and accessible form) by Michael Lawler, "Cohabitation and Marriage in the Catholic Church: A Proposal," in his *Marriage and the Catholic Tradition: Disputed Questions* (Collegeville, MN: Liturgical Press, 2002), pp. 162–192. Criticism is made by Lisa Sowle Cahill, "Notes on Moral Theology. Marriage: Developments in Catholic Theology and Ethics," *Theological Studies* 64 (2003), pp. 78–105, and a response is given by Lawler, "QUAESTIO DISPUTATA," *Theological Studies* 65 (2004), pp. 623–629.

Adultery is treated briefly here, since there is little argument in the tradition, but it is worth pushing students on the question of *why* they are so strongly against it, since it helps expose the foundations of their moral judgments. The discussion of contraception is so sprawling and omnipresent, it is hard to know where to begin citation. The basic argument is accessibly presented by Lawler/Boyle/May. An excellent and comprehensive defense available on the Web is given by Janet E. Smith, "Contraception: Why Not?" at http://www.catholiceducation.org/articles/sexuality/se0002.html (accessed December 22, 2006). Also on the Web is Smith's "Premarital Sex," at http://www.archdioceseofdetroit.org/aodonline-sqlimages/shms/faculty/SmithJanet/Publications/HumanaeVitae/Premarital-Sex.pdf (accessed December 22, 2006). Objections are drawn from the various classic articles collected in *Readings in Moral Theology No. 8: Dialogue About Catholic Sexual Teaching*, eds. Charles Curran and Richard McCormick, SJ (New York: Paulist Press, 1993), pp. 57–167. Rosemary Radford Ruether's "Birth Control and the Ideals of Marital Sexuality," included in the collection, is originally found in *Contraception and Holiness: The Catholic Predicament*, ed. Thomas D. Roberts, SJ (New York: Herder and Herder, 1964).

Chapter 9

These two chapters, on marriage as a Christian vocation, will push both students and professors onto the least familiar territory of the book, but I would argue it is the most important, especially in a post-Christendom context. Reading New Testament texts on marriage (and celibacy) seems to require the context outlined here. The discussion of doing God's will in early Christian morality is found in Wayne Meeks, *The Origins of Christian Morality: The First Two Centuries* (New Haven, CT: Yale University Press, 1993). The importance of the social location of love, as well as numerous other points in this chapter, is drawn from David Matzko McCarthy's *Sex and Love in the Home: A Theology of the Household* (London: SPCK, 2001). Herbert McCabe's discussion is found in *The People of God: The Fullness of Life in the Church* (New York: Sheed and Ward, 1964).

The discussion of the importance of the Kingdom of God in understanding Jesus' ministry runs throughout biblical scholarship, but see especially Gerhard Lohfink, *Jesus and Community: The Social Dimension of Christian Faith*, trans. John P. Galvin (Philadelphia: Fortress Press, 1984); N.T. Wright, *Jesus and the Victory of God* (Minneapolis: Fortress Press, 1996); and John P. Meier, *A Marginal Jew* (New Haven, CT: Yale University Press, 1994). Obviously I am aware of the large-scale debates about this language and message in New Testament scholarship, and unapologetically side decisively with those who read Jesus as a Jewish messiah, or at the very least an apocalyptic prophet. In either case, the eschatology assumed leans strongly in the "realized" direction (without thereby annulling the vertical and future dimension). I cite here W. D. Davies, *Invitation to the New Testament* (Garden City, NY: Doubleday, 1966), and Raymond E. Brown, SS, *Introduction to the New Testament* (New York: Doubleday, 1997). Is this position consistent with subsequent Catholic theology? Obviously a *fully* realized eschatology, or one that expected such a full realization through human activity, would end up turning the Gospel into a purely earthly social program (which is the magisterial complaint with liberation theology), and such a view would be inconsistent with Catholic theology. However, the views of the above authors make much more nuanced claims, and I follow them in my exposition of the Kingdom as inaugurating (if not yet completing) a transformation of earthly relationships and our relationship to God. The later connection to sacraments should reassure those worried about immanentism. Lisa Sowle Cahill's work has also drawn on this notion of the Kingdom, here citing her text *Family: A Christian Social Perspective* (Minneapolis: Fortress Press, 2000). Also cited here is Glenn W. Olsen, "Progeny, Faithfulness, Sacred Bond: Marriage in the Age of Augustine," in *Christian Marriage: A Historical Study*, ed. Glenn W. Olsen (New York: Crossroad, 2001), pp. 101–145.

On this treatment of celibacy, see Peter Brown, "The Notion of Virginity in the Early Church," in *Christian Spirituality I*, eds. Bernard McGinn and John Meyerdorff (New York: Crossroad, 1985), pp. 427–443, as well as his more comprehensive argument along these lines in *The Body and Society: Men, Women, and Sexual Renunciation in Early Christianity* (New York: Columbia University Press, 1988).

Commenting helpfully on singleness in Christian churches is Laura A. Smit's charming (and readable) *Loves Me, Loves Me Not: The Ethics of Unrequited Love* (Grand Rapids, MI: Baker, 2005). Also cited here are Marie Theresa Coombs and Francis Kelly Nemeck, *Discerning Vocations to Marriage, Celibacy, and Singlehood* (Collegeville, MN: Liturgical Press, 1994), p. 120.

The treatment of the context for the divorce saying is found in a number of sources, but see especially Richard B. Hays' chapter on divorce in *The Moral Vision of the New Testament: Community, Cross, New Creation* (San Francisco: HarperCollins, 1996). The reading of the household codes as involving "mutual revolutionary subordination" comes from John Howard Yoder's *The Politics of Jesus* (Grand Rapids, MI: Eerdmans, 1994), pp. 162–192. I often have students read a version of this argument and compare it to Elizabeth Schussler-Fiorenza's treatment of these texts in *In Memory of Her: A Feminist Theological Reconstruction of Christian Origins* (New York: Crossroad, 1983), pp. 251–284.

The sources for the connection of Kingdom language and sacramental language are mentioned at the beginning of the bibliographic note of the prior chapter. The history of marriage becoming sacramental is nicely set out in Joseph Martos' *Doors to the Sacred* (New York: Triumph Books, 1991). A helpful detailing of the conciliar history is given in Joseph Pohle and Arthur Preuss, *The Sacraments IV*, 5th ed. (St. Louis: B. Herder Book Co., 1929). Post-Vatican II sources for the sacramentality of marriage are David M. Thomas, *Christian Marriage: A Journey Together* (Wilmington, DE: Michael Glazier, 1983); Michael G. Lawler, *Marriage and Sacrament: A Theology of Marriage* (Collegeville, MN: Liturgical Press, 1993); and Theodore Mackin, SJ, *The Marital Sacrament* (New York: Paulist Press, 1989). (The Mackin volume also provides documentation for the obligatory character of marriage among Jews of Jesus' era.) Lawler's definition is almost note-for-note from Cardinal James Stafford's explanation of the sacramentality of marriage; see Mackin, p. 557. Karl Barth's treatment of the vocation of the Christian life and the liberation of the individual Christian in the name of witness is found in *Church Dogmatics IV*, 3/2 (Edinburgh: T&T Clark, 1962), pp. 647–680.

The rehabilitation of John Chrysostom on marriage is found in both Cahill's and McCarthy's texts, as well as the anthology *Theology and Sexuality: Classic and Contemporary Readings*, ed. Eugene F. Rogers Jr. (Malden, MA: Blackwell, 2002). The citations here are from "Homily 1 on Ephesians," found in Rogers, pp. 87–92, and "Homily 20 on Ephesians," found in David Hunter, *Marriage in the Early Church*. See also Lisa Sowle Cahill, *Sex, Gender, and Christian Ethics* (New York: Cambridge University Press, 1996).

Chapter 10

The practice of Christian marriage as a sacramental and countercultural witness is the fundamental point of all examples in this chapter, and the explicit practices cited are not necessarily definitive, but rather suggestive. The objection to the anti-family sayings' relevance for today is given by Bruce J. Malina, "'Let Him Deny Himself' (Mark 8:34 and par.): A Social Psychological Model of Self-Denial," in *Biblical Theology Bulletin* 24 (1994), pp. 106–119. The constructive alternative is once again drawn from McCarthy, *Sex and Love in the Home*. The statistics on home size are drawn from *The Carleton Voice* (Winter 2006). On the relative lack of danger of strangers, and further overestimations of threats to children, see Gail Rosenblum, "Worried All the Time," *Minneapolis Star Tribune*, Saturday, January 14, 2006, 1E.

The transformation of the natural ends start off drawing on Judith Wallerstein's *The Good Marriage*. Catholic texts that highlight the conception of marriage as friendship include Michael Lawler, "Friendship and Marriage," in *Marriage and the Catholic Church: Disputed Questions* (Collegeville, MN: Liturgical Press, 2002), pp. 140–161; Bernard Cooke, *Sacraments and Sacramentality* (Mystic, CT: Twenty-Third Publications, 1983); and Enda McDonagh, *Doing the Truth: The Quest for Moral Theology* (Notre Dame: University of Notre Dame Press, 1979), p. 173. The Tertullian quote is from Hunter's collection, as are the later observations from Augustine. The importance of sanctification in marriage is treated at some length and defended in a surprising source: John C. Ford, SJ, and Gerald Kelly, SJ, *Contemporary Moral Theology, vol. 2: Marriage Questions* (Westminster, MD: Newman Press, 1964), especially pp. 138–142. Gaillardetz's observation is from *A*

Daring Promise: A Spirituality of Christian Marriage (New York: Crossroad, 2002).

The rejection of divorce is certainly the most fundamental way in which Christian marriage can witness to something beyond itself. The treatment of current divorce draws on statistics from the following sources: David Popenoe and Barbara Dafoe Whitehead, "The State of Our Unions: The Social Health of Marriage in America 2001: Who Wants to Marry a Soul Mate?" (Rutgers, NJ: National Marriage Project, 2001); www.omsoul.com (accessed December 11, 2007); Paul R. Amato and Alan Booth, *A Generation at Risk: Growing Up in an Era of Family Upheaval* (Cambridge, MA: Harvard University Press, 1997); and *Statistical Handbook on the American Family*, 2nd ed., eds. Bruce A. Chadwick and Tim B. Heaton (Phoenix: Onyx Press, 1999). The data by state and by other categories is available online at www.divorcereform.org/rates.html (accessed December 11, 2007). I follow Barbara Dafoe Whitehead's historical description of the rise of *The Divorce Culture* (New York: Alfred Knopf, 1997). Providing some measured criticism is Pamela Paul, *The Starter Marriage and the Future of Matrimony* (New York: Random House, 2002). Paul's book (she herself had a starter marriage fail) is a study in the ambivalence of these questions—on the one hand, she holds out the ideal of permanent marriage, while on the other hand, she insists that marriage be based fundamentally on emotions and affections, and so cannot be "enforced" by marriage. Paul both wants to retain a moral standard and yet deny moral responsibility. Also illuminating on children and divorce is Judith Wallerstein, Julia Lewis, and Sandra Blakeslee, *The Unexpected Legacy of Divorce: A 25-Year Landmark Study* (New York: Hyperion, 2000). Luther's comments against indissolubility are from *Luther's Works*, American ed., vol. 28, trans. Edward Sittler (St. Louis: Concordia Publishing House, 1973). Eastern Orthodox teaching can be found in John Meyendorff's accessible *Marriage: An Orthodox Perspective* (Crestwood, NY: St. Vladimir's Seminary Press, 1975). The heated debate over annulment is captured in the objections of Pierre Hegy and Joseph Martos, *Catholic Divorce* (New York: Continuum, 2000), and Robert Vasoli, *What God Has Joined Together: The Annulment Crisis in American Catholicism* (New York: Oxford University

Press, 1998). The description of annulment comes from David McCarthy's essay "Marriage, Remarriage, and Sex," in *The Blackwell Companion to Christian Ethics*, eds. Stanley Hauerwas and Samuel Wells (Malden, MA: Blackwell, 2004) pp. 276–288. The address of Benedict is "Speech to the Roman Rota," *Origins* 35 (2006), pp. 599–601.

The section on parenting owes huge debts not only to my (married) friends, but to Julie Hanlon Rubio's detailed and nuanced consideration of these issues in her *A Christian Theology of Marriage and Family* (New York: Paulist Press, 2003). Historical background for Catholic schools is available from Martin E. Marty, *A Short History of American Catholicism* (Allen, TX: Thomas More, 1995); John T. McGreevey, *Catholicism and American Freedom: A History* (New York: W. W. Norton, 2003); and Jay Dolan, *The American Catholic Experience* (Garden City, NY: Doubleday, 1985). The final comment is from Laura A. Smit, *Loves Me, Loves Me Not: The Ethics of Unrequited Love* (Grand Rapids, MI: Baker, 2005).

Chapter 11

The key sources for this account of forgiveness are Dietrich Bonhoeffer, *Life Together*, trans. John W. Doberstein (San Francisco: HarperSanFrancisco, 1954); Gerry O'Hanlon, "Justice and Reconciliation," in *Reconciliation in Religion and Society*, ed. Michael Hurley, SJ (Belfast: Institute of Irish Studies, 1994), pp. 48–67; Herbert McCabe, OP, "The Forgiveness of God," in *God, Christ, and Us* (New York: Continuum, 2003), pp. 119–123; Robert Jenson, *Systematic Theology, Volume 1: The Triune God* (New York: Oxford, 1997); and Rowan Williams, *A Ray of Darkness: Sermons and Reflections* (Cambridge, MA: Cowley, 1995). An excellent novel that illustrates these matters is Oscar Hijuelos' *Mr. Ives' Christmas* (New York: Harper Collins, 1995). I have used this text frequently in moral theology classes, though it does not address the issue of sexual sin directly.

Index